THE CHILDREN WHO SLEEP BY THE RIVER

DEBBIE TAYLOR

D1166989

INTERLINK BOOKS

An imprint of Interlink Publishing Group, Inc.

NEW YORK

First Emerging Voices edition published 1992 by

INTERLINK BOOKS
An imprint of Interlink Publishing Group, Inc.
99 Seventh Avenue
Brooklyn, New York 11215

Originally published in Great Britain by Allison & Busby,
an imprint of Virgin Publishing Ltd.

Library of Congress Cataloging-in-Publication Data
Taylor, Debbie.
    The children who sleep by the river / Debbie Taylor. – 1st
Emerging voices ed.
        p.   cm. – (Emerging voices)
    ISBN 1-56656-102-7 (hb) – ISBN 0-940793-96-2 (pb)
    I. Title. II. Series.
PR6070.A912C45 1992
823'.914–dc20   92-8008
                                                                    CIP

Printed and bound in the United States of America

3 9510 2001 2669 9

For my grandmother
Mary Taylor

This book was written with the support
and encouragement of the World Health
Organization.

PART ONE

Beauty

*E*ustina was watching the night Tendai was conceived. She had seen the young couple making love earlier that evening; and had chuckled at their gaucheness, at the tender, solemn clumsiness with which they pleasured one another. But that was not really what she was interested in.

Though it was good to see their taut young skin gleaming like molasses in the moonlight, and to hear their deep breathing as they slid straight into the heavy sleep of children, her attention was really elsewhere.

She was watching something inside Beauty's body; deep, deep inside, where a fleck of flesh tumbled slowly through a forest of tentacles; where a freckle, a fragment, was being passed like a balloon over the heads of a crowd. On, on it went; to where the first flickering wave of sperm, whipping like fish through fronds of weed, rushed madly and headlong to meet it.

Beauty stirred in her sleep, but did not wake, when fleck and flicker united and the seed of her daughter Tendai was created. But Eustina saw it all.

Partly she was pleased: it was always good to see a new baby in the family – another small voice to swell the sounds of laughter and tears, another stepping-stone from past to future. But partly she was anxious. It was not a good time for this child to be conceived. Beauty's body was not ready. It was too young, too hungry. There was too little blood, carrying too little nourishment to feed the tiny parasite that was soon to lodge in her womb. The bones of her narrow pelvis jutted like blades; the muscles of her arms and legs were hard and bunched like a boy's. Only her small breasts and the rounded contours of her lovely face marked her as a woman.

But, encircled by a slender coronet of pelvic bone, enclosed in the frond-lined fallopian tube, the germ of baby Tendai continued slowly to tumble: cleaving into twin halves, which twinned again so that, tumbling and twinning, baby Tendai was a cluster of four by the time the foreman rang the bell to wake the compound before dawn the next morning.

Beauty woke with a start, jolted out of a dream by the bell. She lay for a few moments staring into the darkness and trying to hold on to the last fading image. It was her great-aunt Eustina, dressed in the spirit-medium's red and black scarf she always wore, standing by a bush studded with small red flowers.

"This is the bush," she was saying. "It's the root that you need. But look carefully at the flowers, and the leaves – so that you can do this for yourself next time." Glancing round to make sure no one else was nearby, the old woman squatted and began hacking carefully at the ground beneath the bush with her hoe.

Hearing Peter roll over and start pulling on his clothes, Beauty shook herself free of the dream and felt for her blouse on the cement floor beside her. She put it on and stood to wrap one of their two blankets round her waist. Still in the dark, she folded the other into a neat square and put it on the plastic suitcase by the wall. As Peter sat lacing his workboots, she picked up a bucket, pushed open the door, and started walking to the standpipe.

Outside the darkness was beginning to thin and, in the gray-blue mists of dawn, she could see other doors opening and other figures, like ghosts, emerging and converging on the open space in the center of the compound. She quickened her pace, hoping to get there before the queue grew too long, and buried a fist in her stomach as she walked to stifle the growls of hunger.

She nodded and murmured a general greeting to the women and children already gathered round the concrete trough. She recognized most of the faces now, though she still could not understand much of what they were saying. And, in the half-light, the pale flashes of their eyes and teeth, their strange blueish facial scars – precise grid-like patterns etched high on their cheekbones – and the foreign babble of their chatter and laughter, welled up and surrounded her like a menace so that she found she was shivering when her turn came to dip the scoop into the trough and fill her bucket.

In daylight these Malawian women were just women. The two she worked between in the tobacco shed could even speak some Shona. But throughout the night and in its shadowy margins, people reverted, regressed, and clung to their own; built a human wall to keep the shadows at bay.

There were two hundred people living in the compound – six hundred if you included the children. And over half were migrants from Malawi. Most of the rest were native Shona, but there were three Mozambican families too – living on the far northern edge, bordering the vlei, the place no one else wanted to live. When one of the two pit latrines had filled up and pressure on the other made it impossible to clean, people had started going to the vlei to relieve themselves. Already some were beginning to straggle over in that direction, reaching up into the branches of the trees that grew there – too spindly to cut for firewood – to pluck a handful of crackly dry leaves with which to wipe themselves.

Beauty shivered again – this time with distaste – then handed the scoop to the woman behind her and bent her knees as a small girl stepped forward to help hoist the brimming bucket on to her head. Tensing her neck muscles under the weight and raising an arm to steady it, she slowly straightened up and started back towards the house.

She and Peter lived in a small round mud-brick house thatched in the Shona way. It was just behind a larger two-roomed brick-and-tin house where the rest of his family lived, his parents and the two youngest children sleeping in the airless room at the back, and the other five older ones unfolding their blankets every night in the larger front room. Before Beauty had arrived, Peter had shared the little round house with two of his brothers. But they had moved out now: the younger going back to sleep in the big house with the rest of the family, the elder moving in with his cousins in another brick house next door. She wondered sometimes if they resented her.

These two brick-and-tin houses were at the end of a row of five that Mr. Johnson – the man who owned the farm they all worked on – had had built three years ago and had allocated to the five men who spoke the best English. Mr. Johnson never came to the compound himself, but used one or other of these five men whenever he had something he wanted to communicate to the rest of the workers. Last week one of them brought the message that Mr. Johnson was sorry but he would not be building any houses this year as he had promised. It was because of the drought, he explained. He could not afford to build any more houses until he felt financially more secure. He hoped they would all be patient.

People were not really sorry. They suspected that when all the permanent workers were housed in proper brick-and-tin houses, Mr. Johnson would start monitoring the comings and goings of the others – the cousins and aunts and friends and grandchildren – who arrived in the spring with their blanket bundles and their suitcases to plant and weed and pick and sort the cotton and tobacco crops. At present they just melted into the compound, like sugar dissolving in tea, as their relatives compressed children into bigger sleeping groups to free a room, or simply shifted over a little to make space for another blanket on the floors of their tiny houses.

At present new homes sprouted haphazardly and stealthily, almost overnight like toadstools, their conical thatched roofs clustered ever more tightly together: difficult to count houses not built in rows; difficult to detect when a makeshift shed or chicken house began expanding then transforming gradually into a home; difficult to calculate how many people should properly occupy each constantly evolving group of buildings. Razing them to the ground and replacing them with square brick houses, numbered consecutively in rows, would make it easier for Mr. Johnson to restrict this ebb and flow of people that maximized each family's survival.

Beauty had been one of this influx four months earlier and it was her cousin, Esther, and her family who had had to move over to accommodate her. But they did not have to house her for long – because she had met and fallen in love with Peter on her first evening in the compound and had moved in with him just two months later.

This was not the way it would have been done back at home. But things were different in the compound: faster, more abrupt, chaotic even – so different from the stately social rhythms of the village. Back at home those rhythms unfolded at a pace that was dictated by the traditional, measured respect due to all branches of the family. But here in the compound, suddenly Beauty was a daughter-in-law, living with her husband's family. Suddenly this compound, miles from her native village, marooned at the end of a long dusty track in the heart of white-owned Zimbabwe – suddenly this strange, squalid, foreign place was her home. As long as her husband's family lived here, she would have to live here too.

Her mother-in-law emerged from the larger house as Beauty approached and the younger woman immediately lowered her gaze, eased the bucket from her head on to the sandy ground, and then knelt and clasped her hands respectfully in greeting, as she had been taught a new daughter-in-law should.

After two months of marriage she only knelt like this in the mornings, when she brought water for Peter's parents to wash with. But when she had first arrived she had knelt whenever she saw them, had fetched water for all his relatives, and only spoke to return their greetings. From the easy familiarity of her cousin's house – into which she had been absorbed so effortlessly, plaiting Esther's shock of unruly hair into neat coils and ridges, carrying her one-year-old baby on her back to the tobacco shed, comfortably adding her long limbs to the tangle that huddled close round the fire in the evenings – from this simple, informal extension of her own home, she had found herself living with strangers.

At her new home Beauty was set apart and scrutinized: her in-laws would have to pay roora to her mother for the services of Peter's new wife and they wanted to be sure they were getting their money's worth.

The first evening of her marriage was the hardest. She had

arrived, with Esther as escort, and had sat down a few yards from her in-laws' house to wait – as tradition dictated – with a blanket over her head like a shawl, until Peter came with some money as symbolic inducement to persuade her to enter his family. On entering the main house itself, she had knelt on the floor, her blanket still over her head, in front of all his relatives – not moving, not speaking, not daring to look up. And there were so many people there – all come to see what kind of woman young Peter had chosen for himself.

Through the folds of her blanket, she could hear them talking to each other in low voices, could hear them chuckling and could feel their eyes on her body: on her bare legs (clean and shining with vaseline – but she knew they would judge them too thin); on her shoes (red plastic and still fairly new); on her skirt (newly washed, neatly mended). Eventually they seemed satisfied and she heard the clink, clink, clink as each adult dropped a coin into the enamel plate Esther held.

This sign of acceptance permitted her to take off the blanket, to eat some of the food they had prepared for her, and to talk if she wanted. But, though she could sense them looking at her throughout the meal, nobody spoke to her at all.

They still didn't talk to her much. But sometimes, when she met her mother-in-law's eyes by accident, she thought they were beginning to soften towards her a little. They did so now as the older woman watched Beauty empty the water into two big bowls and then followed her as she set out again for the standpipe. The back was slender, but straight: that was good. She was strong too, and diligent, and respectful. That was good too. And her nimble fingers were among the fastest in the tobacco shed, so she regularly brought home as much as five dollars at the end of the day: that would be a big help. But perhaps she was a bit too skinny; and that face –

far too pretty for comfort. Peter's mother had noticed how her other sons, and her husband, looked at her lovely young daughter-in-law: it could mean trouble for Peter later on.

At six o'clock, as the sun sent slanting shadows through the dry grass beside the path, Beauty edged round the door of the tobacco shed. Nodding to the overseer, she went to take her place at the long table where the other women were working. She was the last to arrive because, in addition to fetching the family's water, she had had to wash up the breakfast pots and sweep out both houses before coming to work. Since she had married all these extra duties meant her name was often the last to be written in the book where a tally was kept of the bundles each woman sorted and tied.

She smiled quickly at her neighbors, who looked up as she squeezed in beside them on the bench, and grinned across at Esther who raised a hand in greeting from further down the row. Then she bent immediately over the heap of big crumpled leaves in front of her.

Like an oiled machine she began, her hands smoothing and sorting the moist, leathery, semi-transparent tobacco leaves while her eyes scanned each one, automatically assessing its color (a slight greenish tinge, a subtle hint of brown, a faint touch of orange) in the carefully controlled light from the fluorescent tubes hanging over the table.

Everything was carefully controlled in the tobacco shed. The air was cold and clammy from the invisible mist created by a huge humidifier roaring high on the wall above them. In minutes her dress was clinging to her body, her skin felt as oily and damp as the leaves, and her mouth, nose and lungs were full of the heavy humid taint of tobacco. The woman on her left began coughing and the baby asleep on her back woke with a whimper and started to cry. She quieted it by jigging up and down in her seat, her hands continuing their

10

mechanical smoothing, sorting, tying motions without a pause. But as soon as that baby stopped another started, and another, and more women began coughing, so that Beauty's ears were as full of roaring and wailing and coughing as her lungs were full of the cold damp air.

At ten the overseer blew a whistle and the women spilled out of the chilly cavern into the bright morning sunshine. They sat on the ground in small groups: some drinking a thin sweet sadza porridge, others reaching into their blouses for a breast to offer their babies. Beauty spotted Esther's mop of crazy hair and went over to sit beside her cousin.

"How's married life?" Esther teased. "Ready to run away yet? We can always put you up at our house if you change your mind."

Beauty shook her head and sighed. "There's an awful lot of work," she admitted quietly. "But his mother's kinder to me than she was and they have vegetables with sadza, every night."

Esther untied the cloth knotted over her breasts and reached behind to lift a drowsy child on to her lap. "So – enough sadza, a father-in-law with a permanent job and a proper house, a husband who doesn't get drunk every night . . . your ancestors have provided for you well." She picked up a big enamel mug and held it to her son's lips, tipping the grayish sweet gruel into his mouth. "All you need now is a baby," she concluded.

Beauty watched as baby Lovemore swallowed and spluttered, turning his head in a vain effort to avoid the mug. He was tiny, like his mother, with the same huge eyes and a head already smothered in a mass of soft curls that promised to thicken into a dense black mop just like Esther's.

"Don't you breastfeed him any more?" she asked.

Esther put down the mug and patted her breasts with a free hand. "With these useless things? They're empty," she

11

said, opening her blouse to show Beauty how they hung wrinkled and flat against her bony little chest. "I think the milk had gone bad anyway. It can, you know," she explained seriously. "If your baby had diarrhea it can be because there's something wrong with your milk."

She buttoned up her blouse and tipped some more gruel into the mug, which she offered to Beauty. Beauty's mouth stung and tingled as it flooded with saliva. She clapped her hands politely then lifted the mug to her lips. All this extra work meant she was hungry almost all the time and it seemed an age since she had scraped the last of the sadza from the big black pot into her bowl this morning. But, hungry though she was, she only took a few sips before passing it back to her cousin. She knew how scarce food was in Esther's household and she suspected Esther had not had any breakfast at all.

"Maybe the pills you were taking got into your milk," she suggested.

Esther shrugged. "I don't know. You hear so many things." She paused, then leaned forward towards her cousin. "Those pills didn't work anyway," she said under her breath.

"You mean you're pregnant again?" exclaimed Beauty.

"Shh. I don't want anyone to know," she said, looking round uneasily. "You never know what might happen in a place like this."

A group of women burst suddenly into laughter just beside them and the babble of foreign voices seemed to get louder momentarily. Esther clutched Lovemore tight against her and fingered one of the little charms he wore around his neck. "Come on," she said, scrambling to her feet. "Let's go back in. The whistle will go any second now."

The two cousins walked back to the shed together, one graceful and slender with buttocks high and tight as a young boy's; the other nearly a head shorter, walking with short quick steps like a child trying to keep up with its mother, her shock of black hair tangling with her baby's soft curls as he nodded back to sleep on her back.

"Are you going to go on the pill?" Esther asked when they were out of earshot of the other women.

"Peter says I'll run around like a prostitute if I start taking them," Beauty said with a giggle. "Anyway, I want a baby, and I heard they can make you barren."

Esther laughed. "Well they didn't make me barren," she said with a grin. "But maybe that's because I didn't take them at the same time every day like they told me to. But it's impossible to be exact with a family to look after, and the work in the tobacco fields – and this one here" – reaching behind and patting Lovemore's bottom gently – "always needs something."

They stepped into the roaring clammy shed and sat down at their places, blinking to accustom their eyes to the unnatural cold, blue-white of the fluorescent light. As her hands and eyes locked again into their synchronized automatic motions, Beauty's mind could fly free: to the diffident way Peter reached for her body every night, as though he was afraid she'd refuse him; to the way his eyes had narrowed and his face hardened when she suggested she went on the pill: "I don't want people saying my wife's a prostitute," he had said coldly. A prostitute. Could he tell? Esther had said that as long as you made sure you took enough of the medicine to tighten your vagina, it was impossible for a man to tell whether you were a virgin or not. But perhaps there was some other way to find out?

"Come on Beauty, come on baby, this will be our secret. I love you Beauty, I won't hurt you. I just want to show you how much I love you. Quiet now, quiet now, don't struggle, my little Beauty. There's no point in struggling. No one can hear you, and no one would believe you anyway. You know you want me just as much as I want you. And everyone else will think that too if they find out. But you're not going to tell them, are you, my little sweetheart?"

Esther was the only person she told about the school teacher. She was too ashamed to tell any of her friends at school and too frightened to tell her mother. Her mother's quick temper, and the fierceness with which she always confronted anyone who dared to threaten her or those she loved, made confiding in her unthinkable. The thought of her mother – shoulders back, eyes blazing – rushing off indignantly to complain to the headmaster or the village headman – or even the chief himself – was too awful to contemplate. Maybe the teacher would have been fired – and other young girls saved from his big heavy hands and his hypnotic half-wheedling, half-threatening whisper – but that wouldn't have saved Beauty's reputation. No, the whole affair was better kept a secret.

Mr. Lewis – she never discovered his first name – had only taken her twice: on the floor of the stuffy little store-cupboard at the back of the school, surrounded by the musty smells of books and papers. As she lay, rigid and paralyzed, while big fumbling fingers plucked at her clothing, she turned her face sideways and found herself staring at two broken chairs stacked on top of each other just by her head. She concentrated on one splintered break in one leg of one chair – a jagged white wound livid against the smooth brown polished wood – as her own smooth brown body was probed and prodded and broken into.

After the first time she had tried to pretend nothing had happened. But when it happened again a week later, she stopped going to school altogether, complaining she was sick, and spent day after day lying in her sleeping hut with the door closed.

Her body lost all its rhythms as she lay there, and became strangely detached from the pull of sun and moon. Sleep came and went erratically, plunging her from shallow to deep, from doze to dream, regardless of the cycles of light and dark outside. Her periods stopped too, in defiance of the moon's waxing and waning: until at last, after eight weeks of timeless twilight, she awoke with a tearing dragging pain low in her belly, and wet hot blood sticky between her thighs.

Hours later her womb had vomited out the poisoned seed he had planted inside her and she lay, curled and empty as a shell, as her mother – without a word – gently eased the bloodied blanket from beneath her, washed her with warm water and herbs, then silently patted her dry like a baby and left her alone to sleep again.

Though they never spoke of it, Beauty wondered whether her mother somehow knew what had happened, had guessed in that uncanny, magical way of hers that had made lying so pointless when she was a child. But what if Peter found out too? Would he send her home in disgrace? Perhaps his parents would refuse to pay the roora – then everyone would know she had been spoiled.

A subtle change in the quality of the sounds that surrounded her yanked her back to the present: to the big oily leaves and the cold breath of the humidifier on her neck. She looked up from her hands and saw that everyone had tensed slightly and were glancing covertly towards the door, where a tall white woman was talking to the foreman.

It was the first time Beauty had been this close to the boss's wife. She'd often glimpsed her, whisking past the compound in one of the cars, her plump daughter beside her and two or three dogs on the back seat with their noses poking out of the open windows. Now the woman was talking rapidly and gesturing enthusiastically towards where

15

they were sitting. And the foreman was nodding and listening attentively. He opened the book where their names and work totals were recorded, and handed it to her, pointing to something on the page. Lifting a pair of blue-rimmed spectacles to her eyes from where they hung on a chain round her neck, the woman looked down at the book quickly, then raised her head and, letting the spectacles drop to the tip of her long nose, squinted over them at the long rows of women. When the cool blue gaze reached her, Beauty found herself meeting it steadily and smiling briefly before looking back down to where her hands whipped a narrow twist of tobacco rapidly round and round another big bunch of sorted leaves.

After she'd gone, the foreman came back in and beckoned Beauty outside with him.

"Do you speak any English?" he asked abruptly.

"Yes, sir, a little. I finished Grade Four."

"Good. The boss's wife has decided to send someone off for training as a health worker and she wants you to go to her for an interview at two o'clock."

"Why me?" asked Beauty.

He shrugged. "She said you were pretty and had an intelligent face," he said. "And she wanted someone reliable – you haven't missed a single day's work since you started."

Beauty went back to her seat, carefully wiping her face clean of any suggestion of what she was feeling and answering her neighbors' raised eyebrows with a quick shake of her head. She wouldn't say anything until she was sure she'd got the job.

She didn't go back to work after lunch. Instead she ran to the compound, walked quickly to the standpipe for water, then took out the precious sliver of perfumed soap she'd hoarded for special occasions. With her best dress in her

16

hand, she slipped behind the bamboo screen beside the house to wash.

At a quarter to two Beauty stood in the wide gravel driveway of the big farmhouse. Coming from the dusty teeming compound, where chickens and children cackled and chattered and fluttered and toddled everywhere you looked, the big white house seemed silent and still. An unseen bird piped sweetly from a fragrant jasmine hedge – unseasonably green and luscious like a jungle vine – and the faint unfamiliar sounds of crockery clanking against stainless steel came from behind one of the array of closed doors.

So many doors – all painted bright blue, all with keyholes and bolts; some with padlocks hanging heavy like bulky medallions, others half-concealed behind screen doors covered with black netting. Which one should she knock at? The one on the far side of the garage, separated from the house by a row of three cars (freshly washed, with dark stains of water still drying on their tires)? The one flanked by big pots of flowers with a tiny circle of glass at eye level and a little gold button set high in the frame? The one with the pile of plastic bowls beside it? She was just approaching this one when she heard a dog bark from deep inside the house, and veered away – sweat prickling her scalp – to a fourth door, at the side of the house, from where the sounds of someone washing dishes were emanating.

They were coming from a window that was ajar behind its cage of iron – a close-woven grille painted white, that stood proud of the house like an angular eye-patch, one of the many that covered every eye of the house, shielding them from clever black fingers, or knives, or long hooked pieces of wire, that might otherwise pollute or penetrate or pilfer from the Johnsons' big white fortress.

Beauty wiped the nervous dampness carefully off her palms on the back of her dress and stepped forward to knock

17

on the door. A loud clatter and a muffled curse in Malawian drowned her first timid attempt; so she knocked again – loudly – then heard the slop and flap of plastic thonged sandals come shuffling towards her. The door opened silently and she was staring down at the sparse white hair and sharp eyes of an old man, black and bent like a gnarled gnome, in a huge white apron.

He stared at her face for a long moment, narrowing his eyes and nodding his head slightly, just like her mother did sometimes. It was a look that by-passed her damp palms and pretty face and pierced straight to where hope and fear leapfrogged each other in her heart. She dropped her eyes from his but knew he had already found his way inside, whether she wanted it or not.

"I'm Seguro, the cook. You're Mrs. Kanyemba come to see Mrs. Johnson. Come in, come in." Strong bony fingers pressed her down into a chair by the door – afterwards her arm tingled with warmth where he'd grasped her.

"Seguro! –" a sweet high-pitched cry from a long dark polished-wood corridor glimpsed through the kitchen door "– has that girl come yet? – Ah, there you are, dear –" and she strode brisk and smiling into the room. Towering over the tiny cook, a turquoise cardigan draped over her shoulders and the blue-rimmed spectacles swinging against her chest, Mrs. Johnson seemed to fill the kitchen. She surveyed Beauty benignly.

"What's your name, dear? Mrs. Kanyemba? Oh, I can never remember these long African names! What's your other name? Beauty?" She yelped with glee: "How delightfully appropriate! She is beautiful, isn't she, Seguro?"

Without waiting for a reply, she pulled open the door of a huge humming refrigerator and checked its contents quickly.

"The lamb today, Seguro, with some of those green beans and a salad. Potatoes only for the boss, remember. Come

18

along, Beauty, let's go and have our little chat. Oh – and a
Coke for Beauty – would you like Coke or Fanta, dear? – on
the terrace – and tea for me, please, Seguro."

Beauty followed the tall woman back down the polished
corridor past door after open door flashing split-second tab-
leaux – of beds heaped high with pillows, eiderdowns and
soft toys; shelves of books; photographs in ornate silver
frames; fruit in glass bowls; gleaming white porcelain baths
and toilets; furry pastel towels and mats. The last door was
closed and when Mrs. Johnson opened it two dogs bounded
through and jumped up, barking playfully and pawing at
Mrs. Johnson's flowered skirt.

Beauty gasped and shrank in terror against the wall, staring transfixed at their long pink tongues slapping saliva
against sharp white teeth.

It took barely a moment for fawning ecstasy to switch to
snarling sneers, for their lips to draw back into menacing
growling grins as they smelt Beauty's sweat and spotted the
color of her skin.

"Quiet now, down boys –" grabbing their collars and
pulling them away – "Friend, Beauty's a friend – Don't
worry about them, dear. I'm afraid we've had to train them
to be suspicious . . . There's so much stealing, you know."
And she hauled them through into the corridor and shut the
door behind them.

As Beauty walked slowly back to the compound two hours
later the visit settled into a mosaic of disconnected fragments
in her mind: the slavering jaws of the dogs, who slipped back
through the door when Seguro brought the tray; Mrs. Johnson's own narrow pale lips, pursed to sip tea from a sprigged
china cup, opening to laugh her high fluting laugh, or puck-
ering and parting as she uttered the clipped consonants of
Rhodesian English; her long yellowish teeth nibbling ("I
shouldn't, you know") a cookie held daintily in her hand;

the rustle of potted plants towering succulently from the corners of the terrace; the flash and sparkle of a tiny fountain spilling into the swimming pool in the garden; the silent movements of four black men in blue overalls, laying irrigation pipes in rich dark trenches cut across a green sea of lawn between islands of flowers. One of the men was Beauty's father-in-law: so awesome and dignified in the compound, somehow diminished by the respectful silence with which he padded across the sea of green. Beauty watched, fascinated and repelled, as her hostess fed cookies to the dogs, scratched behind their ears and let them lick her chin.

As some point Mrs. Johnson had taken a key from her handbag and had escorted Beauty to the door beyond the row of clean cars that Beauty had noticed earlier. Inside, on a shelf above a small table, was a row of bottles and tins.

"My little dispensary," Mrs. Johnson announced. "I've decided to start a sort of surgery here. So tell your people that if they have anything wrong with them they can come here at eight any morning – only proper illnesses, mind –" she wagged a warning finger. "I don't want people coming with every little ache and pain . . ."

Beauty gathered that she was to attend a training course starting in three months' time at the local clinic and then come and help Mrs. Johnson in her new dispensary every morning.

"I'll pay you fifty dollars a month, all right?" she said, concluding their meeting. "And here's ten dollars now for your bus fares and things. Now run along and come and see me when your course is finished. Good luck – I'm sure we're going to work very well together. Oh – there you are Seguro – show Beauty out will you?"

And the last thing she remembered was the old cook's powerful fingers on her arm again and his voice whispering, in broken Shona: "Go well and go carefully, Mrs. Kanyemba. You have a baby daughter to think about now."

She kept her dress on for the rest of the day (though she had to take her shoes off because they had rubbed a raw patch on one of her heels). It indicated something important had happened. People would ask where she was going or where she had come from. And they did, those that knew her, allowing her to reply demurely that she had been selected by the boss's wife to be trained as a health worker, hiding her triumph behind a modest smile and adding that she hoped her husband would give her permission to go.

Peter grinned delightedly when she told him, thrusting out his hand for her to shake, as he would to another man, then rushing off to tell his parents. And later that evening, when she knelt by the fire with the rest of the family, she could sense a subtle difference in their attitude towards her. Their wall of kinship had dissolved a little and a chink had opened for her. Her mother-in-law complimented her on her dress; Peter's eldest sister rose unbidden to help her with the dishes; and, having seen him tiptoeing across the Johnsons' perfect lawn, Beauty felt less intimidated by the big quiet figure of her father-in-law as he sat hunched, in the only chair, rolling tobacco in a long fat cylinder of newspaper.

Afterwards, when she had folded the dress and laid it back at the bottom of the suitcase where she and Peter kept their clothes, had grappled, giggling, with him in their nightly contest of impulse and restraint, and had whispered "Goodnight, husband" to his "Goodnight, wife," Beauty slipped out from under the blanket. Putting on her old blouse and skirt, she silently opened the door and crept outside.

Usually she was afraid to go outside in the dark alone and tried to control her bladder until morning. But tonight the shadows were friendly as she squatted beneath the mango tree, and its big thick leaves closed protectively over her head. Before going back in she stood for a moment and gazed up at the sky, flung like a jeweled blanket over the sleeping compound.

"Are you there?" she whispered softly. "Can you hear me? I just wanted to say 'Thank you.'" She clapped her hands respectfully and silently to the shadows, and the darkness lifted a little, the stars pulsed brighter for a second, and a little breath of warm air wafted across her face like a feather.

Eustina was there, of course, accepting her share of gratitude with a regal nod of her old head. So were the others – Eustina's five sisters, two of her brothers, her mother and father, her father's three sisters and their mother, and all the nameless ones whose spirits were as strong as ever, though their faces had been blurred by the passing of the years. They all jostled close round their darling child, hiding her slender body from the jealous mists that were already beginning to loop greedy tentacles in her direction.

Once Beauty was back beneath the blanket again, Eustina shooed the others away and sat down beside the sleeping couple, placing a hand, gently as thistledown, on her great-niece's flat girl's belly and gazing deep inside.

All was well. Baby Tendai was now a cluster of cells, just as she should have been: a tiny drop of drupelets, each pink and translucent as a pomegranate seed, which continued its slow-motion, frond-fingered fall toward Beauty's womb; a crystalline fragment of flesh, each rounded facet mirroring each other facet, each reflecting the same message: the predestined destiny of each and every particle of Tendai's baby body-to-be.

Eustina could read this writing and could see already that her great-great-niece would be a light-skinned little seedling, with delicate ears and thick-curled eyelashes like her mother's, and her father's wide mouth and uneven teeth. Her cheekbones would be high, her legs long, her brow a little too broad for beauty. This much had already been decided. But would her heart beat whole and complete in her infant chest? Would those curly-lashed eyes be able to see clearly when they focused first on the world? Would her brain – now barely a blueprint – fill out and function as it should behind the broad brow? Eustina lifted her hand and sat back on her heels with a sigh. She could see trouble ahead for this baby.

It was the end of the harvest season and work in the tobacco sheds had nearly come to an end. The grading tables were empty and big wooden crates, packed tight with bundles of leaves the women had so painstakingly smoothed and sorted, were stacked high by the door. A few of the older women riffled rapidly through a heap of ragged leaf fragments, expertly dividing them between three wooden tubs, while men swept round their feet, hammered shut the last of the crates and hung the metal curing racks back on the wall ready for next year's load of fragrant leathery leaves.

In the rest of Zimbabwe this was a time of plenty: when the maize had been shucked off the cobs and tipped into its compartment in the mud-and-thatch granaries; when water melons, heavy as boulders, round and streaked yellow on green, were rolled to rest beneath chicken houses; when bunches of groundnuts, like misshapen hands, were shaken free of earth and tossed into sacks. But in the compound where Beauty and Esther lived, and in seventeen thousand other farm compounds, the end of the harvest meant the beginning of the season of hunger.

In the rest of Zimbabwe the beer the women brewed from the new stocks of sorghum and maize was drunk in celebration and thanksgiving in those golden weeks of rest at the

23

end of the year; and people laughed indulgently at the men who staggered across the veld, dead drunk in the middle of the morning, or at the old women who toppled tipsily and tripped over their feet as they danced to the mbira in the long lazy afternoons. But in seventeen thousand farm compounds, women watched anxiously as empty Chibuku cartons piled up outside the beer halls. As the women's work came to an end and families were thrown back again to manage on a man's single wage packet, that beer was bought with money that was scarcely enough to buy sadza to last through the month.

Meanwhile Mrs. Johnson had started her surgery, doling out cough mixture and aspirin to the queue that formed daily outside the blue padlocked door. Though her training course had not yet begun, Beauty had been summoned to translate. She stood behind Mrs. Johnson's shoulder, reaching down pills and potions from the shelves as her employer sat making notes in a ledger or peering over her spectacles at the next person in the queue.

They came in sideways like crabs – these reluctant supplicants – the men sometimes holding a hat in their hands. Beauty could occasionally see a glint of resentment in the corner of their respectfully downcast eyes, but Mrs. Johnson went blithely on, noting down names and counting out pills, occasionally stopping to consult a medical book with glossy colored photographs or to write a "letter of referral" for a patient to take to the clinic. With her sweet high voice and gay laugh, Mrs. Johnson's tall linen-clad figure formed a barrier between Beauty and the others in the compound. By asking her to translate their complaints, by forcing her to witness their degrading obsequious sidling, by smiling at her and passing comment about "her patients" to her in their presence, Mrs. Johnson had made Beauty appear to be her creature.

Soon Beauty became aware of a spotlight on her everywhere she went. There was no need to wear her best dress. Everyone knew she was the one who had been singled out by the boss's wife. Curious eyes followed her as she walked to the standpipe, or slipped behind the bamboo screen to wash. She even felt watched as she picked her way fastidiously through the trees in the vlei clutching her handful of leaves in the morning.

"That's the one," she heard, in Malawian, as she passed through their section of the compound with her bucket of water on her head. She smiled uncertainly at the faces she recognized from the groups that peered out from beneath the low overhanging thatch the Malawians favored. But not everyone smiled in return. And, though she never actually heard the words spoken aloud, it was clear that when someone pointed and said "that's the one," there was sometimes another voice asking – in Malawian or Mozambican or Shona – "Why her?" And, though she had basked in the spotlight of attention at first – walking in jaunty steps with her pretty chin held high – now Beauty began to shrink sometimes from its glare, like a hare in a car's blazing headlights, and to long for invisibility.

But it was not until she was washing her clothes one evening, the sinking sun warm on the backs of her legs, that she first felt a prickle of danger. Suddenly – standing, her hands seeped in suds, bent double at the waist over the bowl – she remembered Seguro's warning words: "Go well and go carefully. You have a baby daughter to think about now." As she scrubbed, rinsed and wrung, she realized it was well over a month since she had furtively rinsed out the rags she used to soak up her menstrual blood.

Four weeks had now passed since tiny tadpole Tendai was first spawned. Ten days had been spent tumbling and twinning, becoming a hollow featherlight sphere of cells that bobbed free of fallopian fingers and out into the womb's open sea. For hours she had floated, dipping and drifting to the pulse of her mother's heartbeat, until one bob butted her deep into a yielding cleft of flesh, which opened to receive her and folded snugly around her.

Locked in a warm embrace, the pearl that was Tendai had started to feed, dissolving and digesting the womb wall and growing a faint furring of tentacles with which to suck in the soup that surrounded her. She had been there nearly twelve days now – developing, dividing, defining into layers and chambers – while Beauty slept and dreamed, waked and washed, carried and cooked, smoothed and sorted, carried and cooked and ate and slept again.

Unseeing, but not unseen, baby Tendai rocked in a sea of suffused red light: a tender twist of pink tethered at the heart of a watery pearl, lodged deep in the womb's cushioned wall.

Esther was the first person Beauty told. She found her early one morning, a few weeks later, sitting listlessly with Lovemore fidgeting on her lap and her daughter Violet squatting in the sand, quietly stirring a rusty tin of dust with a stick.

"Look at her, poor thing. There's not enough sadza for her to eat so she has to imagine it –" and Esther laughed a tired and angry laugh. "Sit, cousin. We are not a happy household today. Lovemore has a fever, Violet's hungry, and my back aches from carrying this child." She gestured towards her belly, now obviously swollen with her third baby, and laughed again: "The African woman – one in the dirt, one on her lap, one on the way," she said bitterly. "Come, make me smile. Tell me some good news."

Beauty sat down beside her. "I think I'm pregnant," she said. "Is that good news?"

Esther gave a little whoop of delight and tipped Lovemore

26

on to the ground beside his sister. Ignoring his feeble whine of protest, she hugged her slender cousin so Beauty could feel the belly, high and hard as a watermelon, pressed against her ribcage.

"Good, good, good – the best news! This will force people at home to forgive and forget extra fast! Everyone knows that frowns and angry words are dangerous when a woman is pregnant. How will they dare to be cross with you for sneaking off and marrying without their permission when they see that you're carrying a baby?" Esther laughed gleefully and released her cousin. "I hope it's a daughter," she said. "If you have a girl first there will be two more hands to help you with all the sons you are going to have later."

"Give me a chance," Beauty protested. "Let me have this one first."

But Esther was undeterred. "Yes, a daughter first, that's best. You know Violet already goes to fetch water – she uses that big Lactogen tin – and she can sweep the house and wash the pots. And next year I'll be able to leave this one" – pointing to Lovemore – "with her when I go out to work."

Violet looked up from where she was constructing her elaborate meal of dust, arranging leaves as bowls around the tin she was stirring. She smiled shyly at her aunt then bent again gravely to her task.

"And if you have a girl first," Esther continued, "you can use the roora you get for her to help pay the roora for your sons. Ah, sons, sons, expensive sons – you're nothing but trouble, aren't you?" Lovemore had started coughing, then crying, and she broke off to haul him on to her lap again and wipe his dust-streaked face and runny nose with the corner of a cloth. "Yes, even though your sons will always live near you, somehow a daughter is a greater comfort. Maybe knowing you have to lose her when she gets married is what makes a daughter so precious."

"You know Seguro, the old Malawian cook up at the big house? He said I would have a girl," said Beauty.

Esther looked up sharply. "Did you tell him you were pregnant? How many people have you told?"

"No, no, no one," Beauty assured her. "He just seemed to know without me telling him – even before I suspected it myself. And he warned me to be careful."

"He's a nganga, you know," said Esther, lowering her voice. "People say he's very powerful. But he doesn't do much these days – he thinks there's too much witchcraft in the compound, they say, and he doesn't want to get in-volved . . ." She trailed off and both women fell silent.

Beauty stared at Violet's little stick as she stirred it round and round and round, hypnotically, in her rusty can of dust. Her dress was unbuttoned and fell open as she worked, exposing the whole of the back of her body – her tufty black curls, the dip of her smooth round neck, sharp shoulder-blades and the long, knobby curve of her spine pushing through the dusky skin: a naked shameless five-year-old back, open to the sun, to the air; vulnerable to everyone's gaze. Suddenly Beauty found herself kneeling down and fastening her little niece's dress.

"Seguro's right," Esther said eventually. "You can't be too careful. Apart from you I didn't tell anyone I was preg-nant until it was impossible to hide. We are so far from the graves of the old ones here, it's hard for them to look after us. So I'm wearing chifumuro round my waist to protect the baby. You should do the same. I'll show you how to make it."

Beauty's hands moved involuntarily to the place where her womb ripened and swelled like a strawberry beneath the still-flat planes of her abdomen, then jerked away again quickly as she saw three women walking down the sandy path towards them. They raised their voices in greeting as they approached and Esther handed Lovemore to her cousin before rising to welcome them. He started crying again immediately, giving Beauty an excuse to withdraw from the group to comfort him. The women – big, gaunt and rough-looking, with restless eyes and ragged clothes – were neighbors of Esther's and worked near her in the tobacco shed. Though Shona like themselves, there was something disquieting and desperate about them.

"Have you decided yet?" one of them asked abruptly, leaning forward and staring hard at Esther.

Esther returned the stare levelly, unperturbed. "There's no need to push me," she said shortly. "You know I have no choice – any more than you have. My son's weak and whining; my daughter is learning to cook with dust. When are you going?"

Suddenly all three women glanced suspiciously towards Beauty. "Does she know? She works for the boss's wife, doesn't she?"

Esther waves a dismissive hand. "Oh, she's okay. She's my cousin; she won't say anything. I'll ask her if she wants to come too."

After they'd gone Beauty turned wide-eyed to her cousin. "You can't go! It's stealing. You know it's wrong. And it's so dangerous. What if you get caught? What if they give Darwin the sack and throw you all off the farm? Please don't go."

Esther's face hardened. "Don't you tell me what's right and what's wrong. What choice do I have? Look at this baby of mine: he cries all the time – not because he's bad, but because he's hungry. He's thin and he's miserable and he's sick. So I take him to the clinic. 'He's underweight,' they say, 'that's why he's sick. You should feed him better.' On what, Beauty, on what? 'Give him beans and peanut butter and cooking oil with his sadza,' they say." She was speaking

29

fast, her chest heaving. "Darwin earns fifty dollars a month. They should try buying beans on fifty dollars a month!"

At the sound of her raised voice, Lovemore started grizzling again and held out his arms to his mother. Beauty handed him over and Esther cradled him against her. "Ssh, baby, ssh. I'm sorry I shouted. I know, I know, I know – you're hungry." She turned again to Beauty. "Violet doesn't even complain. She just gets quieter and quieter – and I know she's trying to be good, and it just breaks my heart."

Beauty was silent; shocked. The women were planning to steal maize from one of the outlying fields. The big cobs had been cut and collected weeks ago and the long dry stalks, with the small shriveled secondary cobs still attached, were piled up waiting to be collected and stored as winter fodder for the cattle. Their plan was to go, at night, and take a heap of the small cobs into a little wood by the field. If they shucked off the grains there, they decided, they'd be able to carry more food home and hide it more easily. But doing it that way would take more time. And that meant more danger, more chance of being caught red-handed by one of the guards.

"It's still stealing," said Beauty again. "That maize belongs to Mr. Johnson. You know it's wrong to take it."

Stealing: it went against everything they had ever learnt. As children they were taught that anything you stole became bewitched and stuck to your hands like glue, so everyone would know what you'd done.

"What's worse? To steal some maize or to let your children starve? You wait till you have your baby, then you'll understand," said Esther wearily. "Look at his arms. You know what a baby's arms should be like: fat and shiny and strong. Look how thin they are. And the skin's so dull and dry." She stroked his arm soothingly as he lay against her, quiet now, and sucking his thumb. "It's Boss Johnson who's the thief: stealing food from my children and giving it to his cows; spending his money on cars and dogs and his two fat children, while my daughter learns not to complain about her empty stomach."

"Couldn't you go to a different farm to get the maize?" Beauty suggested. "The Johnsons are kind people; they try to do things for us. What about Mrs. Johnson's surgery? She gives us all those medicines free. And she told me they're planning to build a school in the compound next year, and a crèche to take care of the children when the older ones are working."

Esther snorted derisively. "Pills and books! You can't feed a child on pills and books. Now – if you were to tell me they're planning to give us a sack of mealie meal every month; or that they've said we can use one of their fields to grow food in; or that they've changed their minds about letting us fish in the lake – then I'd think about it. No, you wait till you have your baby and have nothing to give it but sadza gruel – then you'll understand."

Would she? Would the curled-up creature growing in her womb give her eyes the same hard glitter that she saw in the eyes of her cousin and the other three women? Beauty watched Esther bend over Lovemore now, running her fingers through his wild curls as his head nodded dully against her breast and his thumb slipped, slimy, half out of his sleepy mouth. Her face was no longer the face of the girl Beauty had grown up with. Though her body was still as slight and unformed as a twelve-year-old's, Esther's face had grown old. Without Beauty being aware of the transition, the quick-spirited, light-laughing young girl, whose dancing footsteps Beauty had chased after when she was a child, had been shaped and honed sharp by responsibility. Esther was a woman now: watchful and wily as an animal, wise and determined as a stone. By bearing and caring for her children, she

31

had gained the fierce grace that would earn her a place among her ancestors when she died.

But the hunger that gnawed at the compound now that the slack season was here lent a bitter touch of desperation to the faces of all the women. There was a continual thin wailing from the children that were too old for the breast but too young to have learnt patience, as the porridge grew thinner, the portions smaller, and as the hours between meals seemed to stretch longer. In the evenings the poorest families scattered their children like leaves round the compound where they hovered, eyes big with hunger, hands newly washed, mouths fixed in polite smiles, waiting for a nod of invitation. And the relatives and friends, as always, would nod; would move over; would make space, again, for another small hand to pull mouthfuls of sadza, again, from the steaming white domes in their bowls.

In Beauty's new household things were better. Two men brought in wages at the end of each week: good men who kept away from the beer hall on Sundays. So her mother-in-law was one of the few who could nod to the children lurking in the doorway like shadows. But that didn't mean they weren't hungry. And Beauty – still doing most of the housework, still one of the last to be served, still politely taking less than she wanted – Beauty was growing thinner.

"I have to go," she said, breaking the uncomfortable silence that had fallen between them after Esther's angry outburst. She put out a hand to touch Esther's shoulder, seeking the warmth of flesh on flesh, trying to reach across the chasm that had opened between the woman and the girl.

Esther looked up and smiled sadly at her. "Welcome to motherhood," she said.

That evening was still and calm and the compound basked in the rich copper light of the sinking sun, soaking up the last moments of warmth before winter's twilight lowered its chilly gray veil. The air lay heavy and yellow like oil over the houses, hushing the evening's bustle and coating everything with a film of gold. The dull duns and browns of the round mud huts blushed russet, and the thatch – neat sharp cones in the Shona section, flatter floppy-brimmed hats where the Malawians lived – glowed a deeper yellow.

Beauty was sweeping the ground round the house – like women and girls in every household: backs bent, arms swinging rhythmically with bunches of fine twigs in their bare hands, feet shuffling backwards in the wake of wide arcs in the dust. Swish, swish: the sound mingled with the clank of buckets, the clatter and squawk of chickens, and the ceaseless rising and falling of human voices as the compound prepared for the night.

The drumming began hesitantly: so that, at first, it was difficult to pick out the sound from the usual twilight noises. But soon it was unmistakable – an urgent galloping rhythm coming from the hill just beyond the beer hall.

Beauty stood up and squinted into the sun, looking for the source of the sound. And, one by one, the other sounds faded as sweeping, pouring, carrying, chopping, pounding and washing stopped, conversations were abandoned in mid-air, and soon everyone was gazing across to where the sun's last red rays glanced at crazy angles off the jumble of huge rocks at the foot of the hill, casting long black shadows towards the compound.

"What is it?" Beauty whispered to her mother-in-law who had come to stand beside her.

"They begin every year at around this time: drumming and dancing until they're exhausted. The dancers wear masks so you can't tell who they are – they're possessed by evil spirits. People say they eat raw intestines of chickens and drink their blood while it's still warm. And they have to open a new grave and eat the heart of the dead person before they're allowed to touch the drums. Can you hear the singing? That's the children. They go to watch and learn the songs. . . ."

Together the two women gazed at the hulking black rocks as the drumming rolled like thunder around them and the blood red sun was sucked slowly down behind the hill. Instinctively they stepped closer to one another as the children's voices, eerie in their innocence, chorused mysterious Malawian phrases into the night.

The singing continued all evening and the family was quiet as they sat around the fire, drums numbing their brains like a narcotic, making them incapable of speech. Beauty could not eat her supper. The solid white sadza seemed to cling to the roof of her mouth and to swell so she could not swallow it. Nausea welled up in her stomach and nudged at the back of her throat and she excused herself politely then hurried out of the house.

Outside, the drumming was louder, but a cool wind blew in her face as she leaned against the wall, lulling the sick heaving of her stomach.

"Are you feeling better?" asked a soft voice beside her. "The first child is always the worst. But the sickness means your baby is taking hold strongly in your womb."

Beauty stared at her mother-in-law in amazement. "How did you know?"

"When you've had ten children, you learn to recognize the signs. And I've been watching you, wondering when my son's wife would give me a grandchild. You've made me very happy, Mrs. Kanyemba," she said with a smile, using Beauty's married name for the first time. "Come, sit," she added briskly. "Someone else can clean the pots tonight. We have things to discuss."

As they talked, sitting alone together in the darkness,

while drums thrummed on in the distance, Beauty's vague fears were formed into firm shapes. Her good fortune, said her mother-in-law, at marrying into one of the better-off families in the compound, and at being chosen as the new health worker, already made her a target for jealousy. Her pregnancy exposed her to even more danger.

Those women in the compound who had lost babies, or who had never borne a live child at all, were described in great detail to Beauty. These were the women who were rumored to be witches and whose homes it was wise to avoid. Beauty knew well enough that such people tended to be envious of a pregnant woman and might try to steal her child's soul, or make it grow deformed in her womb. Some had already eaten their own babies, enslaved their souls and turned them into malevolent spirit creatures whom they dispatched at night to harm their enemies.

Some of the other dangers she had heard of already: that she should not gaze on ugly or misshapen people, nor look too long at a monkey or baboon, lest her child take on their characteristics; that she keep away from graves and refuse to eat the meat of a pregnant animal, lest she have a miscarriage. And the importance of secrecy was impressed on her again and again. It was so easy for an ill-wisher to harm an unborn child: sitting or loitering in her doorway could cause a long labor or still-born baby; building the cooking fire badly – with the thick end of the wood burning first, or with the sticks overlapping wastefully rather than set to meet at a point in the center – could cause the baby to be born upside-down.

She was also cautioned against going to the clinic too early, lest people suspect she was pregnant. "And if you give birth here on the compound, don't let any other woman near you. I was far away from my mother when my first baby was born, so I had to be delivered by a neighbor. I thought she was someone I could trust. But my child died and it must have been her doing. So I had all the rest of my babies alone: I cut their cords, buried the afterbirth, washed them clean all by myself. It was better to be safe. And all my other children lived."

The drumming continued intermittently the whole of the following month: sometimes starting in the middle of the afternoon; sometimes not until long after sunset. Often the big rocks at the foot of the hill were silent for days and people held their breath during the lull, bracing themselves for the next assault so there was no peace to be had even on quiet nights. Already irritable and short-tempered with hunger, people's taut nerves were stretched still tighter by the drums, till the whole compound was electric, hissing with resentment and suspicion.

Anxiety fed on hunger, fed on infection, fed on imagination; phantom ailments became real; real ailments became harder to bear; and the queue outside Mrs. Johnson's surgery grew longer each day. Esther and the three other women had begun their night-time raids on the maize fields, adding their own shifty-eyed wariness and constant fear of discovery to the general air of disease. And Beauty was caught up in it all – as securely as a fly in a web – strung out on the tension, vibrating with every movement of every other fly in the compound.

She saw danger everywhere: in the eyes of the people waiting patiently when she and Mrs. Johnson arrived to unlock the door to the surgery; in the faces of the women who went with Esther to steal maize; and in the gaze of every woman who did not have a child of her own.

Esther helped her make a chifumuro belt and she wore it night and day beneath her clothes, gaining a measure of comfort from feeling the little cloth package of roots chafing against her skin, rubbing its protective goodness into her. But it was such a small thing: no match for the bad airs that swirled round the compound that winter. She needed the power of her mother, and the spirits of the old ones, to keep her and her baby safe.

Sometimes, in the evening, when the drumming began, she would shut her eyes and try to recapture that feeling of security and well-being, of being surrounded and cared for by nurturing ghosts, that she had the night she first went to the big house. But it was impossible. She could tell there was no one there; she had been abandoned; they were all far away and she would not be with them again for months yet – not until she went home, as tradition decreed, eight weeks before her baby was due. But by then it might be too late.

But still Tendai continued to grow: a curved pink maggot, still only the size of Beauty's smallest toe, feeding on her flesh, growing fatter and rounder, eyes bulging beneath transparent skin, soft spine segments running the length of her little worm's body, arms and legs budding each side.

And so Beauty passed the days: sleeping and waking; dreaming, by night, of women's faces mad with blood-lust, tearing her baby from her womb with their bare hands, ripping it apart and gorging on its flesh; seeing, by day, those same women's faces waiting in the queue for the standpipe or meeting them unexpectedly on the path near her house. Her appetite faded to nothing, and her rounded cheeks began to flatten, then to hollow, beneath her curly-lashed eyes.

Seeing her growing so gaunt, her mother-in-law became suffocatingly solicitous, slyly serving her the best portions of food and gradually passing some of Beauty's chores on to her younger daughters. Peter, too, had noticed how thin and distracted his pretty young wife had become, how unmoved by his smiles and caresses, how she muttered and twitched in her sleep.

Then one night she woke with such a start, catapulted into consciousness with such violence, that she was sitting up trembling, the blanket clutched round her, before she had even opened her eyes. Peter rolled over, tugging the blanket away and leaving her shuddering and shivering with cold and terror, certain something was wrong, every sense straining for a clue in the dense darkness of the little hut.

With shaking hands she struck a match and lit the stump of a candle. Immediately the darkness retreated, replaced by jumping shadows as the little flame dipped and guttered. Then an instinct made her look down, and what she saw stopped her blood and tightened the skin on her scalp so her hair rose up like an animal's.

A cross had been cut in her pubic hair. There was no mistake. The flesh glowed pale amber, a living wound, in the thick black bush at the base of her belly.

Paralyzed with horror, she stared at the cross for a long time, as the shadows leapt round the room and an owl screeched from the mango tree outside. Eventually the spluttering of the candle, as the wick burnt down into a pool of spilt wax, brought her back to life. Like an automaton she reached for her clothes and set off into the night to fetch water. She fixed her eyes on the ground as she walked, closing her ears to the squeaking, scrabbling and rustling in the grass by the side of the path, and the whirr and whisper of wings overhead.

Back again at the hut, she quietly picked up a new candle, searched for and found Peter's razor, and – still moving as though in a trance – went behind the bamboo screen outside to shave.

Next day she was like a hunted animal: starting at sudden movements, cowering and cringing when looked at or spoken to. In her haste to remove the stigma from her body she had grazed the skin with the razor and the sting of her raw flesh was a constant reminder of the witch's brand that had appeared on her pubis.

How had it got there? Who had done it? She suspected everyone now; trusted no one. Perhaps her mother-in-law had been feeding her poison, covering her crime with false concern for her health. To make her sleep that deeply, so she would not wake when evil fingers etched their sign on her skin, there must have been a drug in her food. Or a spell cast on her by a witch. Everyone knew that a witch's most powerful skill is plunging her victims into a hypnotic sleep during which they will do whatever they are bidden.

And why had it been done? As a warning that she had earned someone's displeasure, perhaps. Or a sign that her child had been cursed. Perhaps the baby was already a gargoyle – had already grown horns, or hair on its face; a third arm, or scales on its back. Perhaps the baby was dead, waiting to be vomited.

Like the last time she was pregnant.

She had almost forgotten the school teacher. She had lost that baby too. At the time she was pleased; glad her body had expelled the weed that sprouted from the spore of her alien invader. But perhaps the rejection had been mutual. Her body had been sullied; her purity polluted. Perhaps no child would consent to grow there now; a punishment for submitting to those fumblings and poundings on the school storeroom floor; and for keeping them secret from her husband.

Somehow she carried out her duties: presenting herself at the big house as usual, smiling at Mrs. Johnson and doing her work in the surgery; then back to the compound, to fetch water and sweep floors, to wash clothes and collect firewood, to sweep floors and fetch water again. And so Beauty passed through the hours, with a stinging in her groin and a whirlpool of thoughts in her head, oblivious of the raised eyebrows that followed her haunt-eyed figure as she shrunk and slunk through her day.

At last, near the end of the afternoon, she found her feet taking her back towards the big house. Without consciously weighing up the choices – take time off to go home to her mother, ask Esther to recommend a nganga, risk confiding in her mother-in-law, confess about the school teacher to Peter – she had decided to go to Seguro, the old Malawian cook. She had not spoken to him since that first day, but had remembered the warmth of his hand on her arm and his concern when he warned her to take care. And, though his power to look inside her was unnerving, there was something familiar and reassuring about it: because it reminded her so much of her mother.

Seguro was sitting on the kitchen doorstep when she arrived.

"Ah, there you are Mrs. Kanyemba," he said, jumping nimbly to his feet and peering up into her face. "I was wondering when you would arrive. Come in, come in. The bosses are out so we will be able to talk in peace."

Wordlessly she followed him inside and he handed her the mug of tea he had waiting for her. Then he pushed her gently into a chair – just as he had the day she first met him. "Drink that, child. There's no hurry. I'll just finish clearing up, then we can go to my room."

She clasped the hot enamel in both hands and sipped the sweet liquid while his tiny wizened body darted busily round the kitchen – opening and shutting drawers and cupboards, piling pots and pans, clanking cutlery; then whisking a damp cloth over every surface till all was clean and gleaming.

The heat of the tea, the normal friendliness of his greeting and the mundane thoroughness with which he went about his chores made her feel better immediately. And when he nodded to her to follow him and led her round to the back of the house, she felt able – for the first time that day – to look around her without dreading what she might see.

He led her to a row of small rooms screened out of sight of the big house by a tall hedge. The doors of the rooms faced away from the main house too, so the Johnsons need never see the place where their servants lived. Seguro took a key from his pocket, opened one of the doors, and ushered Beauty inside.

"You know I don't usually like to get involved in trouble at the compound. I'm too old. And there's too much suspicion. You know, people here are far from their homes: it makes them afraid. They are surrounded by strangers, are tired from working too many hours, or hungry, or drunk on Chibuku – and they start imagining things. They think someone has buried a hexing charm in their house. Or they awake to find dust on their feet and imagine a witch has been making them walk in their sleep. And so they go to a nganga to get a spell put on whoever they suspect as their enemy . . . then that person goes to buy a stronger spell . . . Ah –" he shook his head – "there's no end to it. I'm too old to untangle all those knots."

While he was speaking, he pushed Beauty down again on to a filthy old sofa that took up the entire wall of the tiny room. Then he turned to a ramshackle table propped against another wall beside the bed and began ferreting about among some little piles of leaves, roots and sticks collected there. Beauty had not uttered a word. There had been no need. And she continued watching him in silence as he took one of the leaves – a big purple leathery one – and cut it into a rough circle with a knife.

"No, I don't throw bones like some of the other ngangas," he said in answer to her unspoken question. "This is what my father told me to do. He was a nganga too, before he died, and he taught me everything. Now he comes to help me whenever I have a new patient. He told me you were coming. But he hasn't said yet whether we can help you."

He paused for a moment, concentrating on cutting some careful slits in the leaf. "I'm not a crook either," he went on with dignity. "Sometimes there is nothing we can do and I have to send people away."

She started to interrupt. "And don't worry about paying me," he said, as if she had spoken. "I know none of you people have any money to spare. Just bring the baby to see me when she's born. That will be payment enough."

He filled a hollow gourd with water, gave it to Beauty to hold, and placed the slit leaf like a lid over the opening. Then, attaching it by a hook to a chain hanging from the ceiling, he upended it suddenly. Beauty's eyes grew round as she saw the gourd swinging upside-down, the water kept miraculously in place with the perforated leaf, barely a drop seeping out.

The old man did a little skip of pleasure. "Excellent, excellent. I thought as much," he grinned at her. "Now, let's get to work."

At last he let her speak and, without omitting a single detail – what would be the point? He would be sure to know she was lying – she told him she had woken to find a cross cut in her pubic hair, that she thought people resented her because she had been favored by the boss's wife, that she had miscarried a previous baby two years ago, but that she had pretended to her husband that she was a virgin and that now – in a very low voice, hardly daring to let the words pass into the air lest they turn out to be true – now she was worried that the child she was carrying was dead or de-formed and that she would never be able to bear children like a normal woman.

He listened, perched on the edge of his bed, eyes bright as black beads, head tilted to one side like a bird's. His bony skull was covered with sparse white stubble and there were ragged triangular holes cut in his big long-lobed ears. His hands – strangely smooth and large – lay still on his knees, as though age had shriveled and shrunk the rest of him leaving his hands untouched.

When she finished they sat in silence for a while, as the gourd swung gently on its chain between them, dripping slowly on to the rough cement floor. Beauty started to speak again but he held up a hand to stop her. His head was still on one side, listening, his body still tense with concentration, his eyes on her face still, but a little glazed and focused beyond her. She listened too. But all she could hear was the drip, drip of the water from the swaying gourd and the afternoon noises outside: sparrows chirruping in the hedge, a tractor starting up in the distance.

Eventually he relaxed. "Have you been bleeding?" he asked abruptly, focusing on her face again. "Good, very good. Your daughter is still growing strongly inside you."

Beauty felt her lungs expand as the iron clutch of anxiety was released and allowed her to breathe deeply again. But he reached out quickly across the space between them and grabbed her knee hard with his hand. "Don't think you're safe yet, child," he said, staring urgently into her face. "You have let yourself grow weak. You were right to think you are not fit to carry a child. It's true. Your body has no flesh on it; your mind flutters with fear; you have lost nearly all your protection; you're far away from home. No wonder this kind of thing happens!"

He let go of her knee and shook his head disapprovingly. "Nothing is as it should be on these compounds. The old ones are neglected; the old ways are forgotten; people are lost. There is evil everywhere. You have to make yourself

43

strong to withstand it. Unburden your mind to your husband; eat and sleep well; be gentle with yourself. And make sure you make peace with your family and go home to deliver your baby. You will need all your ancestors' help. You have grown weak," he repeated warningly. "This will not be an easy birth."

"Aren't you going to take the spell off me?" Beauty asked.

"There's evil everywhere," he said again. "What else can you expect? I will give you some medicine to make sure you don't lose the baby. But it's protection you need, not more spells. Now go away and do as I say."

She walked back slowly, thoughtfully, to the compound, clutching a glass bottle of brownish clear liquid in which floated – miraculously, since the width of what it contained was far bigger than the neck of the bottle – a neatly-tied bundle of roots and twigs.

The rasping wounds in her groin still stung, but the sand was warm under her bare feet and little grasshoppers, sunning themselves on the path, flicked away like bullets from a pistol as she approached. She passed two Malawian women starting out on the long walk into the bush for firewood. One of them – the younger – was massively pregnant, waddling sway-backed with the weight of her belly. Beauty found herself smiling sympathetically at her and was surprised by the warmth of the grin she received in return. She was still smiling when she got back home.

The hair grew back eventually: first an itchy stubble, then soft bristles, finally corkscrewing again into a bouncy mat of tight black curls. And, as it grew, and as the level in the bottle of brown liquid sank, so Beauty's appetite returned, her fears began to fade and, slowly, her mind started to turn outwards again. With the resilience of the young, her footsteps grew jaunty once more, she opened her arms again gladly to her husband and began to look forward to the day she would board the bus to Chikombera for her first lesson in health care at the clinic.

She had learnt a lot in her time with Mrs. Johnson. In fact it all seemed rather easy – just a question of matching symptoms to the row of jars and bottles on the shelf. And if someone had a symptom which did not tally with an available remedy, then Mrs. Johnson simply packed them off to the clinic in Chikombera where, presumably, they had a larger supply of medicines. She already knew what to give people for the commonest ailments and was eager to learn more; eager, too, to prove her worth to those unheard voices that questioned her selection in the first place.

She saw the looks of grudging respect Mrs. Johnson received from her patients and could tell she enjoyed playing doctor: flicking importantly through the pages of her medical books (there were three now) with her glasses perched on her nose; shaking pills into little brown envelopes; finally entering name, ailment and treatment almost triumphantly in her big blue record book. Beauty wanted to feel some of the satisfaction that emanated from her employer as she flipped shut the big books at the end of her morning sessions; and she wanted those looks of respect to be directed at her too.

And so a little halo of calm settled round Beauty in the weeks following her visit to Seguro: an oasis in the midst of the ferment that continued in the compound – as the nights grew colder and longer, the drumming more frequent and frantic, the children wailed louder and the women's raids on the maize fields grew more and more daring.

"Be careful, please," Beauty warned Esther each time they met. But there was the spark of recklessness in her cousin's eyes, and she shrugged off the caution carelessly.

"Why don't you come with us?" she teased. "It's easy. The guards hate patrolling when it's as cold as this, so it's not so dangerous now."

So Beauty had to content herself with pushing a ten-dollar note into Violet's small fist – she would walk to Chikombera for her training sessions, she decided, so that she could let Esther have her bus fare.

"Just stay away one week, for me," she pleaded, as Violet knelt respectfully, in the traditional way, to give the money to her mother. Esther slipped it quickly into her blouse.

"All right. I promise. One week," she said.

Beauty set out before the rising bell on the day of the first training session. It would take four hours to walk there and she wrapped a blanket round her body and put her shoes and a covered bowl of cold sadza in a bundle on her head. The cold sand chilled her feet, making her shiver, so she quickened her pace trying to get warm, fixing her eyes resolutely on the lightening horizon and refusing to think about the restless ghosts winging back to their graves after a night of mischief.

Soon her footsteps took her on to a single-track tarred road: kinder to the feet but impossible to walk on when the sun was high. This was the way she would have to come if she had her baby at the clinic; the way every woman in labor had to walk if there was no money to spare for a bus fare and if they wanted to be delivered by a nurse. Four hours – maybe in the searing shimmering heat of the mid-summer sun: stopping to sit out each contraction; praying you got there in time. No wonder so many gave birth to their babies at home. Perhaps she'd be able to help them soon.

As the darkness lifted and a red arc of sun crested the hills in the distance, she began to pass people walking in the opposite direction: men mostly, some in tattered felt-brimmed hats, some wobbling on heavy-framed bicycles; and children, with blankets draped round their bony shoulders and buckets balanced on their round tufted heads, on their way to a tap by the roadside.

When the sun was high and yellow, the clinic finally came into sight – a cluster of white buildings shaded by an ancient syringa tree. She stopped for a moment to fold her blanket and slip on her shoes, then walked shyly to join a group of people waiting under the tree.

Six hours later she was on her way home again: a tall slender figure, all boy from behind, a thoughtful frown creasing her pretty girl's face as she walked along the sun-warmed tarmac. It had not been at all what she had expected.

"Forward with development!" they had all chanted exuberantly at the end of the lesson. "Forward with good health and happiness! Forward with full stomachs and clean water!" And then – deeper, full of disgust and determination – "Down with bad housing and low wages! Down with hunger and dirt! Down with cruelty and exploitation!" No mention of drugs and doctors.

And as she walked Esther's words came back to her: "You can't feed a child on pills. . . . They say he's underweight – that's why he's always sick." And she remembered Lovemore's arms as Esther caressed him: thin like a monkey's, the skin gray and lusterless as tree bark. And Seguro's words too: "Your body has no flesh on it; you've lost your protection. It's protection you need, not more spells."

One foot after another on the warm black tarmac; four hours of footsteps; four hours to think before the tendrils of smoke from the cooking fires came into sight winding upwards over the compound.

Next day as she stood behind Mrs. Johnson, handing

down boxes and bottles from the shelf and mechanically translating Shona symptoms into English, she tried to look differently at each person who sidled into the room.

"Cough and fever," she translated for Mrs. Johnson – but her eyes saw a ten-year-old shivering, dressed in shorts and a man's shirt with the arms torn off at the shoulders.

"Diarrhea for three days," she said, looking at a baby's tearless eyes, at the skin stretched tight over his skull, and at the hungry hollows in his mother's dark cheeks.

"Diarrhea and vomiting": an older child this time – old enough to totter into the vlei and play by herself in the dirt, but too young to wash her hands, even if there was money to buy soap.

And so on down the queue: patients shuffled in, pages were turned, names neatly written down, bottles taken down, opened, screwed shut and replaced.

Suddenly there was a hubbub of noise outside and the orderly, respectful queue broke up and clustered excitedly round a woman who had just arrived from the compound. Mrs. Johnson raised her eyebrows exaggeratedly at Beauty and clicked her tongue with exasperation.

"*Now* what's happened? Oh, go and find out what's the matter, dear," she said to Beauty. "And tell them to calm down or we'll be here all day."

Beauty could hear for herself what had happened.

"The guards caught some women stealing maize early this morning," she reported, her voice as expressionless as if she were still translating symptoms. "And the police have arrived to take them away."

PART TWO

Miriam

*M*iriam stared down at the baby and she didn't know what to do. How many times had she knelt like this – on beaten mud, cement, or in the open bush; at midday, midnight, or in the deathly haunted hours before dawn? A hundred, two hundred times? But now she didn't know what to do.

It had not been a difficult birth. The mother already had five children: her body had been stretched and moulded by the passage through it of their big round skulls and impatient flailing limbs. There was pain, of course. But, like a plough – oiled and put away for the long summer months – it was the pain of a good, strong machine easing into well-remembered motion after disuse. Already her breathing was steady and she was struggling in the arms of her old mother-in-law, who had supported her for the last tumultuous hours, and straining forward to see the sex of her new baby.

It was a boy: genitals dark reddish-brown against the creamy pallor of his body; tacked on like a comical after-thought; disproportionately large and swollen, lest there be any doubt that this child was male. Satistified, the mother

51

subsided back against the old woman kneeling behind her on the mud floor.

Then they waited, the two women; the mother and the grandmother: one reclining backwards like a beached whale, naked from the waist down, belly still bloated, thighs streaked with blood and mucus, the thick white umbilical cord protruding obscenely, like a huge parasite, from her vagina; the other dark as a shadow, face crumpled with exhaustion, shrunken and wizened like the cast-off husk of the powerful fruiting body she held in her arms. Together they waited expectantly for Miriam to do something. But Miriam couldn't move.

Minutes passed. Miriam stared at the baby, who had begun to writhe around energetically on the sack she had spread on the floor between his mother's legs. He was probably cold, Miriam thought vaguely: thrust from the heat of his mother's straining body into the chill air of a Zimbabwean winter's night, skin still damp, hair plastered to his little head.

"The newborn baby cannot shiver. He should be wrapped immediately. Cut the cord with a new razor blade and tie it in three places with boiled cotton thread."

The cord. Miriam stared at the cord.

"On no account must anything be put on the cord. It must be kept spotlessly clean. A dirty cord can kill a newborn baby."

The cord was dangerous: that she knew. It could coil round a baby's neck like a snake, throttling it so that, even as the child's mouth was opening to suck in its first lungful of air, that first gasp was a gasp of death not life. How many times had she slipped her fingers in past the hot folds of vagina circling a baby's neck as it was born fighting for breath? How many times had she grasped the evil white tentacle wrapped round the child's throat and eased the slimy thing back over its head?

Or it could kill by letting in malevolent vapors that would circulate round the baby's body causing all kinds of illness as the child tried to vomit or cough or shit out the badness. Oh, she had seen the cord kill. She had held them in her arms, the children who sleep by the river, held them as their little bodies battled on the boundaries of life and death, their untutored muscles in confusion – breathing vomit, shitting water, swallowing blood. Or just locked solid, rigid with terror, unable to cry, lips pulled back from bare gums in a grotesque paralyzed grimace.

That was how she had lost her second son. He had grimaced and grinned, twitched and clenched, as fever burned through his brain like an electric current and jerked his tiny muscles into the spastic spasms that killed him. And they had taken him out of her arms, her mother and her aunt Eustina; had washed him and wrapped him in a blanket; and had laid him to rest in a clay pot that they buried beside the river, where all the dead babies are buried; where the water can wash them clean of the ill will and bad magic of the adult world and lull them into the sweet sleep of innocence.

It was the cord that killed him, Eustina told her then, all those years ago. The medicine she had put on it had not been strong enough and the evil had managed to penetrate. But now they were saying it was the medicine itself that was evil; that the cord should not be touched; that it should be left naked, open and vulnerable to the air, with just a bit of clean cotton tied round it for protection.

Miriam had the cotton and the razor blade beside her, still wrapped in the little plastic bag they'd given her at the clinic. And she had the medicine mixed ready too: soot from the family's cooking fire to help the cord stump dry quickly and to seal its passage against the air; and dust from the entrance to the house, where people had walked, each leaving a trace of their spirit which would protect the baby from any future harm they might want to do to it.

And still the two women waited: respectfully, patiently, trustingly. The old woman pulled a blanket up round her daughter's shoulder and began massaging the back of her neck. The wood in the fire shifted and settled, billowing smoke out in great fat clouds. The baby started to cry – an urgent panic-stricken wailing – jabbing his tiny fists blindly at the smoke, his movements tugging on the cord that still linked him to his mother.

His cry cut imperiously into the silence, demanding attention, and his mother started immediately into action. She heaved her tired body forward and lumbered over on to her hands and knees ready for the final animal effort of the long night. Miriam didn't try to stop her. She could not bring herself to tell this woman, whose experienced body had already delivered itself of six babies – could not bring herself to suggest, as they taught in the clinic, that she really should lie on her back to give birth.

The big body squatted in labor as she had always done, and then turned over and knelt to expel the afterbirth as she had always done. And Miriam was expected to do as she had always done too: wait for the afterbirth to be delivered, then cut the cord and apply the medicine she had prepared. But the clinic people said to cut the cord immediately: "Attend to the baby first; then look after the mother." As if to emphasize the point, the baby's cries took on an hysterical note and Miriam finally opened the plastic bag and took out the cotton.

Having made that decision, the actions were simple and familiar. In less than a minute the cord was tied and cut. The she hesitated again, looking at the severed stump lolling pale and heavy against the darker skin of the baby's belly: a dead lump of foreign flesh – neither part mother nor part baby – and it was the work of a moment to smear it with the thick brown mixture she had ready.

Swaddling the infant snugly in a blanket, Miriam then turned back to the mother who had started grunting as her muscles responded stoically to the last contractions of her womb. Miriam picked up the cord that hung down loosely between her legs and pulled gently on it, urging the mother to push harder. Lowering her head to the floor and bracing her knees apart with the effort, the woman did as she was asked. But nothing happened.

Normally Miriam would not have been alarmed: it sometimes took as long as half an hour before the placenta came out. But this time she was uneasy. It was the first time she had ever cut the cord while the afterbirth was still inside; the first time she had felt it swing, rubbery and empty, from her hand, like a length of pallid hosepipe. What if severing it early made the placenta adhere like a limpet to the womb instead of sloughing off smoothly and cleanly as it should?

That was the thing she feared most. If it was the cord that killed the babies, it was the afterbirth that killed the mothers. It was as though the two half-human pieces of flesh – neither really a part of any body – resented coming to an end of their usefulness, resented being cut off like spent meat, and wanted to steal back some of the life they had given. The cord sucked in vile vapors or strangled the infant it had nurtured; the placenta ripped itself apart like a rotten bloody rag, leaving fragments stuck fast to the womb wall which continued to drink precious blood by the cupful and to spill it wantonly into the cavity where the baby had lain.

At first all would seem normal. A lusty child would lie screaming on the floor and faces would start to relax, almost forgetting about the placenta. But gradually the mother would stop straining and would collapse on her side, heart racing, face gray, forehead clammy and cold. And a hand placed on her belly would feel it soft and swollen instead of tautly contracted, spongy instead of hard and tight, as her

55

heart slowly and secretly pumped it full of blood through the rags of flesh that hung in tatters from the lining of the womb.

Miriam had only seen one woman die that way. But the ghost of that woman's bloodless face would sometimes pass for a second or two over the faces of some of the older women she delivered. Earlier that year she had seen the dead woman's shadow on her own darling Alita's face as she slumped exhausted in the last stages of her youngest son's birthing. Desperately Miriam tried every trick she knew to stem the stealthy seepage of blood: first massaging the ominous softness with her hands; then pouring salt water down Alita's throat and holding her tongue down with a spoon to make her gag and vomit, praying that the violence of her guts' convulsions would cause her womb to contract too. Then, when that failed, throwing herself again on to her sister-in-law's belly and kneading it with all her strength to force it physically to close tight on those treacherous open wounds inside. And all the time heaping curses on her aunt Eustina – for allowing this to happen.

"You old witch," Miriam had shouted as she pummeled the deadly soft flesh of Alita's belly. "Where are you when I need you? Come and help, you lazy old woman. Don't you dare leave my sister to die." And, finally, Eustina had come and had told Miriam to give Alita rapfumo – a herbal preparation that contracted the womb so strongly that Miriam hardly ever used it. And Alita had lived; though she had been taken to hospital next day and given a transfusion to replace the blood she had lost. Six months later she was still weak and pale.

Suddenly, kneeling in the dark hut, the dead cord dangling from her hands, her eyes stinging from the smoke, Miriam felt a surge of anger against her aunt Eustina – for not preparing her for this. She had trusted her aunt, believed everything she had been taught about safeguarding the

health of mothers and their babies. But now the clinic people were saying it was all wrong; that the old ways were
primitive and dangerous. Who was right? How was she to
decide? And why wasn't Eustina here now to help her?

The woman ducked her head and grunted again, trying to
expel the afterbirth as another contraction took hold inside
her. Her buttocks seemed mountainous in the ruddy glow of
the fading embers: great globes of flesh thrust shamelessly
upwards as she rode the wave of pain. And then, just as
Miriam was looking around for a spoon to ram down her
throat to make her gag, the vagina gaped open once more
and out slid the placenta – whole and unbroken, sly and
slimy, like a seal slipping out of an underwater cave.
Miriam reached forward just in time to catch it and cradled
the shiny cushion of red meat with relief and a brief prayer
of thanks.

Eustina had been there all the time, naturally; fidgeting with
frustration as Miriam paused and hesitated over each stage
of the birthing procedure. She had tried again and again to
get her niece's attention, but Miriam's senses were closed to
her. Instead Eustina was made to endure the one-way tirade
with no opportunity to defend herself.

"Silly woman, silly woman," she shouted as loudly as she
could in Miriam's ear. "Whoever said I was infallible?"

But Miriam couldn't hear her. So Eustina just stood quietly and watched the familiar firelit tableau: one pair of
woman's hands clenching and unclenching with pain;
another pair caressing and soothing; a third pair cutting and
binding, probing and pulling, washing and holding.

"There, you see? That was all right, wasn't it? What was
all the fuss about, you great goose?" Eustina said later, as
she walked home beside Miriam in the darkness just before
dawn. Miriam didn't say anything, but steadily quickened

her pace until she was striding furiously along the path with her face set in a mask of anger.

"Come on, come on, I know you can hear me," gasped Eustina breathlessly as she scuttled along trying to keep up on her bent old legs. "I never pretended to be perfect. If you believed I was, that's your fault, not mine. And whoever said change would be easy, eh? Eh?" And she prodded Miriam in the ribs with a long bony finger. Her niece winced, but didn't slow down. And eventually Eustina gave up and let her go.

"Go on then, you stubborn goat," she called, sitting down on a rock to get her breath back. "But don't come crawling to me next time you need help – because I won't be there – do you hear me?" she shouted after Miriam's determinedly receding figure. "You're on your own now."

It wasn't true, of course. Eustina would never abandon Miriam. Their souls were twinned, entwined with one another; linked together as closely as the two wings of a butterfly: where one flew the other had to follow. Miriam was her aunt's window on the living world; Eustina was her niece's light piercing the recesses of the past. Physically they were twins too, their faces like the heads on two coins issued fifty years apart but from the same mint: the same long thin upper lip, cleft chin and heavy eyebrows; the same small broad nose and graceful neck; the same chameleon eyes, at times so dark they seemed like fathomless sightless holes, at times all glittering, flashing brown surfaces.

Miriam's eyes glittered and flashed now as she walked briskly down the path. It had been such a straightforward birth: no complications; no delays; no breath of witchcraft. She should have been able to do the delivery in her sleep. Yet she had been paralyzed with indecision. Should the woman be made to lie on her back? When should she cut the cord? Would the placenta come out safely? Would the woman bleed to death? Would the baby die because she'd dressed the cord stump with medicine? But if she had left the mixture off, would she have exposed the child to even more danger . . .?

On she walked, shaking her head, furious at her own confusion. Usually she was so sure. So familiar were the contours of a pregnant woman's body, it was like running her hands over her own skin. Her slender fingers could sense instantly – from hints of hardness they found buried in the springy cushion of a mother's flesh – the exact shape or angle of the baby beneath. And if she discovered something unusual – a convex hollow instead of a concave bone, the knob of an elbow or knee where a buttock or forehead should be – she would take a deep breath, close her eyes for a moment, and abandon her hands to Eustina.

Eustina had never let her down before. Oh, sometimes the two of them had been defeated: by a pelvis whose bones would not open wide enough for the baby's head to pass through, or by a spell that sucked all the strength from the mother so that she had no power to push, despite the herbal potions Miriam gave her to drink, and her child suffocated waiting to be born. But Eustina had always been there when she'd called, ready to hiss instructions into her ear or simply to step into Miriam's body and take over completely, moving her long-fingered hands for her.

Not realizing that it had been she, Miriam, who had refused to respond to her aunt's frantic attempts to make contact, she let her resentment grow as her bare feet pounded on along the dark dusty paths that forked and converged round the trunks of trees, or dipped and climbed out of little dry creek beds.

Eustina had made her look like a fool, she thought angrily. People expected her to cope confidently when they summoned her to their dim smoky huts in the middle of the night, or when they carried their sick children to her house. They trusted her, respected her. But if she felt lost and confused, unable to trust her own judgement, how could she expect other people to continue offering their bodies and their children's bodies to her when they needed help? She had fought long and hard to build her reputation. Was Eustina going to let her lose it all now?

On she walked, until she reached the river itself: just a trickle after the months of autumn drought; a narrow ribbon of water, pearlized with the rippling reflection of the distant dawn horizon, creeping silently over its bed of flat stones. Miriam stopped and sat on the bank, staring out across the dark expanse of stone and gravel either side of the sliver of silvery water.

It was a hushed and sacred place; a place to lower your voice and tiptoe through, for fear of waking the sleeping souls nestling beneath your feet. Dominic, her son, was here somewhere, limbs folded neatly, his fever-glazed eyes closed for ever. But she was never shown exactly which stone had been raised then replaced over his little clay coffin. The elders said it was better kept secret; it would not do for a mother to mourn too long for a dead child when there were so many living ones who needed her.

She pulled her blanket shawl tighter round her shoulders and breathed deeply, letting the peaceful air flow into her lungs. Slowly her body relaxed, her senses opened again, and she could hear them – hear the rising and falling of a hundred tiny chests, hear their faint whimpering, chortling and snuffling, as they slept.

The tender stillness of the place soothed the turbulence in her head and took the edge off her anger. Anger would not help these spirits now. She had seen so many die: scarcely a woman in the village had reached forty without having to watch the pulse flutter and fade in a smooth brown forehead, or to feel the warmth of a beloved body grow cold in her arms. Though she had seen it happen so often, it was something she could never get used to: a child, a blameless child – eyes wide and greedy for experience; excited, delighted with the world – all that bursting new life quenched and quelled for ever. All these small deaths, the snuffing out of all these infant candles: this was the reason she was so troubled. Had Eustina really misled her for all these years? Were the clinic people right? Could some of these deaths have been prevented?

Wearily she struggled to her feet and, as the sky glowed a pale rosy mauve, set off on the last half-mile of her homeward journey.

The woman she had delivered lived in one of the outlying households, close to the fence marking the boundary between black and white land. On the white side the dry bush was deserted, save for cattle that wandered thigh-deep placidly munching, through a waving silver sea of dry grass. On the black side the sea was shallower and sparse, with patches of red earth showing in places where the goats had nibbled to the roots so often that the grass could no longer gather strength to thrust yet more tender green shoots up into the sunlight. Here the trees were fewer and clusters of thatched houses dotted the landscape like shells on a shore. Here and there were the uneven fenced enclosures where cows and goats were herded for the night, penned securely away from the carefully tended vegetable plots beside the open wells.

As Miriam approached the cluster that was her home, she could see that the twins – her grand-daughters – were already up. Through the kitchen door she could just make out the silhouette of one of them – she could not tell which – squatting down to blow the dull embers of the fire into a bright yellow flame. And she glimpsed the back of the other disappearing into the bush with a tall cylindrical bucket on her head. The door to Daniel's hut was shut, so perhaps he had left for school earlier, while it was still pitch dark.

She sighed as she surveyed her home: once humming with activity and life, the doors of its four sturdy huts once constantly opening and closing as her sons and daughters cheerfully and chaotically bounced through their days. Now it seemed almost desolate. There were no young boys to bed down in the kitchen at night; only Daniel was left in the older boys' hut; the twins – still only six years old – barely filled a quarter of the girls' hut; and she, Miriam, slept alone in the big square marital room, with only heaped bags of fertilizer for company.

She walked towards it now, opened the door, and leaned against it for a moment looking inside. It was just as she'd left it at sundown the previous evening. The blankets still half-folded, where she was interrupted in laying them out for the night; the candle still on its side where it had fallen when she hurriedly blew it out; the big clay pots of beer still bubbling gently as they fermented in the corner. Well, of course it was just as she'd left it. Since Fidelis had died no one but she ever came in here.

Suddenly a wave of mourning and loneliness broke over her: for baby Dominic, asleep by the river; for the other five babies, now grown, who had each slept for two years by her side beneath the rafters of this big old hut; for Fidelis, dear departed husband, patient partner; for Eustina too, cantankerous double, pain in her side, her weakness and her strength. And for herself: midwife, child doctor, neighbor, mother of two generations; a woman who could speak with spirits but could not write her own name; who could turn a breech baby in the womb but didn't know the date of her own birthday; who had studied childbirth's secrets for two decades, piling up bits of knowledge like grains of rapoko in a basket, only to have her hoard tipped over and trodden into the dust.

And she had another lesson at the clinic today: another two hours of walking to do, another three hours of contradictory information to absorb, before she could lie down to rest on the blankets waiting ready on the floor. She turned her back on the bleak room and sat down in the doorway, leaning back against the frame again with her eyes shut and letting the first thin rays of the winter sun warm her face.

After a while she heard tentative footsteps approaching and opened her eyes to see her two grand-daughters smiling uncertainly at her. They were not really twins – one was Maud's eldest daughter, the other Lilian's youngest – but they were born within days of one another and looked so similar that they were always referred to as "the twins." The taller of the two, Patience, had a battered enamel bowl of hot water on her head which she lowered carefully to the floor in Miriam's hut. The other one, Margaret, was carrying a clean cloth, a bar of soap, and a mug of sweet gruel. There they stood, two small, slim six-year-old figures, stiff with the effort to comfort and please their fierce and mysterious grandmother.

At the sight of their sweet anxious faces, Miriam melted. Opening her arms wide, she cuddled the two bony litte bodies close to her.

Three hours later her feet were again walking briskly along the maze of narrow dusty paths that threaded their way from household to barn to well, from road to school to beer hall, skirting boulders and bushes, arcing widely round the bases of looming kopjes. As usual she tied her red, white and black-patterned scarf round her head to set her apart from the others attending the course and to remind the nurses that they were not simply dealing with an ordinary grandmother, but an established spirit medium, a nganga, with a certificate of registration with Zenata, Zimbabwe's official Institute of Traditional Medicine. But today it felt like an empty gesture, a vanity. She didn't feel like a nganga any more and she no longer trusted the advice of her familiar spirit. In fact, were she not haunted by a myriad tiny ghosts and by the pale face of a woman she had watched bleed to death, she would never have registered for the course at all, would never have chosen to place her skill and reputation beside those of the nurses or dared have them compared and judged so publicly.

When at last she arrived at the clinic she was absorbed immediately into a cordial and orderly round of greetings as the other middle-aged and elderly women gathered there bowed their heads and clapped their hands, some even curt-seying to one another. The stateliness of these ancient courtesies – often skimped or shrugged off by the young, but enacted with such dignity by this motley collection of grand-mothers, all dressed in their very best clothes – restored a little of Miriam's self-confidence. Rich and poor, in ragged cardigans and fray-toed sneakers or lace-trimmed blouses and neatly zipped skirts, these women all knew Miriam and respected her. Some had even called her to help them deliver their own daughters' babies – the greatest compliment one woman could pay to another. Warmed by their approbation, Miriam held her chin up and squared her shoulders, ready for her next confrontation with Sister Tekedi.

The lesson that day began with a repetition of the main points they had covered the previous week. Sister Tekedi stood like a squat sergeant-major in the center of the clinic delivery room, which had been converted into a cramped lecture theater by lining the walls with benches from the waiting area outside. The bed had been pushed into the middle and served as a stage on which various parts of the delivery were mimed. Sister Tekedi patted a big cardboard box on the bed with her hand and smiled importantly round at her audience, asking for a volunteer.

A short fat woman got up readily and, amidst murmurs of encouragement, pretended to heat some water into which she dropped some pieces of cotton. She then spread out two empty plastic fertilizer sacks in front of the cardboard box that represented the laboring mother's torso. Repeating, word for word, the previous lecture, she carefully wiped – from top to bottom, one side at a time, with some little pieces of cloth – round a hole cut in the side of the box, and finally delivered the baby itself – brown nylon stockings knotted and sewn into a passable baby shape – through the hole. First the head appeared and was duly wiped with more bits of cloth. Then the rest of the baby's body, followed by a sizable length of plaited rope representing the cord.

"On no account should any medicine be put on the cord," she intoned, pretending to tie the boiled cotton threads round it.

Miriam didn't need to watch. She knew the sequence by heart; had even practiced it in real life just the previous night. The difference was that the woman she delivered had squatted on the floor in the traditional way and was not conveniently displayed on a waist-high clinic bed; her torso was tilted half vertical, half reclining – not spread-eagled on its back the way the box on the bed was – so Miriam had to kneel on the cold beaten mud and bend right over to catch the first glimpse of the baby's emerging head. And then there was the mixture she had put on the cord – in direct contradiction to the clinic's teaching.

The women applauded as the first volunteer lowered a cotton sanitary towel over the gaping hole, like a curtain coming down at the end of a play, to mark the end of her demonstration. Sister Tekedi stood up again, smiling her approval, then, turning away from Miriam's corner of the room, she asked if there were any questions.

Miriam hesitated, intimidated by the way the nurse had so pointedly averted her stocky white-starched figure. But she caught the eye of the other nurse – a gentle, willowy woman in glasses who occasionally brought her own children to Miriam for treatment. That nurse nodded encouragingly and Miriam put up her hand.

"Yes, Mrs. Zvidzai, what is it this time?" Sister Tekedi sighed, like a harassed parent addressing an irritating child. Miriam asked her question. She was worried about the cord, she said. In her many years of practice – and she tried to stress the length of her experience – she had come to recognize several abnormalities of the umbilical cord, each of which could make a baby dangerously ill if it were not treated promptly by the application of some preventive potion. Everyone knew – and here she looked round at the circle of old women who were listening attentively and nodding – that a baby was very susceptible to diseases carried by bad air. Bad air could enter the child by many routes, but the fontanelle and umbilicus were the most vulnerable points. If they were forbidden to put anything on the cord, or give the child any medicine when it was born, how could they stop the bad air entering and the baby falling ill?

What exactly were these abnormalities of the umbilicus? Sister Tekedi wanted to know, indicating by a raised eyebrow that she did not really take Miriam seriously. Undeterred, Miriam went on to describe in great detail certain subtle changes in skin color and texture and in the outline of veins and arteries. She had studied these painstakingly over the years in an attempt to account for subsequent ills suffered by the children in her care. She was convinced that there was a pattern.

She did not convince Sister Tekedi, however, who stood –

starched seams straining to contain her plump body – and smiled indulgently.

"All the conditions you describe are perfectly normal," she pronounced kindly and dismissively. "There's no need to treat them at all."

Miriam kept standing for a while, wanting to continue the discussion, but Sister Tekedi ignored her and went on to repeat her warnings about cord hygiene and eventually Miriam sat down again.

Sister Tekedi went on to warn them against attempting to deliver what she termed "abnormal presentations": babies in an unusual position in the womb – with forehead instead of crown pressed against the opening, for instance, or twins, or babies lying upside-down so a foot or buttock rested against the outlet. The latter two cases should always be delivered by an expert, at the clinic, she said, puffing her ample chest out proudly.

Another woman put up her hand. How could they tell whether the woman had an abnormal presentation until it was too late to do anything about it, she wanted to know. Sister Tekedi surveyed them all sternly with her hands on her hips. It was absolutely vital, she said, that every pregnant woman came to the clinic for at least one antenatal check-up before they delivered. Ideally they should come five or six times, so that they could have their blood pressure monitored and be given their anti-tetanus injections plus any medication they needed. The nurses at the clinic – and here she smiled conspiratorially at the tall willowy nurse – would then examine them and would be able to detect whether the baby was lying abnormally or whether there was any other reason why the mother needed special treatment.

But what about those women who had not been for an antenatal check-up, the questioner persisted. She lived in a village nearly three and a half hours' walk from the clinic and some of the older women there regularly went the entire nine months without consulting anyone about their pregnancies. And what about the ones who went into labor unexpectedly early, or in the middle of the night when there was no transport to take them to the clinic, or those who had no money to pay for transport or bus fares?

The others murmured their agreement.

Sister Tekedi frowned. It was a problem, she knew. Most families did not have easy access to a car or truck, and the buses were so infrequent and only ran during the day in any case. She told them she would teach them how to examine women earlier in their pregnancies, so that they would be able to identify difficult cases and make sure they got to the clinic in time.

The old women exchanged uneasy glances. At one of their first lessons, when they were learning how to feel for a contraction to establish that labor had really started, the nurses had asked a couple of pregnant women from the morning's antenatal session to wait behind and serve as guinea pigs for the old women to practice on. But none of the grandmothers wanted to touch them. They were afraid, for one thing, of harming the unborn baby by the necessary firm kneading movements. But, more important, they were wary of laying themselves open to blame for subsequent difficulties in the birth which people might then attribute to their having touched the mother's abdomen.

That was the main reason why, apart from exceptional occasions, they only ever delivered the babies of their close relatives. Only a niece, a daughter or a grand-daughter would trust that they were innocent of witchcraft if any ill befell their baby. Only a woman – like Miriam – who came from a long line of trusted midwives and healers, would dare come into such close contact with an unrelated mother and her baby at such a vulnerable time of their lives.

The Children who Sleep by the River

Miriam put her hand up again. Why, she wanted to know, didn't the nurses teach the women how to deliver some of the difficult cases themselves? Then they would know how to cope when it was impossible to get the mother to the clinic. She herself, she pointed out proudly, had already success-fully delivered three sets of twins and numerous breech presentations. Another murmur of approval greeted her suggestion, and Miriam felt she had regained some of the ground she lost when Sister Tekedi snubbed her earlier.

Everyone knew that her magic hands had untangled babies – like so many miniature Houdinis – from the most complicated internal knots, or extricated them unharmed through the tightest of pelvic gateways. And perhaps they also remembered the babies that the clinic itself had lost over the years: the breech babies strangled by their own cords; the white babies and the blue babies with the color of life extinguished; and the women who had been bundled into the ambulance and rushed to hospital forty miles away, with a foot protruding from their vagina, a drip attached to their arm, a child whose faltering heart could no longer be heard inside their womb.

"Who are the real experts?" was the unspoken question Miriam wanted to see hanging in the air. And there it was, faint and tenuous: the shadow of a doubt in the assumed superiority of the two nurses rustling crisply in their starched white uniforms.

Sister Tekedi looked uncomfortable, aware as anyone of the clinic's imperfect record. But she refused to concede the point. No, all unusual cases were to be referred to the clinic: as were all first births and all women who had six or more previous babies. So the lesson continued, with a demonstra-tion of the delivery and examination of the placenta. They were also taught how to massage the woman's belly if it felt soft after the placenta was expelled and warned for the umpteenth time against dosing the mother with any medicine. But there was no mention of making her gag or vomit to make sure the placenta came out in the first place – nor of the importance of burying it behind the door to ensure no evil-doer could get hold of it.

There was an expectant silence when Sister Tekedi again paused for questions. But this time Miriam did not put up her hand. She was exhausted after her sleepless night and felt she had fought enough battles for one day. So the rest of the lesson passed uneventfully, with the old women separating into groups as usual to practice, miming what they had learnt and then laboriously going through it all again in a series of public demonstrations to the rest of the class.

Faint from lack of sleep, Miriam watched the solemn enthusiasm of the other women with a kind of hazy detachment. They held the imaginary placenta tenderly in their hands; recited their lesson as reverently as a prayer. She was envious of the simple faith with which they accepted the new ideas; they seemed so grateful that their traditional role of midwife had been recognized by the government. It was not that they were passive: far from it – by no means all of the debates had been initiated by Miriam. But, because they had not dedicated their whole lives to this work, they had much less at stake than she. And if the old ways were criticized? Well, they would argue the point to start with, naturally. But, once convinced, most of them would be happy to change.

For once Miriam slipped away before the singing that marked the end of the sessions. She did not have the heart to raise her voice with the others, stamping and swaying to the rhythms of the new health songs they had learnt at the start of the course.

Tired, she was so tired. Her feet felt like lead as she

threaded her way back through the dusty brown lace-work of paths spread out across the golden afternoon. Even the little eddies of greetings, that marked her progress past the homes of the many women she'd delivered, failed to lift her mood as they would normally have done. She barely saw the unruly escort of "her" children who danced along behind her or ran shrieking off ahead, manic little outriders to her drag-footed progress through the village. But, nearing her own home, she did look up when she heard Alita's gentle voice calling her name, and turned gladly off the path towards her sister-in-law's big rambling homestead.

"Don't ask me about the lesson, sister dear," she said, subsiding gratefully on to a little stool beside the open kitchen door. "I just want to sit quietly near you for a while and let some of your calm rub off on me." Alita nodded, understanding, and knelt again over the big flat stone where she was grinding rapoko.

Her body began undulating rhythmically to and fro once more as she leant her weight behind the smaller stone she held loosely in her hands: pulling it backwards over the smooth surface of the big stone, trapping a pinch of small red grains, then pushing it forwards over them, crushing them to a puff of pinkish-white flour. And back again; and forwards; with a hollow rasping sound, white the heap of hard red grains near her knees gradually shrank and the heap of soft pale flour away from her grew.

"Did I do right by you, Alita?" Miriam asked silently, watching her sister-in-law's long oval face and serene slanting eyes as she bent, madonna-like, over her task. Baby Alfred, five months old, slept on her back tethered securely in a blanket knotted over her breasts, his head nodding as his mother rocked fluidly forwards and backwards, grinding the red grains to white.

"Is it my fault you've grown so weak?" Miriam silently

71

questioned again. There was a languor about Alita that wasn't there three years ago: every movement was a little slower; every task took a little longer – as though she was moving under water or had her hands and feet weighted with iron. When she spoke or laughed her gums seemed almost transparent, as though there were no blood left in her body. And sometimes Miriam would catch her wincing with pain as she reached round to hoist her baby higher on her back.

Eleven pregnancies. It was too many for one body to bear – even one as strong and stoical as Alita, with her maddening refusal to rush and her quiet, economical movements, measuring energy out in sparing portions so there was always just enough to last to the end of each day. Miriam used to tease her as they slowly got to know one another in the early years – two young girls newly married to two brothers; each far from home, each trying her best to please her exacting new in-laws.

"You are like an ox ploughing a field," Miriam used to say, "plodding steadily backwards and forwards across the land. And I'm like a chicken: madly squawking and clucking as though each egg I laid was my first. Whose is the best way sister? Slow and careful or quick and impulsive?"

But Alita just used to smile her sweet peaceful smile. "Only time will tell," she would say enigmatically.

Now time was giving its answer: prudence was not enough. Though Alita had hoarded her energy carefully through the years, she had miscalculated the amount she would need. Eight children were all she'd wanted; all her body could carry and recover from in comfort. It was not so much a plan as an expectation: after two years a baby would be old enough to sleep away from its mother and she, in turn, would be ready to conceive another; would be beginning again to look forward to holding another new life in her arms. No urgency; no rush; just the calm unfolding of a continuous slow-moving cycle that would leave her with eight children by the time the tides of hormones ceased ebbing and flowing round her body.

But her slow cycle had been disrupted, contracted. Samuel, her husband, had banished the babies, one by one, from her blanket, before they could walk – and planted a new one in her womb before she had regained her strength. So now, with her eleventh child nodding heavily on her back, Alita's store of energy was finally running out.

They had discussed it so often, the two sisters-in-law, sitting together round the fire in the evening, in low voices so the children couldn't hear. There was no question of Miriam giving her something to wear round her waist, as many other women did, to stop her conceiving: Samuel would rip it off as soon as he saw it. So Miriam had traipsed far out into the bush in search of a rare plant, which she ground into a powder and gave to Alita to drink with water every time she and Samuel had sex. But he had caught her drinking it one day and had beaten her so badly she never dared take it again.

Three months later she came to Miriam late one evening, a half-mad look in her eyes and tears on her cheeks, begging for help to get rid of the latest child growing in her womb.

It was a shocking thing to ask. If anyone suspected them of killing the unborn child, they would both – mother and midwife – be shunned and branded as witches. And if the deed were reported to the police, people said the penalty for inducing a miscarriage was hanging. Despite the dangers, Miriam did not utter a word of protest or rebuke. She did not know of a herb that would do the trick, she said, but she would help Alita to find the right kind of twig and – though the thought made her wince – she offered to help insert it into her vagina and plunge it through into her womb.

So they went out together one sleepy afternoon and picked

a bunch of the small twigs. Alita held them in her hand fearfully, as if they were the sharpest of knives.

"No, I'll do it myself," she insisted bravely. "I don't want you to get blamed if anything goes wrong. Don't even mention the subject again. Pretend it never happened."

So Miriam never asked if she had managed to pluck up the courage to thrust those evil-pointed twigs into her tender pink vagina. But two weeks later Alita miscarried her child.

That was just one baby, however. There had been two more since then: two more to drag on her belly and her breasts, gorging themselves with the life they drained out of her body. Would it have been any different if she'd delivered at the clinic as Sister Tekedi instructed? Had Miriam been wrong to give her the rapfumo? Could the nurses have stopped the bleeding any faster than she and Eustina had done?

On an impulse she scrambled to her feet and knelt down in front of Alita. Startled, Alita dropped the stone into the heap of flour and put out a hand to Miriam's shoulder in an instant, instinctive gesture of concern and comfort. Miriam covered the hand with her own and gripped it hard, staring deep into her sister-in-law's anxious eyes.

"No more babies, Alita. Promise me. It's got to stop. The next one will kill you, I'm sure of it. You're fading in front of my eyes."

Alita shook her head then, laughing ironically. "And who will deliver this message to my husband, sister? That's what they told me at the hospital too. They said I should have an operation that would stop the babies for ever. But they won't do the operation unless Samuel agrees. He has to sign a form giving his permission. And you know he'll never do that." She shrugged. "So I'll just have to trust in God to look after me."

Miriam put both hands on Alita's shoulders and shook her roughly.

"Don't laugh about it, please." But she released her again almost immediately, knowing it was useless to get angry with Alita – it was like punching your fist into a sponge.

"Oh, if ever there was a man to make me turn to witchcraft . . .," she muttered, then laughed as a look of horror came over Alita's face.

"Don't worry, sister. Your man's safe with me – though why you should want to protect him is beyond me. Is a man like that really better than no man at all?"

This was familiar ground: the widow arguing with the wife.

"He's the father of my children," Alita said stubbornly.

"Precisely," Miriam agreed with a grin. "You have your children now. What more use could you possibly have for a man?"

Alita was smiling too, glad to see the tension dissolving from Miriam's body. "Talking of children," she said, to change the subject, "how is your errant daughter?"

Miriam had had a letter from Beauty the day before and Daniel had read it to her. "She's following in her mother's footsteps," she said proudly, "being trained as a health worker. She's a good girl, and she says her husband's family seems to be a respectable hard-working family . . ."

"But it was so sudden . . .," objected Alita, interrupting, referring to the speed with which Beauty had got married.

Miriam smiled. "Which way is better, sister dear? Slow and careful or quick and impulsive? Perhaps some things are better done quickly," she said mysteriously.

And with that she got up, bid Alita a swift farewell, and walked briskly away. She had seen Samuel approaching in the distance and did not want to have to face his wary hostility on top of everything else she had been through in the last twenty-four hours.

In fact, she did not want to have anything to do with

Brother Samuel at all – on any day. In the ten years since Fidelis had died the distrust and dislike between them had grown up and thickened like a hedge of thorns. He was particularly suspicious of Miriam's close friendship with his wife; knew it was she who had given Alita the traditional contraceptive potion, and guessed – though he had never accused her directly – that she had something to do with Alita's last miscarriage. She knew he was waiting for an opportunity to get his revenge.

The battle for control of the womb: that age-old battle between man and woman. But at the moment this man was winning, thought Miriam grimly, and killing his woman in the process.

At home the early evening domestic routine engulfed her and stopped her reflecting any further: a neighbor wanted a remedy for her child's fever; there was the kitchen and her bedroom to sweep, the twins' clothes and Daniel's to wash, sadza to prepare, pots to clean. But eventually Miriam was free to relight the fallen candle, lie down on the blankets and close her eyes. Within seconds she was asleep, oblivious to the rustling in the thatch above her head or the continuous gentle bubbling of the pots of beer fermenting in the corner.

A moment later Eustina appeared and stood looking down at her niece, arms folded sternly, a look of fierce determination on her face.

"Aha, now I've got you!" she crowed gleefully. "You can't escape me now, not when you're asleep. I'll make you listen, just you wait." And she crouched down beside Miriam's body and began viciously pinching the muscles of her back and neck, her upper arms and right down the back of each leg. When she was satisfied, she squatted down beside Miriam's head and sighed.

"Oh, Miriam, Miriam. Stubborn, confused Miriam. I wish we didn't have to go through all this again. But really, you've given me no choice. You've got to listen to me, trust me. We can't work together if you don't trust me."

She was there the following night too; and the one after that. For eight nights, as soon as Miriam relaxed control of her consciousness in sleep, Eustina leapt on to her prone body like a wizened old jockey on a racehorse, bruising it mercilessly with knuckles and knees. And in the mornings Miriam would awake with her limbs stiff and aching, after dreams where she cowered inside a dark hut, hiding from an invisible pursuer who was trying to break down the door. In her dream she longed to open the door and admit whoever was outside – simply to put an end to the terrible noise that filled her head, tied her muscles in knots and made her whole body throb with pain. But each day she forced herself to get up as usual, her stubborn spirit triumphing over her reluctant leaden limbs.

It was her practice – her duty – to visit the mother and baby she delivered to check on their progress every day until the cord stump dropped. It was during this period that she would administer the appropriate protective potions to the baby, advise the mother about caring for it, and watch for any unusual developments, which she would then treat. Usually it was a joyful time: a time when she would see her small charge thrive under her care and would bask in the warm appreciation of the grateful mother. In some of the more traditional households only the mother, grandmother and midwife were permitted to touch the newborn baby at all, or were even admitted into the hut where the birth had taken place. So Miriam would sweep past the proud father and all the other relatives who had gathered outside in a boisterous group, uniquely privileged to witness these first intimate, vulnerable days.

Often it was the atmosphere of the relations outside that

gave her the first clue that something was wrong with the baby inside. She would see them in the distance as she approached, and her heart would sink. Instead of swaggering, drinking and slapping each other on the back, the men would be hunched together in a group on their stools, smoking moodily and silently; and the children would be going about their chores with extra care, as though their own diligence would somehow sweeten the air and protect their new brother or sister from harm.

But on this occasion things seemed to be entirely normal. The mother recovered well – there was no bleeding; no foulness round her vagina; and no tear to worry about: just the usual brownish-red fluid, flowing slowly and steadily, clean-smelling, flushing the last traces of the pregnancy out of her womb. Without Miriam instructing her, the woman had massaged her breasts to rid them of the watery liquid that accumulated before the proper milk came. Everyone knew that this strange fluid – neither milk nor water – was bad for the baby, giving it colic and a kind of green diarrhea. And the baby transferred smoothly from being spoonfed warm cow's milk to taking milk from the breast.

On the second day Miriam brought a black oily mixture with her, made from seeds that she'd roasted and ground with some herbs. This she smeared on the child's fontanelle, covering the soft downy skin that concealed the gaping hole in the skull beneath. The black mixture would seal this access to the child's brain and protect it from the bad vapors that hung in the air. She also inspected the cord stump each day, and the skin around it, alert for any of the signs she had come to dread.

Though Sister Tekedi had been so scathing of her observations of the cord and her conviction they portended future illness for the child, she could not consider questioning, let alone abandoning, what was one of the cornerstones of her practice. Oh, many women – especially the younger ones – went to the clinic now to deliver their babies. But they all came back to Miriam for her special medicines to prevent the diseases that entered the baby through the cord.

This baby's cord stump was drying nicely. But she was concerned to see that the skin around it was a little red and inflamed. Perhaps she had hesitated too long before applying the dust-and-soot mixture? Or perhaps it was true – that the mixture itself was harmful. In some ways it hardly mattered. Over the years she had developed a potent cocktail, with ten different kinds of root, leaf and bark in it, which would protect the baby against the worst effects of all common childhood diseases. She unscrewed the top of a big glass bottle she carried and tipped half a capful of brown liquid into an enamel mug of water and slowly fed it to the baby, spoonful by spoonful, every time she came to visit.

And so it was all over Zimbabwe, and had been for hundreds of years; inside thousands of huts with their circular black mud floors, polished to a shine with soot and candle-wax. A trusted midwife visiting her clients – bringing with her the legacy of her mother, aunt or grandmother; of their mothers, aunts and grandmothers too: a mixture of certain knowledge and probable guesses, of priceless skill and cunning intuition, of painstakingly tried and tested preparations and desperate potions that were part drug, part psychology, part prayer.

On the last day, when the red inflammation had gone and the cord had dropped, Miriam spent an hour fashioning a chifumuro charm for the child to wear. This was her final duty: to shave some of the downy "ghost hair" from the baby's body and sew it with the discarded cord and a sliver of a particular root, inside a small piece of cloth which she attached to a string round the child's neck or waist. With the chifumuro in place, it was now safe to allow the baby out of

Debbie Taylor

the hut and into the dangerous wide world with its jealousies and grudges and whirling vile vapors.

Inside, breathing woodsmoke, regarded with respect as she put the finishing touches to the precious little packet of chifumuro, Miriam was the midwife. Outside, blinking in the sunlight, with the twins waiting patiently for her and a two-hour walk ahead, she immediately became the grandmother again.

Bidding farewell to the family, of which she had become an honorary member for the past eight days, Miriam set out with her two small companions. The mother had slipped a ten-dollar note into one of the twins' hands before they left and Miriam knew a chicken or a brace of pigeons would follow soon enough, delivered to her house by the sister or brother of the new baby.

She had brought the twins with her that day because she wanted to collect firewood from where it was still relatively plentiful – on the white land just over the fence. This particular boundary was not patrolled very carefully – there were no crops growing there for hungry black hands to steal and the penalties for cattle rustling were severe enough to deter all but the most foolhardy. With three pairs of eyes scanning the landscape for guards and three pairs of hands pulling the dead branches from the tangled nets of pale grass beneath the trees, they should be able to collect a big bundle in less than two hours. Normally she would have hesitated to expose the twins even to this slim danger of being caught, but the muscles of her arms and legs had become progressively more and more painful as the week wore on and she did not think she could manage the task on her own.

She had only felt this kind of pain twice before. And both times it had meant the same thing: that Eustina was displeased with her and was demanding acknowledgement, respect and access to her mind. It was always the way: when

80

one of the ancestors wanted to open a path to the living world, they caused pain in the person they had chosen as a gateway. Taken together with the recurrent dreams Miriam had been having, the signs were unmistakable: there would be no relief from the dragging ache until she gave in, organized a proper bira and formally – publicly – invited Eustina back into her life.

But meanwhile there was wood to collect. Miriam turned her attention to the twins bobbing dutifully and quietly, long-limbed and barefoot, beside her. She had taught them good manners; had schooled them in most of a woman's domestic tasks; and they had already spent one whole season out in the fields with her building the beginnings of an understanding of cotton and peanuts as well as of maize and rapoko. Now it was time they learnt something about some of the wild plants that grew in the bush.

This was the part played by every grandmother. For a slice of every child's life, she took over the duties of motherhood. Just when a child was growing rowdy and curious, when its mother was tearing herself in two trying to keep up with the demands of the latest babe at her breast as well as the plaintive wails of the two-year-old toddler ahead of it, it would be time for the grandmother to step in and whisk the third child out of the way. It was she whose job it was to transform that child from a raw little ruffian into an orderly respectful representative, guardian and exemplar of the family's reputation.

They had come, Miriam's grandchildren, in ones and twos, aged anything from two to six years, taking over almost imperceptibly from her youngest children as they had grown up past the mischievous puppy stage. Along they came to fill the vacant spaces left by their mothers on the floors in the sleeping huts, to lay their heads in Miriam's empty lap while she combed their hair, and to bob along dutifully beside her, carrying firewood home from the bush.

The sun was behind them on their way back, so their shadows strode ahead of them, tall and ungainly, each with a big spiky bundle on its head. Her last son Daniel was standing in the kitchen doorway swinging a dead chicken by its legs and grinning at them when they arrived. And suddenly time turned and ran backwards thirty years. And it was Fidelis standing there, his eyes glinting copper in the setting sun, his feet planted firmly apart, his shirt open at the throat. And it was her two eldest daughters – mothers of the twins – who returned with her now to this same homestead laden with wood.

*   *   *

That evening they ate well. There were cowpeas – a rare dish these days since they took so long to prepare and used up so much scarce firewood – and two kinds of sadza: the usual glutinous white mounds made with maize flour ground at the mill, and the gritty pinkish-brown sadza from hand-ground sorghum. There was a dark green vegetable relish too, from leaves that Alita's children had grown in their garden by the well. And the chicken, of course, the reason for the feast: stringy brown flesh, creamy puckered skin and bright yellow fat floating in a delicious gravy glistening with droplets of oil. Alita's family and their old mother-in-law, Chengetai, were there too, sitting in a circle round the fire, faces glowing gold, chins and fingers shiny with chicken grease.

Miriam knelt up by the fire doling out portions with two big wooden spoons: presiding over her kitchen, a twin on either side. Familiar faces watched her; familiar voices laughed and teased one another, or snapped out a sharp word of rebuke. Even Samuel, sitting near the door on the low bench of polished mud that circled two-thirds of the wall, his big angular legs bent uncomfortably, ankles dusty and bare above his shoes, fingers digging hungrily into his bowl – even Samuel's festering enmity was familiar. There is a Shona saying: "Be kind to those you live with – it's dark where you're going next" – better the devil you know than the danger of a stranger.

Here they were all known, each face composed of the same finite set of features. Over there were Alita's softly slanting doe-eyes repeated in her eldest daughter, the sad and stony, the barren, Cornelia; and twinkling above three-year-old Millicent's dimpled cheeks; and staring out from Taona's solemn, elfin eight-year-old face. There were Fidelis's hands: broad and strong – bull hands, bear hands – at the end of Brother Samuel's arms, and gesturing in the air as her own son Daniel told a joke; and there they were again – jabbing at the bowl that Fidelis's nephew, eleven-year-old Peter, shared with his brothers, the doe-eyed Taona and six-year-old Nelson. Those same hands had also been bequeathed to Cornelia, tall and gaunt, and to Rena – the pretty fumbling filly, whose fifteen-year-old face bore a look of wide-eyed dismay at the way her limbs had lengthened and her hands and feet were growing almost as big as her father's.

Yes, the man's seed was stronger. Alita could give her eyes and long sad face to her children; and Miriam's babies had inherited her own firm chin and heavy-browed black eyes. But they all – both Alita's and Miriam's children – bore the common stamp of the father-clan – of Fidelis's and Samuel's blood, and the blood of their father and grandfather and uncles – the stamp that marked them as issuing from the same family: those heavy hands, a particular set of the shoulders, the rangy long limbs that so discomfited Rena. The mothers were all strangers, brought in like breeding mares from a dozen different stables, to the same stud of blood-brothers. The mothers' blood was weaker, its influence more dilute than the blood of the clan fathers and brothers with which it was mixed. It was the fathers whose features finally branded the babies and claimed their allegiance to the man-clan, and it was the fathers' totem clan-name they adopted and lived by.

Yet, though she had not been born here, this was Miriam's home – had been for over thirty years – and Alita's home; and Chengetai's home too, for even longer. Looking at Chengetai, her mother-in-law – the ancient one, mother of grandmothers – it was hard to discern any features now. She was a mass of folds and wrinkles, like brown crumpled paper; and her bones had lost whatever family form they ever held, all knobbed and gnarled now, the flesh stretched loosely over them like skeins of sheep's wool strung out on a wooden fence. With unsteady hands and eyes misted with blue, she straddled the space between life and death: today an elder; tomorrow, perhaps, an ancestor.

Soon Samuel – sole surviving architect of this family edifice – nodded to one of the twins and washed his hands in the bowl of clean water she brought to him. Then, reaching into his jacket for tobacco, he unbent his long legs and went outside. The older boys followed a moment later, and the women and children were left – as they were every evening in huts all over Africa – sitting in the orange light of the fire, surrounded by discarded bowls and plates with, here, an untouched mound of sadza, there a half-eaten chicken wing and a dark scrape of relish.

Outside was the men's fire, on the leeward side of the hut: low stools ranged round, big feet shifting in the dust, deep voices, a growl of conversation, barks of laughter, haloes of tobacco smoke. Inside Miriam sat in her adopted home, with her adopted family. And, oh, her body hurt. Now the main work of the day was over there was no ignoring the pain. It nudged insistently at her, fists in her flesh, every time she moved. A drowsy dimpled Millicent crept up beside her and snuggled a soft curly head against her breast. Miriam lifted an arm to put around her niece, but even that movement made her wince. She closed her eyes.

"Yes, yes, all right. You win. A bira. I'll hold a bira. Yes, all right. Soon. It will be soon, as soon as the beer is ready. I promise."

But where? By rights it should be where the last two had been held – at her home village: the place where she was born, the place where Eustina's bleached bones, and the bones of all her ancestors, were buried. But that village was hardly a home for her any more. Her father had been dead twenty years; her mother for six. Her sisters had been scattered like chaff, whisked apart and away to flavor the thick male blood of as many tight-knit neighboring man-clans. And her brothers had long since brought home their own hand-picked stock of new women to breed the next dynasty of brothers. No, she only belonged there while her mother was still alive, still powerfully spinning at the center of her web. With her gone, the last threads were cut and only the graves were there to call her home.

It was the same for all women. They were just temporary residents in men's homesteads, just passing through, lodgers with no rights. First they were daughters in a father's house, learning to spin love and laughter with a mother and sisters, a grandmother, aunts. Then they were cut adrift, threads severed, and set down as wives in alien households to start weaving that web all over again with a new group of women, who had themselves been severed and cast adrift, or soon would be in their turn. Meanwhile the men stayed together, safely anchored, secure; fishermen standing solid on home shore, reeling in drifting lissom females or tossing them back for another safe-rooted fisher to catch.

85

So, here in this hut, which Fidelis had built; under this smoke-blackened thatch, which Miriam and her daughters had cut and brought back from the bush: this was where she would hold the unruly séance that Eustina demanded as her right.

A candle by a cracked mirror; a yellow flame dipping, guttering; ghastly hollows appearing in temple and eye sockets as the red-patterned scarf is tied. Whose eyes reflect the flame from those deep black hollows? Whose coarse graying curls are pulled back from the high forehead and thick brows? Earrings – heavy, silver – are slipped with numb fingers on to her neat ears. Rows of black beads and red beads and white beads, each flecked gold with a myriad minute reflections of the faltering, flickering flame, are wound round her slender throat, dropping cold between whose hanging breasts?

Snuff the candle. Walk out under the stars and stare up at the sky, breathing cold air, shivering as the spirits brush past the hairs on her bare arms. The heart thuds in her chest; blood sings in her ears; her eyes scan the shadows.

Fat clay pots of beer squat ready in the dark kitchen, in the dark, fearful, phantom-filled hours before dawn. Fan flames from red embers and the polished black mud glows dully; the red clay pots blush forwards out of the darkness.

Figures and faces appear, shuffling slowly and quietly in through the door, kneeling reverently by the fire. Whose figures are they, those of the living or the dead? The features are the same: the phantom form of the father, or the firm flesh of the son? The wraiths of a lost mother or aunt, or the warm bodies of breathing daughters?

A ladle is dipped and beer poured – some into the hard metal cups of the living, some into the miasmic cups of the dead, falling through the air on to the floor. Dipping, tipping, sipping, spilling: the first pot is empty.

A second pot is broached; the fire stoked higher; two men – sons, nephews, uncles, fathers? – carry brimming cups outside to the men's fire, take up their instruments and begin to play: a soft repetitive rising and falling rhythm like water trickling over stones, as fingers flick the bent ends of sprung metal keys fixed inside a big hollow gourd. The mbira: tinkling bells ringing at the entrance to the spirit world, calling the dead to drink with their daughters and sons.

Hours pass. Dawn creeps across the veld, breathing a cold light through feathers of grass and rattling the dry-leaved trees. Graves gape vacant beneath the heaps of red earth, marked with white stones that absorb the weak wisps of light and shine startlingly bright – ghostly beacons – in the blue-gray gloom.

The music continues, rising and falling, ringing endlessly round and round, spiraling up into the blue air, looping cadenzas backwards and forwards, winding time on its reel and letting it run free again as more clay pots are emptied and the fire flames flare and leap.

The sun rises and reaches warm fingers through kopje crevices, bearing jumping purple shadows to tie to stamping dancing feet. Singing begins now: a thin yodeling, a braided refrain of three voices; someone shakes a gourd maraca; bottle-top bangles clatter from jerking ankles above scudding feet.

More hours wind by as memories and mirages start to surface, lassoed and looped up from the past by the timeless continuity of the music. Old voices speak with young tongues; young faces crease with old grievances. And some simply drink – half seeking a piece of eternity, half making a bid for oblivion.

Was it last year, or ten years, or twenty years ago that Miriam last left her consciousness in trust like this, last let herself be dissolved and remade through a day and a night of flame and flowing beer? Eustina's prancing spirit had not aged. She still capered and cackled today as sprightly and mischievous as when she lived. And soon Miriam shook off her pain and capered and cackled too, her face ageless, her voice cracking and wheezing in the tremulous tones of Eustina's last years.

During the bira, past, present and future were blurred and blended; time preceded and shadowed itself: eclipse on eclipse on eclipse – moon across sun across earth across moon. The filmy curtain that hangs – invisible as a cobweb on an autumn morning – between the worlds of the living and the dead, was drawn back and the ancestors thronged around their loved ones, soothing, berating, confirming, refuting: calming the seas of confusion; letting a soft silt of certainty settle in the minds of their children. And when it was over, all fog of doubt was dispelled and things slotted into their places like dislocated joints blessedly released and sprung back into alignment.

Miriam walked with a firm step in the weeks that followed: reassured, confident. In her bedroom, folded carefully away with the coils of ceremonial beads, was a new black and white wrap and a crown of plumed ostrich feathers that, as Eustina, she had claimed as her right – her confirmation of senior spiritual status – towards the end of the bira. She did not need to wear them. Everyone knew they were there. Her eyes commanded; their eyes obeyed, paying homage to this woman who was two women in one.

With her senses open to Eustina again, Miriam regained her solidity, the still center at the eye of her stormy soul. Her hands moved with a surer grace over the women who came to consult her and she added the evidence of her fingers to the testimony of their faces with such skill and depth of understanding that her name was suddenly on every woman's lips and the nurses at the clinic found first one, then two, then three, four, five pregnant women who were expected to deliver their babies there had called Miriam to their homes instead.

A pair of girl twins was extracted pink and kicking from their frightened teenage mother; and a woman, whose babe was wedged sideways in her womb and whose belly bore the scar of the surgeon's knife from her last pregnancy, cried with gratitude when Miriam edged the child out safely. Later the mother paraded him proudly at the clinic to ask why Sister Tekedi had insisted it would be necessary to cut her open again. If Miriam could deliver her child normally, without having to resort to the knife, why couldn't the nurses do likewise?

Sister Tekedi pressed her lips together and said nothing. But she was worried. Each day brought more news of Miriam's activities: a child cured miraculously of fever; coughs soothed with a touch of her hand. And she began seeing children with fresh wounds on the skin of their wrists and ankles where herbs had been inserted to reduce a swelling or release bad air.

"That nganga's a stubborn and dangerous woman," she complained to her soft-spoken colleague. "And she's not very clever either – it's almost impossible to teach her anything. She just doesn't seem to grasp what I'm saying."

The other nurse raised her eyebrows. "I'm sure she understands what we're teaching. The trouble is she doesn't always agree with it. And sometimes I wonder . . ."

"Not you as well! Don't tell me you approve of two-year-old children having that muck cut into their skin, or newborns being dosed with whatever poison it is she carries around in that filthy old bottle? And as for her miracle deliveries – it was sheer luck that the woman with twins didn't have complications. And as for that woman with the history of Cesarean section: she should never have had her baby outside the clinic. What if she'd ruptured her uterus?"

Her quiet companion turned away guiltily. She didn't want to argue; didn't know how to explain why even she – trained and experienced as she was – still took her youngest child to Miriam from time to time. Sometimes cold clinic medicine just did not seem enough: often a fretful sickly baby was calmed quicker by the fiery dark-eyed nganga than by two aspirin four times a day. Sure, clinic cures were fine for a purely physical disease. But how many diseases had only a physical cause? Aspirin or streptomycin was no match for pain caused by a hexing charm or for illness resulting from incest, infidelity, neglect of the ancestors or excessive ambition.

Meanwhile the training course continued and the next lesson was about the care of newborn babies. Miriam brought her bottle of brown liquid to the class and plonked it down loudly on the steel trolley next to the bench where she sat. Sister Tekedi spotted it – grubby and incongruous among the trays of shiny instruments and white cotton-wool puffs – as soon as she bustled into the room. But she made no comment and launched straight into the lesson, beginning with breastfeeding and the importance of putting the baby to the breast as soon as possible.

"The mother's own milk is the very best food for the baby," she said, puffing out her own tautly corseted bosom and patting it fondly. In particular she stressed the value of the watery liquid, colostrum, that came out of a woman's breasts before the milk proper began to flow.

"It's not true that colostrum gives the baby colic or diarrhea," she said, as a faint murmur of objection rippled round the room and the old women began to whisper to each other and fidget in their seats. "In fact, giving babies colostrum helps prevent them getting ill because it contains antibodies against many common infections."

Miriam stiffened, digesting this information. She had been advising women to throw away the strange liquid – that was neither water nor milk – for as long as she could remember. They all had. She could not believe that something most women in the village had been doing for generations could be bad for their babies. She put up her hand. "What is an antibody?" she asked.

Sister Tekedi hesitated, unwilling to embark on an explanation of how a woman's immunity to disease could be passed to her baby. She was sure her class of mostly illiterate, sun-blackened pupils, whose clothes smelt of woodsmoke and whose feet were unaccustomed to shoes, would never understand the kind of information she had learnt during her training.

"An antibody is a substance in the mother's blood that makes her strong. If her baby drinks the colostrum it will be strong too."

"If this substance is so powerful, why do babies fall ill then?" Miriam wanted to know.

"Because it's not powerful enough. A baby needs all kinds of preventive medicines to make it strong. Mothers should bring their babies to the clinic to be immunized against diseases like polio and diphtheria as well."

Miriam picked up her bottle and shook it. "Well, my medicine *is* powerful enough. If a baby has this, it doesn't need any of the things you've been talking about." She shook it again, and a thin beige foam appeared on the surface. Sister Tekedi looked at it and curled her lip with disgust. She turned back to the other women.

"Don't listen to her," she said. "It is very dangerous indeed to give traditional medicine to a small baby. These medicines haven't been tested properly, they don't work and they can be poisonous. I've told you before – if a baby gets sick it should be brought to the clinic. How many children do you think have died because they've been poisoned by your so-called wonder medicines?" she asked finally, turning back to where Miriam was sitting.

"And how many have I saved?" Miriam retorted.

Sister Tekedi's expanded bosom seemed to deflate a little and she pressed her lips together, as she had so many times in the last couple of weeks, silenced by her knowledge of Miriam's legendary midwifery skills.

Miriam placed the bottle back again on the trolley and crossed her arms firmly, putting an end to the discussion. In the silence that followed the old women looked at the scuffed bottle with its muddy brown contents and worn screw-top lid, and at the other bottles on the trolley: clear bright glass holding clear bright liquid. They looked at Miriam's stubborn angular figure with her fierce black eyes, her red, black and white scarf and the single string of red beads that cut across her dark throat like a wound. And they looked at Sister Tekedi, in her stockings and lace-up shoes, with her starched cap pinned primly on her curls. She crossed her arms too – the shiny brown flesh quivering slightly, crumpling her crisp white uniform like thin cardboard – then, taking a deep breath, she continued with the lesson.

But the class was distracted. She could tell that, although they listened in silence to what she was saying – about the treatment of diarrhea with a solution of sugar and salt – and turned their faces towards her politely, as usual, they were not really concentrating. A part of their collective mind was drawn, like green leaves towards the sun, to the tall figure sitting stubborn and dignified by the trolley with her bottle of murky brown medicine and her sacred string of blood-red beads.

These were the driest days of the year, the days before the rains, when the dust – rusty or ochre in the hollows by the kopjes, grayish yellow on the rough-rutted fields by the road – rose up like spirit spinning-tops in the wind and danced madly across the ground, whipping dead leaves and maize stalks into wild pirouettes and spitting grit at the legs of the children. The grass, nibbled threadbare, clung to the shifting ground like gray lichen on a rock, rustling and pricking the feet as people walked. The air was empty of life, as though birds and insects had been sucked dry too and their dead husks were caught up and whirled into the skidding dust-clouds.

Inside their houses the women all but abandoned the attempt to keep the dust at bay. It rushed in through the doorways in hysterical gusts, scattering the ashes of the cooking fires and sending smoke lurching in ugly billows. In vain did they take down their tiers of painted clay pots – small balanced on medium on large, like fat brown wedding cakes – and clean the red and white markings of their film of dust; in vain did they wipe inside each chipped enamel bowl and mug, or reach up to the top shelves of the molded mud dressers with small twiggy brushes to sweep down their loose gray layers.

The dust crept into every cranny: peppering the sadza with grit that crunched against the teeth, collecting in sticky black runnels in the folds behind babies' knees and beneath women's breasts, floating like muslin on the surface of the water jars. The hens grew sulky and ill-tempered and refused to lay; the cattle dropped their heads and nuzzled the arid earth listlessly, their soft nostrils cracked and caked. Only the goats seemed oblivious, trotting busily from bush to bush and tugging at the brittle foliage with their teeth.

Those with oxen watched anxiously as their hides lost their shine and sagged into dirty hollows on their flanks while the herdboys drove them further and further afield, scouring the land for every sparse patch of grazing and searching out watering places where there was still a small pool of evil-smelling brown water at the center of a sea of churned up mud and dung.

The wells were low too and the twins had taken to going together to fetch water so that one could hold the legs of the other while she upended herself into the dank muddy opening to reach the tin scoop down towards its reflection in the surface. And one day Patience – or was it Margaret? – lost her grip, letting Margaret – or Patience – slip headfirst into the well, where she struggled and spluttered, clawing frantically at the sheer slimy bank while her double screamed for help.

Miriam tried to suppress her smiles when they came home, abashed and bedraggled, shivering from shock and cold, their clothes still wet from where they'd tried to wash the mud out. She shook her head sympathetically while they poured out the story, but a dimple kept appearing in her cheek and her black eyes held a laugh in their sparkling depths. She was still chuckling quietly to herself when she saw Alita walking slowly towards her across the stretch of land that separated their two homesteads.

She was carrying Alfred on her back as usual, but something in the way she walked – studied and steady, with a hand held behind, under her son's bottom – drained the smile from Miriam's face. She got to her feet and went quickly to meet her sister-in-law, holding out her arms to receive the little body Alita was releasing from the blanket tied above her breasts. A sudden gust of wind stung their skin with sand and wrapped their skirts tight around their legs. A corner of the blanket was whipped out of Miriam's grasp and flapped behind her like a broken wing as the two women walked back to her house.

The Children who Sleep by the River

Inside, out of the wind, Miriam sat on the floor by the fire with her feet outstretched and lay the child across her lap. He was dressed beautifully, as usual, in a little striped jumper and a pretty blue hat that Cornelia had knitted. But his legs, in their matching blue bootees, were unnaturally limp and still; and the eyes that stared up into her face seemed flat and dull, like the eyes in a newspaper photograph.

Alita, kneeling beside her, reached across and gently unfastened the bow securing the little blue hat. "It's his nhova," she said, easing off the hat and passing her hand briefly over the top of his head, as though unwilling to expose it to the air. And indeed, without the hat – which placed him in the world of magazines and knitting patterns, where children are always healthy and smiling – baby Alfred seemed suddenly very naked and lost: a little changeling soul, in a body no longer his own, clad in garments from another world.

The two women looked at the place where the perfect circular shape of his head was marred by a slight dent – more of a flatness than a hollow – like the moon just on the wane, with only a sliver missing from its sound round surface. Beneath the brown skin with its light scraping of curls they knew that this flatness marked the place where the bones of his skull gaped open, like the bones of every child's skull. Normally that vulnerable spot was hidden from sight, revealed only to probing or caressing fingers. But sometimes, as now, the skin sagged and sank treacherously, targeting that place for all to see – an open invitation to evil.

"I noticed it first this morning," said Alita. "He's had diarrhea for four days – ever since I took him to the clinic to be weighed. They made all the mothers take everything off their babies, even their beads and chifumuros. One of the women complained, but the nurse said she couldn't weigh the babies accurately if they were covered in beads. So I thought it would be safe – if all the other mothers were doing it too. I thought that if all the babies lost their protection they would be less able to hurt Alfred. But some of the mothers whipped their baby's chifumuro on again so quickly I'm sure that's why Alfred's sick now. There must be some powerful children in this village to have affected him so quickly – he was only unprotected for a couple of minutes."

Miriam undid the top button of the striped jumper and hooked out the two chifumuro charms with her finger. She had made them herself, with even more care than usual, adding a separate perforated disc of sheep's bone to the normal root and umbilicus packet, specifically to protect the baby against diseases of the nhova, or fontanelle. Sometimes an ordinary shirt button was used for this purpose, its hardness being transmitted to the baby and compensating for the secret space in the skull. But Miriam had searched for a real skull instead and had spent hours carving the charm. She sighed: just a moment's carelessness and all her effort might have been for nothing.

"Have you given him anything yet?" she asked.

"Only the usual," said her sister-in-law. "I gave him the diarrhea medicine, but nothing for his nhova."

Miriam nodded. There was a certain kind of grass that grew on the termite mounds. People often boiled it in water as a cure for diarrhea. She stroked the child's legs gently, noting the lack of resilience in his flesh. Like dead meat, it held a faint imprint of her fingers when she pinched it: springy still, but sluggish and slightly flaccid.

After a few moments he started to wriggle and to wail feebly, flexing his arms and legs as his guts spasmed painfully, clearly uncomfortable stretched out flat on his back. Miriam lifted him and he curled up instinctively against her like a puppy protecting the soft underparts of its body. A sour stench seeped from his diaper. She could half feel, half hear the liquid churning chaos as his coils of inflamed intestine, their walls weeping like running sores, tried to flush out the invading badness.

She slipped a cool hand beneath his clothes and rested it against the hot skin of his tummy. The fevered churning beneath seemed to quieten momentarily and his little hunched body relaxed a fraction as she handed him back to his mother. But the signs were not good: that she knew only too well. Once the nhova had begun to sink, the spirit seemed to sink as well, leaking out as surely as the liquid was leached from his bowels.

Alita unbuttoned her blouse and pulled out a breast for her son. "I don't know whether I should be feeding him really," she said anxiously. "But he seems so thirsty. Do you think it might be my milk making him sick? You know what Chengetai and the other old women say." She lowered her head in embarrassment: sex was said to make a woman's milk thin and watery and to give her baby diarrhea.

Miriam shrugged. "I don't think so. But it does seem to me that a man who respects his wife should leave her alone when she's breastfeeding anyway. Haven't you got enough to worry about without the prospect of another child to look after?" And she paused, watching, as her gentle companion crooned a quiet lullaby to the sick child at her breast, watching as the liquid flowed from mother to son – from one weakened body to another – and the dry wind outside flayed the trees free of leaves.

The remedy was one she'd used many times: leaves pounded with salt, then fried and added to a foaming bowl of egg and milk. While Alita was feeding this to baby Alfred for the diarrhea, she began to make the medicine for his sunken fontanelle: big brown seeds, roasted and crushed, then smeared on his head to suck out the hollow. She put some on her thumb too and pressed it to the roof of the child's mouth, willing the deadly dent in his scalp to reflate.

But as she was concentrating, eyes closed, on the shrinking spirit in her little nephew's body, Eustina's voice came to her clear as a cock crowing on a still winter's morning:

"We're going to lose him if we're not careful. Remember, we've lost them before, these babies with their hot dry bodies, shrinking and shriveling, leaking liquid endlessly. Remember the lesson. Remember what they said about a child losing liquid."

Miriam took her thumb out of the child's mouth and opened her eyes. Had she heard right? Was Eustina really telling her to follow the clinic's instructions? She closed her eyes again, listening.

"You know I've never really had much confidence in that particular remedy," Eustina remarked. "But we had to do something, didn't we? We couldn't just watch them die without trying something – and sometimes they got better."

It was true: sometimes they did get better. And when they didn't, Miriam assumed that some stronger evil was being wrought: a father having secret sex with a neighbor; a maternal spirit taking revenge for nonpayment of the roora for that child. It was the same with every one of her remedies: sometimes they worked – and sometimes they didn't, because the powers they were fighting were too tenacious. If she lost her faith in this one remedy, she would have to question every aspect of her practice. And that was absurd: she was the most skilful midwife in the area, could deliver a baby better than any so-called professional nurse. Her body stiffened and her chin tilted upwards at the memory of her conflict with Sister Tekedi.

Closing her ears firmly to Eustina's words of protest, she opened her eyes again and reached for the pot that still sizzled on the corner of the grate with the remains of the herb mixture. Too late, as her hand closed around the smoke-blackened handle, did she realize it had been resting directly above a brightly burning length of wood. With a cry of pain she let go, dropping the pot sideways so its sizzling contents splashed on to her bare ankle.

Next day her right hand and shin were just a mass of orange blisters, full of watery pus, like bulbous fungi feeding on her skin. The pain was terrible – burning, throbbing – preventing her doing anything with her hand and making her hobble stiffly round the homestead.

"That'll teach you to be so arrogant," Eustina crowed gleefully. But Miriam just scowled, then winced as her hand brushed against her skirt.

Baby Alfred seemed a bit better, however. His eyes had lost their piscine glaze and his scalp's concave patch had rounded out once more, concealing the void beneath. But he was still very weak, and his bowels still gurgled and wept water. Alita had to change him hourly, smearing his angry red bottom with Vaseline and taking down another barely dry diaper from the fence. He only had four, so she and Cornelia were constantly scrubbing and wringing them out. And, for once, they blessed the wind that filled their eyes with dust and peeled the skin off their lips, because it dried the diapers so quickly.

But they were still washing diapers the next day, and the day after that, so that even Samuel noticed and insisted they take the baby to the clinic. "I don't want my son treated by that witch Miriam," he said. "Take him to someone who's been trained to treat babies."

"What do you think about this remedy?" Alita asked Miriam after she'd come back. She was holding a tin mug to Alfred's lips and urging him to drink the solution of sugar and salt inside. "They said he needs liquid to replace what he's losing in the diarrhea."

"Did they give you something to stop the diarrhea itself?"

Miriam asked cynically, then – not waiting for an answer – "What do you think? Do you think it will cure him?"

Alita took the mug from Alfred's lips, looked at it doubtfully, then put it down on the floor. "That's enough, I expect. He's already had half. Let's see if it does any good."

Another day passed. And another. The wind dropped, but the air was still dry as tinder and the sun glowered through the dusty haze: a white sphere in a white sky. Here and there in the fields men started burning maize and millet stubble ready for ploughing. Elsewhere fires started spontaneously as the sun glanced off a fragment of flint or a piece of glass lying in a patch of long gray grass. Soon black ash floated in the air like spots before the eyes, nostrils filled with black scum, and smoke hung in dense gray curtains across the veld.

Miriam's blisters burst, one by one, but her raw flesh – refusing to harden and heal – continued to ooze clear liquid, like salt tears, in a steady stream. Alfred's insides kept weeping too and gradually his fontanelle sank again as the fluid in his brain seeped away and his eyes dulled once more as his tear-ducts dried up like the well by the vegetable plot.

Again Alita brought him to Miriam's house; again she laid him on her lap, smeared the nhova ointment on his head and pinched the flesh of his legs. And once again, like a succulent flower cut and dropped on the ground, his flesh felt limp because his cells had lost their plump loads of water and had collapsed, slack and flaccid, against one another.

He was dying, Miriam knew it. His very substance was leaking out before her eyes and soon his body would be a husk too: empty, vacated by its small spirit tenant. Hopelessly she banked up the fire and heaped a mound of pungent leaves on to it. Then, wincing with the pain of her wounded hand, she lifted the child in her arms and held his

100

frail body – light and dry as a weaver bird's nest – in the dense fragrant smoke.

Her eyes wept for him. The stigmata on her hand and leg wept for him.

Alita never reproached her. There was never a hint of blame in those sad-slanting eyes during the days that followed. Her oval madonna's face – yet more transparent and bloodless in mourning – was a mask of quiet defeat as she sat – expressionless, motionless – amidst the frenzied grieving ululations of the other women. And Miriam was so grateful for that silent statement of support because the reproaches she carried in her own heart were pain enough to bear and there were many other eyes turning in accusation towards her.

Long years of experience let her stand straight and meet those suspicious eyes with a steady stare of her own, but inside her spirit was quailing. And when she came face to face with Samuel, his face crazy with anger and grief, it took every ounce of her strength to match the fire in his face with a blaze of her own, and to roar the witch's words of defiance when he stepped towards her with fists clenched:

"If you touch one hair of my body, we will meet – you wait and see – we will meet again."

And so the body was buried: old women and old men with picks on their shoulders stepped and skidded gingerly down the scree-lined bank to hack and shovel the stones aside. And another infant grave was dug in the gravel of the dry river-bed, and another infant body lowered into it beside his brothers and sisters, his cousins, his aunts and uncles, his great-aunts and great-uncles – the ones who never walked or talked or bore children; who simply smiled and cried, kicked, sucked and dribbled, then simply died.

The next night thunder rolled in the distance and lightning hissed: silver snakes in the sky. Heaving clouds mounted one another like a herd of bulls and advanced their black bulk towards the moon. The smell of rain was in the air, sharp and peppery, and soon big fat drops splashed down, making craters in the parched dust. People stood in their open doorways when they heard the rain and stared out at the sparse drops that fell like golden coins through the shafts of yellow lamplight.

Miriam stood alone in the kitchen doorway looking out at the rain. It was late; the twins were asleep, but a faint line of light under Daniel's door told her he was still awake, studying she guessed, on his stomach on the floor with a book and a candle by his head. The rain was falling harder now, glittering needles stabbing the ground, piercing the puddles that formed on the compacted clay paths linking hut to hut. Out by the river the water would be rushing over the pebbles: a thousand rivulets converging, carrying leaves and twigs, feathers and bones – debris from the long dry months – and whisking them away, leaving the stones bare and shining. And soon the water would start seeping down through the layers of gravel, reaching cool soothing fingers towards the small sleeping souls resting there.

She turned suddenly, back towards the shadowy interior of the hut, and began to dismantle the towers of painted pots that held her stock of dried roots and herbs. Then, convulsively, she started tipping them, one by one, on to the red embers of the fire in the middle of the room. Flames flared yellow as wizened wood and crumbling leaves were instantly incinerated. Her cheeks burned with the heat and the air was studded with showers of blazing red fragments as she threw handful after handful of fuel on the pyre.

"Stop!"

The command could be heard even above the roaring of the rain and the crackling of the fire.

"Stop!"

Again – and Miriam froze: a tall slender woman, with fire in her eyes and tears in her heart and a handful of crumbling leaves.

She sat, flushed and panting, and let the dust of crushed herbs trickle through her fingers. The fire subsided as suddenly as it had started so only winking red embers remained.

"Miriam, Miriam, proud stubborn daughter, what are you doing? No amount of destruction will bring that babe back to life. And one failure doesn't mean all of our work is worthless. It just means that we have to try harder: be ready to accept new knowledge, learn to sort the good sense from the bad."

Miriam stared at the fire as the words filled her head and her ears were full of the hissing and roaring of the rain outside the open door.

"You know where our strength lies. I don't need to tell you. Trust in that strength: in your magic hands, your eyes that can read souls, your way with a word or a look. These potions aren't the source of your power. Potions are for weak healers. A strong healer helps the body heal itself."

Sister Tekedi could barely conceal her triumph. "This week we are going to discuss traditional medicines and midwifery practices. These are not illegal, but some – as you know – can be dangerous. . . ."

She did not need to look at Miriam, who sat and listened in silence while the other women described the various things they used to do before their training: agreeing, disagreeing and correcting one another, bursting into gales of laughter at the ignorance and naïveté of the past. In just two hours ten centuries of trial and error, faith and hope, were shrugged off like an old blanket from the shoulders.

And a week later, when the grass had already started sprouting and the bare ground was flecked brightest green with new leaves, there was a graduation ceremony at the clinic. An enormous pot bubbled with sadza on a fire outside and the room rocked with music and singing as the women swung their rumps and stamped their feet to the words of the new health songs they'd learnt. The white doctor from the hospital had come to distribute certificates, and everyone applauded his stumbling Shona greetings. Then, amidst more hilarity and applause, a group of women mimed how they used to deliver women before their training; and another group showed off what they had learnt on their course.

Back at home, in her bedroom, Miriam opened the suitcase that held all her treasures – the black-and-white wrap and her new ostrich-plume crown, her red-black-and-white scarf and her coils of bright beads, her official nganga's certificate from Zinata – and she slipped her midwife's graduation certificate inside, beside them.

PART THREE

Esther

*T*he bus swerved to a halt fifty yards down the road and the little crowd of would-be passengers gathered up their belongings and ran towards it. Two young men arrived first and swung up easily inside; followed by the first of the women – pregnant and balancing a big blanket bundle on her head. Next came a group of three old women, scuttling stiff-legged, breathless and anxious, one with an enormous basket of fresh greens, the other two dragging metal trunks across rough ground.

Esther – seven months pregnant, half waddling, half running, with a bundle on her head, a carrier bag in her hand and Lovemore tied in a blanket on her back – was last of all. Little Violet ran along beside her, struggling with a suitcase, while the bus-driver revved the engine impatiently and engulfed them both in evil black exhaust fumes. Kind hands reached down to help the two dimunitive figures clamber aboard as the bus jolted forwards into motion again and threw them sprawling against the hard chrome-and-plastic seats.

Crammed, finally, into a seat by the window, with Violet's bony buttocks digging into her lap and Lovemore's sleepy body forcing her to sit forward, right on the edge of her seat, Esther leaned her head against the greasy glass and closed her eyes. She could barely move, hemmed in as she was all round with her arms pinioned to her sides, her legs wedged tight by the luggage on the floor, and her body weighed down front and back by children. But at least, for three hours, she could rest.

Children, her precious children: it was to fill their stomachs that she had raided the maize fields. It was their little hunger-pinched faces that had sent her creeping like a shadow across the stubble in the moonlight to rip the small dry cobs from the piles of harvested stalks before retreating quickly into a little thicket of trees with her booty. As she and the other women tore away at the outer leaves and frantically thumbed off the lines of grain into their baskets, the crackling and rustling noise they made had covered the sound of the guards' feet crashing through the undergrowth towards them.

Esther was the only one they caught. The others had frozen for a second in white-eyed horror, then scattered in all directions, leaving Esther desperately scrambling to her feet from where she had been kneeling, hampered by her seven-month belly and the weight of baby Lovemore tethered as usual on her back. A rough hand had gripped her shoulder and forced her back down on to her knees until her eyes were level with a gun pointing straight at her forehead.

Children, precious children; how they slow a woman down. If she had not been pregnant and carrying Lovemore she might never have been caught. Without a child on her back she might have earned half as much again in the cotton fields. If Violet had not fallen sick she could have worked ten extra days in the tobacco sheds. Then, perhaps, she would not have been forced to forage like a rat in the cattle fodder of the white man; not scrape and scrabble and scuffle through the undergrowth, pursued like vermin by black men carrying white men's guns.

They had taken her to the big house and stood guard over her outside one of its many blue doors until early the next morning. And it was there that Mr. Johnson, the boss, found her when he unlocked the locks and unbolted the bolts to release himself from his luxury prison the next day.

"What have we here?" he asked, glancing curiously at Esther as she stood with her mop-head bowed, no taller than the breast-pockets of the two guards beside her.

"Stealing, boss. From one of the west boundary fields," one of the guards announced proudly, erecting his gun and standing to attention.

A look of irritation flicked across Mr. Johnson's face at this ritual and clumsy show of respect. "Well, man, is that all? What happened? Was she the only one?"

The guard subsided slightly and his shoulders slumped: "There were six of them, boss, all women, but the others got away."

Mr. Johnson raised his eyebrows in exasperation. "Well, now," he said sarcastically. "Shall I give you a clue about what you should do now? You should take the woman into my office and – can you guess? Yes! – find out the names of the others. And can you think what might be a good idea then? Right" – with slow and exaggerated patience – "call the police. And can you tell me what else you should do? Good! Clever boy! Go and round up the others. God help me – talk about buy a dog and have to bark yourself . . ."

Esther winced on the guards' behalf and for a moment the bond between black and black was stronger than the rift between captor and prey. Her eyes blazed hatred at the tall white man with his bullet-head and clean-shaven jaw; at the great, red, meat-fed thighs and knees that protruded from his new-pressed khaki shorts; at his enormous freckled hams

109

of arms with their repulsive golden fur of hair. Beside him the guards, fidgeting uncomfortably in their ill-fitting navy overalls, looked like brittle blue saplings bowing before the pink and blond breath of an elephant.

How could those guards, humiliated so casually and routinely, keep a strong and humane picture of themselves in their minds? What vengeance smolders in the heart of someone whose livelihood depends on his deference to a man who despises him? Was it surprising that so many should try to quench that fire with Chibuku at the end of the week; try to damp down the embers of anger; try to stop them from burning the people they loved? And was it surprising if the flames sometimes burst through the mists of alcohol and the women in the compound bore bruises where fists and workboots had found their mark?

The guards pushed her into the room Mr. Johnson had just vacated and made her kneel on the floor again. She looked at their feet, at the steel caps of their heavy boots; and at their hands, pale-knuckled, itching to lash out. They towered over her as she knelt there, no bigger than a child, with one hand on her belly and the other reaching behind to protect the baby asleep on her back.

It did not even cross her mind to stay silent as they questioned her. Instead she used words as a shield, pouring them out into the air to keep those feet and fists at bay. And soon enough the five other women were pushed into the room and made to kneel down beside her, while the guards lit cigarettes and swaggered up and down, laughing and jeering while they waited for the police to arrive to take them away.

Mr. Johnson had decided to press charges, one of the policemen told them after the six women had been ushered into a cell. Stealing was a very serious offense, he went on. Mr. Johnson had decided to make an example of them to dissuade other people in the compound from following their lead. They would be required to come back here in three weeks' time from where they would be taken to the court-house in Kwekwe to be tried.

Esther, almost fainting with hunger and trying in vain to quiet Lovemore's piteous wailing for food, was only dimly aware of what he was saying. Just one bowl of sadza and a cup of water for the baby – was that too much to ask? In some ways she was more concerned about the resentful, angry looks she was getting from the women she had betrayed than she was about the fate that the magistrate might have in store for her.

They were kept another five hours, without food, while the life of the police station continued around them. Two typists with straightened hair, stockings and high-heeled shoes tapped desultorily at the big heavy manual machines. More policemen in spotless khaki uniforms came and went, sat at desks and answered the phone, or wrote reports laboriously in their round childish writing. Finally, at four o'clock, the prisoners were released – without busfare – to make their way home.

Esther walked alone, dizzy with hunger, for the first two hours, shunned by the others who strode off ahead. But later, after sunset, when the shadows began to reach out black feet to trip her and black hands to tangle in her hair, she found two of them waiting by the roadside for her and one touched her arm while the other lifted Lovemore gently off her back.

The road to Chikombera police station was wide and dusty: a broad red runway for trucks and tractors carrying fertilizer and pesticides, cotton and coffee, between the railway and the white man's fields. Esther and the others had to walk the length of it three times before their case was over: along the wire fence that bounded the fields either side; over cattle grids to stop the herds wandering and mixing; past the signs, miles apart, nailed prominently to gates, painted white on black and proclaiming "Freshwater Farm Estate" or "East-wyke Tobacco" or simply "J Anderson Esq."

The hearing, in the light airy courtroom with its polished wood benches and parquet floor, was attended only by the magistrate and the policeman who'd questioned them. Beneath portraits of Comrades Mugabe and Banana, who gazed solemnly and benignly down from the wall, the six women were fined thirty dollars or three months' hard labor apiece and given four weeks to come up with the money.

Back at the farm their sentence had been harsher: notice to leave by the end of the week and a warning never to come back again.

On the bus now, with her forehead rubbing against the cool window, Esther was simply grateful Mr. Johnson had let her husband and his family stay. She opened her eyes and stared unseeing at the landscape: at the jets of water spurting and spitting from irrigation pipes like sparks from a catherine wheel, casting rainbows of spray in the air and fattening the rich green lines of tobacco plants; at the men perched high on tractors grinding forwards through a sea of yellow stubble, leaving a wake of raw red ruts behind them; at the sleek white Brahman bulls nodding and munching through thigh-high grass; and at the clouds of maize dust that billowed over silos where human food was ground into cattle fodder.

Eventually the landscape changed and, though there was no sign proclaiming the end of the white man's realm, suddenly it was clear that the road was now passing through what were once called the Tribal Trust Lands but which the new government, oddly, now referred to as the Communal Areas. Gone were the sturdy lines of fenceposts fronting acres of empty space. Suddenly a white clinic building or a school, and short terraces of shacks with a grocery, bottle-store and butchery appeared across the wide ditches that flanked the road. Parades of school children in green or navy uniforms straggled along laughing and chattering together. And homes could be seen: sometimes just two thatched huts and a mango tree; often three or four to a cluster; occasionally even five or six, with tin roofs and a car parked outside. Homes: mushas, homesteads; places where the land was owned by the family who farmed it; places where a visitor was welcomed and invited to stay for supper.

Esther nudged Violet awake and prepared to disembark.

It had all happened so quickly – the arrest, the trial, the eviction – that there had been no time to write. So nobody at home was expecting to see the two small dusty figures that trailed tiredly down the path towards the homestead. Cornelia spotted them first and stood for a moment squinting into the sun before giving a shout and breaking into a big-footed lolloping run towards her pint-sized sister.

Tears flooded Esther's eyes when she saw this great horse of a woman galloping over the sparse scrapings of new green grass. Cornelia, dearest Cornelia: sister, mother, beast of burden; with her heavy bones and her long sad face; her full heart and her empty womb – how good it was to see that sight again. She dropped her bag and bundle to the ground and reached out her arms.

In no time she was sitting in the kitchen by the fire, with her mother, Alita, on one side and Cornelia, with Lovemore on her knee, on the other; and sadza bubbling and water steaming in two big black pots on the fender. She leaned against Alita's body, just as she had when she was a little girl, nudging the other children out of the way so she could nestle against her mother's big doughy breasts and smell the

113

smoky sweet-and-sour perfume of her skin. Just sitting next to this so-familiar body with its aura of calm was a comfort, even though this homecoming had proved even more bitter than she had expected. She signed deeply and gazed into the fire, trying to absorb the news.

Baby Alfred was dead. Just two weeks ago. While she was dodging from tree to bush to hedge to shed, in the darkness with her basket of stolen corn, her mother had been watching the life leak out of her baby brother.

Strange. This had been a baby she had hardly known at all. Both Alfred and little dimpled Millicent had been born after she had married and gone to live on the farm. She had not carried them and washed them, felt them as part of her own flesh, as she had her other brothers and sisters. Now he was gone it was as though he had never existed. Except that, for once, Alita was without a child at her breast. That was the thing Esther missed: not baby Alfred's unique personality, unfolding as his lips started to form words and his hands to grab at chicken bones in a bowl, but his anonymous infant's body, the latest of many, occupying the space nearest her mother.

Alita looked smaller, somehow, without a child continually clinging to her. Esther had not realized how slender her mother was, a fragile bird-like wraith with a graceful neck and sharp shoulder-blades showing through her blouse. And there was a kind of restlessness underneath her mask of quiet mourning. Her eyes would flicker around the smoky hut as if looking for something; her hands would start reaching round behind her or would finger the opening of her blouse where, for almost the first time in twenty-six years, there was no knot of blanket digging into her chest. She could not seem to get comfortable, was continually changing position, trying to adjust her body to a loss as tangible as an amputated limb.

Still, it was good to be home; to be coddled and fussed over and fed like an honored guest after all the hardship of the last three months; and to see Violet's eyes grow round with delight as she watched Cornelia sawing through the throat of the chicken they killed in honor of her homecoming. The poor child had not tasted chicken for nearly a year.

The three women had exchanged the bare bones of their news within seconds of their coming together. Now, while the afternoon shadows grew long outside and the children embarked on their evening chores, they settled down by the fire to luxuriate in talk, embroidering anecdote and detail until their intimacy was rewoven and Esther was absorbed once again into the fabric of the family.

She heard how her father was threatening to call in a powerful muuki from the next village to investigate Alfred's death. He suspected that Miriam had killed the child with witchcraft, but he did not dare to accuse her to her face. And she heard of how Miriam herself had grieved – more than anyone in the family – and how some people were saying they would not let the black-eyed nganga deliver their babies or treat their children any longer. "But they're wrong," said Alita firmly. "Miriam's my sister. She did everything she could. Sometimes a child dies and there's nothing anyone can do. It's God's will."

Then they asked her about Beauty, about her new husband and the health course she was on; about her own court case and how much she'd been fined.

"Thirty dollars. More than half of Darwin's monthly wage. We can't possibly pay it. But if we don't I have to go to prison." She paused and looked at her mother. There was a silence as the unspoken request hung in the air.

"You'll have to ask him yourself," Alita said at last, shrugging her narrow shoulders. "I don't know how much money there was from the maize this year. We harvested twenty bags and he sold ten. There should be enough, but I don't know . . ." She trailed off.

"You mean he might have spent it all already?" Esther asked, amazed. "What about your housekeeping money? Surely he lets you have enough for soap and sugar?"

Alita shrugged. "Yes, yes, of course. He always gives me whatever I ask for. And he's paid the school fees for the younger ones." She paused again. "He just doesn't like to talk to me about money," she finished lamely.

"She means he's spent half of it on beer," said Cornelia bluntly, "like all the other men. Where do you think he is now? Someone's been brewing over on the other side of the village. He's been gone all day."

"Don't talk about your father like that," said Alita. "It's his money and he is the one to decide how to spend it."

Cornelia turned on her. "That's the whole trouble isn't it? Who does all the work in the fields? We do. All the planting and weeding. And the harvesting – and remember how long it took us to shuck all the grain off the cobs? Twenty bags! Have you forgotten how long it took us to fill them all? All father did was a couple of days of ploughing – but just because he was the one registered with the Grain Marketing Board he got all the money."

"A man is the head of a household," said Alita with dignity. "He is the one who owns the land. It's only right that he should be in charge of the money."

"Is it right that he would spend it all on beer and prostitutes?" Cornelia retorted. "I know, I know. Father's not as bad as that," she added quickly as her mother's eyes began to flash and her chest to heave with anger. "But some men are like that, aren't they?" She turned to Esther for support. "If the husband is the only one to look after the money, the wife is powerless. All she can do is pray he will use it responsibly and make sure she always has enough for the housekeeping. Ah, you're lucky sister," she said bitterly. "You have a good husband."

The three women fell silent. Cornelia's husband, Mlambo, was a bad husband. Twenty years her senior, he had mistreated her as soon as it was clear she was not going to give him the children he so desperately wanted. At first he beat her and accused her of using some kind of contraceptive behind his back; then he simply ignored her, leaving her to do all the work on their small plot of land and giving her only the minimum of cash to buy the things she needed to keep the household going. Finally he disappeared altogether, off to Harare where it was rumored he had found a job and was living with another woman.

Cornelia resumed her task, ripping the feathers out of the dead chicken as though she were tearing at her own husband's flesh. And soon the four youngest children materialized, as if by magic, and squatted down by the fire to wait while she unwound the coils of intestine, washed them and squeezed them clean of their muddy green contents, then rewound them again around four little sticks which she set to roast over the fire.

"Here you are," she said, when the white coils had sizzled and browned. "Violet first – you know what this is for, don't you?"

Violet held out her hand eagerly for the little smoking stick of meat. "To stop me being afraid of the dark," she recited solemnly.

"Right, good girl. And why shouldn't you eat this?" she asked, brandishing the bloody bony stump of gizzard.

"Because it will make me neglect my parents when I grow up."

Cornelia nodded. "Excellent. Your mother has taught you well. Millicent, Nelson, Taona – you heard what she said: here's your share too, so mind you always take care of your mother and father." And the four children danced out of the hut into the evening sunshine brandishing their little sticks while Cornelia gazed wistfully after them.

Esther and her mother exchanged glances. Sure, Alita had just lost a child, but she had eight more to care for her when she grew old and – perhaps even more important – to keep her spirit and memory alive when she died. Esther, though still only twenty-four years old, had assured her future too, with two children already, and another on the way. But Cornelia, at twenty-eight, had been marooned in mortality by her barren womb. Her breasts had never felt the sweet ache and tingle of a baby's greedy grasp. Derided and deserted by her husband, she was destined for a hard and lonely old age and a dismal empty eternity.

They could not remain gloomy for long, though. The excitement of the children – delighted to be reunited – who dashed, screaming and laughing, round and round the courtyard and kept popping their bright-eyed faces round the door to check on the progress of the feast the women were cooking – all that unbridled gaiety was infectious.

Soon Rena, Esther's fifteen-year-old sister, came back from school, dressed in the blue and yellow uniform she'd inherited from Esther. Esther scrambled to her feet and hugged her.

"How is my favorite little sister?" she asked fondly, then all three women burst into gales of laughter – because Rena was already at least half a head taller than Esther: the dress she was wearing barely buttoned across her big plump breasts and a band of darker blue showed where the faded skirt had been let down to accommodate her long legs.

Eleven-year-old Peter arrived home a few minutes later and was shooed out of the kitchen amidst more laughter.

"You're a man now," Cornelia teased him, while Rena pushed him towards the door. "Don't you know that a man will grow big ugly bushy eyebrows if he looks into the pot while the women are cooking?"

"Yes, out you go," Esther agreed, laughing. "Only women and children allowed in this room – we're discussing big secrets not fit for a man's ears," she joked, frowning ominously then grinning at her brother.

Samuel came back just as the meal was ready, opening the kitchen door on a scene of cheerful chaos, with newly washed brown limbs glowing in the firelight and teeth and eyes flashing with merriment. Esther struggled hurriedly up from where she was sprawled, giggling, between her two sisters. She stepped carefully over the legs of the other children, then fell to her knees, bowed her head and clapped her hands respectfully in greeting at her father's feet.

He stood swaying drunkenly in the doorway, bloodshot eyes blinking, then collapsed heavily on to the mud bench by the door.

In retrospect Esther realized she had chosen her moment badly. She should have approached her father in private, some time the following day, when the effects of the beer had worn off. But, emboldened by her afternoon with the other women and encouraged by the benign smile that spread over Samuel's slack features after he had finished eating, she broached the topic of a loan to pay her fine.

Instantly the atmosphere changed. His soft-focused eyes hardened and his body tensed up and back like a cornered hyena. The rest of the family fell silent and busied themselves clearing up the remnants of the meal as though it were the most absorbing task in the world. Then he exploded, launching into an ugly angry tirade against both of his elder daughters.

"Unnatural," he called them; "nothing but a burden"; "cursed with bodies like men's." "I marry you off, but your

119

husbands refuse to support you and back you come to me whining for help. You can't even bear children like normal women; one has to be cut open every time she delivers; the other can't even get pregnant." So he went on, as the children slunk outside into the darkness, and the women sat staring dully at the fire. He would have to pay back the roora he had received for Cornelia if her husband divorced her for not bearing children, he complained. And where was the roora he was owed by Esther's husband for her last baby, he wanted to know. "Daughters, useless daughters," he spat out finally, storming out of the hut.

"Father's right about the roora." Cornelia's voice, coming clearly out of the darkness later that night, startled Esther just as she was falling asleep. She rolled over towards her sister, cupping herself around Lovemore underneath the blanket and putting a hand on his little curly head.

"Mlambo has threatened to divorce me and throw me off the land. I think he wants to bring a new wife home," Cornelia went on, with panic and pain in her voice. "Esther, what can I do? I don't want to be buried with a dead rat in my grave . . ."

Esther reached out a hand to touch her sister's shoulder.

"I've tried everything," Cornelia went on miserably. "Last month I even went to the hospital in Kadoma. I heard there was a new white doctor there who could cure jeko and help women who can't have children. She was very kind; asked me lots of questions about Mlambo – if I thought he ever went with prostitutes – and about how long I'd had jeko and if I'd ever been with another man. She gave me some medicine for the jeko too. But she said she could not help me have children because I'd left it too late. She said if you have jeko too long it's impossible to have children. She said I probably caught it from Mlambo and that he'd got it from a prostitute. She said he had to come for treatment too or he'd give me jeko again next time he came home."

Lovemore wriggled in his sleep and nuzzled his face between Esther's breasts like a puppy. She bent her head and buried her nose in his curls, inhaling his warm animal smell and listening to Cornelia's sad, disembodied voice coming out of the darkness, coming from her cold, lonely blanket on the hard mud floor.

"When I came out of the doctor's room a woman started screaming and slapping my face. 'Prostitute! Prostitute!' she was shouting. She said she was possessed and that she could tell, just by looking at a woman, whether she was a prostitute or not. Then she started slapping all the women waiting to see the doctor, screaming 'Prostitute! Prostitute!' at everyone, accusing them of stealing her husband . . ."

"I knew she was wrong about me, but there were a few other women there, dressed – well, you know – dressed like prostitutes, in expensive dresses and high-heeled shoes. We were all there for the same reason – the wives and the prostitutes – we all had jeko and none of us could have children. Dirty, we were all dirty, all of us . . ." Her voice wavered, wet with tears, and Esther reached out across the cold floor again and felt for her sister's hand beneath the blanket. Cornelia sniffed, then swallowed hard.

"The medicine cost a dollar and the doctor said I should go back for more, and bring Mlambo with me, a week later, to get some more medicine," she continued, with a bitter laugh. "At first I thought she was joking. I had to borrow money from Mother to get there in the first place, and even if Mlambo was not away in Harare I know he'd never agree to go to the hospital . . ."

Esther laughed too, squeezing her sister's hand sympathetically. "Men!" she snorted derisively. "You'd never get a man like Mlambo to the doctor in case she discovered that he was infertile too!"

Cornelia sniffed again in the darkness and wiped her face on the blanket. "That woman was right, though. Some prostitutes put a magic potion inside their vaginas. Once a man has that potion on his penis he never wants to make love with his wife again. I think that's what happened to Mlambo – this new woman of his has bewitched him with some medicine. What can I do Esther? I can't go on living like this. A woman must have children. No one ever loves you the way a child loves its mother. A woman can't rely on a man; she only has her children to rely on – and if she doesn't have children . . ."

She was crying properly now: great raw sobs that convulsed her big bony body. The naked intensity of her grief was shocking, even to Esther, who had slept with her sister in this very hut for most of her life and had witnessed her reaction to every kind of childhood and adolescent crisis. Even when Cornelia had been told, at fifteen, that she was to marry Mlambo, against her will – so that Samuel could use the roora to pay off a debt – even then she had not sobbed like this, as though her heart was breaking, as though despair would wrench her big body apart.

After a few moments the storm passed and the brute force that had taken hold of Cornelia released her, like a wave beaching a piece of driftwood on a shore.

"There is something else you can try," said Esther quietly. "There is a powerful Malawian nganga at the compound." And she told her sister about Seguro and how he had led Beauty back to health. "Come back with me, when I go to pay my fine. I'll take you to see him."

Esther lay awake for a long time after Cornelia's jagged breathing had smoothed into the long slow ripples of sleep. She put a hand on her belly, where her unborn child was flexing his tiny arms and head-butting her diaphragm. If she, Esther, were to die tomorrow, the elders would slit open her belly before they buried her, so her dead child's spirit could escape – just as they would soon be slitting her open at the hospital in Kadoma to allow her living baby to escape from the narrow body that would otherwise trap it in a coffin of unyielding bone and smother it before it was born.

They had told her she had the pelvis of a man, with bones that had grown over the opening that the baby should pass through. She was lucky: it was only her pelvis that was affected. Her curse was light compared to the one that Cornelia carried. Cornelia's whole body was cursed. Her whole body had been taken over by a man – by a restless infertile ghost, spirit of a man who had died without children. This was the way with many barren women: their bodies were appropriated as vessels for unhappy wandering spirits who'd had no chance to win a place among the ancestors in the hereafter. Only by lowering the self in the raising of a child can a person attain that state of spiritual maturity that earns a place beside their mothers and fathers after death.

Oh, the elders tried to prevent it happening; tried to prevent the blight of barrenness from passing from the dead to the living. A woman who died without children would be buried with a mealie cob in her vagina and a rat by her breast as a way of convincing her ghost that she had not died barren. A man without children was interred with a dead rat too, to still his lonely wandering and make him sleep soundly in the earth. But these precautions were not always sufficient. Sometimes the despair of the childless could not be thwarted so easily and took its toll on the loins of the living.

What must it be like to share your body with an alien spirit? Esther rolled over on to her side again and stared at her sleeping sister. All she could see was the vague outline of a body under the blanket: tall enough to be a man's, with a man's heavy shoulders and thighs. What did Cornelia see

123

when she looked down at that body, with its flat boy's belly and firm breasts, its big broad feet and the continual, dirty, dragging pain of jeko pulling at her poor empty womb? Did she feel the same faint flicker of fear and repulsion that all mothers felt when they met a woman without children?

Witchcraft. The mantle of witchcraft enshrouds the barren woman, woven by the fears of the fertile. Understanding how envious a childless woman must feel, how bitter despair must run deep in her veins – that understanding makes those lucky enough to be blessed with progeny suspicious of their childless neighbors and afraid for the safety of their own good fortune. Esther could feel it herself, despite her love for her sister. If she let the thoughts take hold, she could conjure a darker black shadow, peeling itself away from Cornelia's sleeping body and lifting itself to hover above her.

She shivered and reached out her hand once more into the darkness. As she touched the warm skin of her sister's tear-streaked cheek, the shadow disappeared.

The rains were slow to start properly that year. For weeks the clouds banked up in the sky, rumbling with thunder, swelling with the promise of deluge. But only a few staccato showers fell, like a child with a stutter trying to speak fluidly but able only to utter a single short syllable at a time. Smears of green grass, no more than skidmarks, appeared in the hollows where puddles had lain briefly before being sucked into the thirsty ground. And a sparse moss of seedlings, that had ventured out at the first sniff of rain, withered from green to gray as the greedy sky held on to its load of sweet water.

Then at last, like a sigh, the sky yielded and released its hoard in a steady, solid outpouring while the land abandoned itself to gobble up the glut of water. Soon the drought-starved dust was bloated into thick red mud and tree skeletons swelled with fat fleshy buds on their diet of rain. The relief in the air was almost tangible as memories of past droughts were washed clean for another year by the hissing gray curtains that swept heavily across the countryside.

Suddenly all movement was towards renewal and rebirth. The ghosts of the old year were swept away and buried in the mud. It was time to start again. All over the land ploughs were brought out of storage and the winter's rust was scraped from their blades. Sacks of seed were hauled up from the granary or offloaded from donkey-drawn carts. And the trucks of the Grain Marketing Board, piled high with sacks of fertilizer, began hiccoughing and roaring over the rutted rural roads.

One of the four set-down points in the village was beneath a big syringa tree on the edge of Miriam's homestead and, when Esther came back from her twice-daily walk to the well to fetch water, there was a small crowd gathered, and voices raised in argument, around the big mud-spattered truck parked there. She deposited the bucket on the ground, hitched Lovemore higher on her back, and hurried over to see what was going on.

It was Miriam, as usual, at the center of the fray. Esther smiled at the familiar sight of her tall fiery aunt wagging her finger and vehemently shaking her head at the two GMB officials with their clipboards and pencils. Cornelia was standing beside her, stooping slightly with nervousness, but with a stubborn frown on her long sad face. Miriam finished what she was saying and some of the other women in the crowd gabbled a chorus of corroboration and agreement while the men muttered angrily in the background.

"They're complaining about wives not being allowed to register with the GMB," one woman on the edge of the crowd informed Esther when she arrived. "If it's just the husband's name on the registration form, then the check for the maize you sell at the end of the year goes to him too – even if he's away; even if he doesn't even come home to plough . . ."

"It's not fair," complained Miriam later, when the truck had roared off leaving great angry wounds in the soft muddy ground. "Why should a man get the money if it's his wife who does all the work on the farm?"

She was yoking two oxen together in a worn wooden harness while Esther and Cornelia stood by their heads to discourage them from moving out of the way. It wasn't really necessary: there was no fight left in them – they were old and tired and had done this a hundred times before. Miriam fastened the last buckle and slapped one of the beasts on its flank.

"You know a widow is sometimes better off than a wife. At least she can keep what she earns. What is the point in doing all that weeding if you never see the money for the crop?" She moved round to the rear of the animals and attached the yoke to the plough.

"That was what I was going to talk to you about," said Esther, with a twinkle in her eye. "I need to get my hands on some of that money to pay my fine at the police station next week. Could you give me some sorghum and lend me a few dollars to buy sugar? I'm going to brew beer at grandmother Chengetai's house. I'll let you have the money back when I've sold the beer."

Miriam laughed. "Well, that's the best way I know of to get money out of a man: sell him a couple of mugs of beer. The wives won't bless you though," she warned.

"Let them brew their own beer the following week if they're worried," Esther retorted, standing back while her aunt steered the oxen round towards the track that led to her fields. "If all the wives brewed beer too, the maize money would soon be back in the hands of the women!" She grinned mischievously, then waved at the departing procession: Miriam in front leading the two big lumbering beasts; Cornelia behind, holding the plough straight. The following week their positions would be reversed as Miriam helped Cornelia to plough her small plot of land with the same pair of elderly oxen.

Two women at war: pitted against the land; pitted against the men; pitted against tradition. For Cornelia and Miriam the battle never ended. They were anomalies – the barren wife and the widow – standing out as starkly as the naked termite hills around which they maneuvered the plough.

Once it would have been unthinkable for a woman to plough: rather let a twelve-year-old boy do it, or wait until an uncle or brother-in-law was free. But these days a woman who had to wait for a man's help was a woman who might wait for ever. Some of the men were away in the city, digging trenches, humping crates, driving taxis; many found work on the white-owned estates, tending the tobacco-curing fires or binding up bales of cotton; others had been claimed by the war and an empty sleeve or trouser leg stopped them from working. So today it was not unusual to see a woman's colored scarf and skirt at the head of a team of oxen or to hear a woman's voice calling out directions in the cool morning air as she leaned her weight behind the plough.

Esther watched the winner and the loser in the battle of the sexes plod steadily up and down, as the oxen nodded their lumbering heads and the plough blades sliced slowly through the rain-flattened ground. Miriam, the winner, against the odds: undaunted, indomitable, leading the way across the field, walking confidently in a straight line through the stubble, laughing and tossing comments back over her shoulder. There was a woman who never stopped fighting.

127

She'd lost her husband, but hung on to her land and her independence. Esther could still remember the day when Miriam had dug in her heels and said "no." Though nine years had passed, the tremors of that long moment still reverberated through the family.

It was one year after Miriam's husband, Fidelis, had died: time for the kurova guva – the ceremony that would summon and soothe his spirit and lay it finally to rest in his grave. When the ceremony was over, tradition decreed that Miriam should marry Samuel, Fidelis's only brother, so there would be no danger of Fidelis's land or children passing into the hands of another family. But Miriam had refused to become a second wife. The gourd of water she was required to drink, to signify her acceptance of Samuel as husband, remained untouched on the ground before her. The family waited for her to reach for the gourd and raise it to her lips, but her hands remained quietly folded in her lap. And Samuel had never forgiven her.

Miriam had fought and won. But Cornelia, following in her aunt's steady footsteps across the freshly turned earth, Cornelia was beaten already – because she was without children. Children make all the difference. Children, sons, give a woman roots and help anchor her firmly to the land that her husband inherits. They carry his name and his likeness and inherit his land when he dies. But a woman without children is rootless. She does not even take her husband's full name when she marries – the clan name that signals her acceptance into the lineage of his family under the watchful gaze of his ancestors. So, having failed in her duty to provide heirs, the barren woman can be easily discarded.

Already there was something defeatist about the way Cornelia moved: clumsier than Esther remembered, with her rangy limbs shrugged closer to her body, as though she felt

unworthy even to occupy that small piece of extra space –
like a dog cringing on its belly waiting for the stick to fall.
And she had taken to spending most nights at her old family
home, as though she had already been thrown off her husband's land.

Esther watched a moment longer, with her hands resting
gently on the hard living mound of her pregnancy while
Lovemore wriggled restlessly on her back. Then she turned
and walked thoughtfully back to the homestead.

It took eight days for the beer to ferment. And, though there
was no real need, Esther checked on its progress every
morning. It was really an excuse to visit Chengetai, her
grandmother, the woman who once was the hub around
which the wheel of the family turned.

The prospect of a beer party had brought a sparkle to the
old woman's milky faint-sighted eyes and new energy to her
stiff knotted limbs. Together they peered into the pair of
brimming tin drums: the grand-daughter with a belly round
as a chicken's breast, the grandmother stringy as a stand of
maize.

On the eighth day they sieved it through a fine-meshed
flour sieve, pressing the gray sludge from the bottom of each
pot with the heels of their hands to extract every last drop of
liquid. Then, after toasting each other with a mugful of the
thin sour brew, they dispatched the children off round the
village to announce that the beer was ready.

Soon the customers began to arrive: first the old men, too
frail for work, trailing slowly, in ones and twos, from households all over the village. In they came, fumbling in their
pockets for coins, then shambling outside with mugs of
sweetened beer to ease their creaking frames down on to
stools in the morning sunshine and pass round a polished
cow's horn of snuff. Three or four old women came too, a bit

later, when the bulk of their morning chores were finished. They stayed inside to drink their beer, kneeling by the fire with grandmother Chengetai, like a cluster of bats chattering and rustling their dusty dark wings.

The old people drank slowly, savoring each sip, mindful of the number of coins in their pockets. Gradually, as their faces were warmed by the sunshine and the glow of the fire, and the alcohol seeped gently into their blood, they grew merry, garrulous, quarrelsome – arguing in cracked, angry voices, then rocking and wheezing with helpless laughter.

Then came the first of the younger men, taking a break from a day of ploughing. They tossed their coins into Esther's hand more carelessly than the old folks and, just as carelessly, threw the foaming gray liquid to the back of their throats before holding out empty mugs for more. And later, when the oxen had been unyoked and left with the young boys to be grazed and watered, these same men came back, for a more prolonged bout of drinking.

Inside her grandmother's kitchen, Esther listened as the noise outside grew louder and the weight of coins in her pocket grew steadily heavier and heavier.

It was twilight now and some of the men had settled in for the evening. They had built a fire outside and there was much knee-slapping and great bursts of drunken laughter. Every so often someone would stagger unsteadily in through the door and stand, red-eyed and vacant, while Esther re-filled his mug.

Cornelia and Miriam arrived, tired from their labors in the field, and settled down beside the old women, while Esther passed them mugs of beer and sugar and Chengetai served them with a mound of steaming white sadza from a pot on the fire.

Miriam grabbed Esther's skirt as she passed and shook it to make the money jingle. "The sweet sound of success!

Now you can make your peace with the police – but how will you make your peace with the wives of that crazy crowd outside?"

Chengetai – her slow old blood quickened and her tongue loosened by alcohol – jabbed a big wooden serving spoon towards Miriam. "You leave her alone. She's doing well. A woman needs money these days and she has to get it however she can." She shook her bony old head, making the long torn lobes of her ears quiver: "Ach – money," she spat into the fire. "Father Paul is right – it's the root of all evil. I remember in the old days, when no one had any money at all. People were kinder to each other. Men used to help their wives . . ."

This was the signal. Everyone had an opinion on this subject.

"Now people want to be paid for everything. You can't even get a cup of milk for the children without someone asking you for money."

"You even have to pay people to plough for you. The men have been spoilt; they don't want to work any more."

"And even when they do get money they don't always give it to their wives. Some women are really suffering because their husbands keep the money for themselves."

A man from the rowdy group outside appeared at the door holding two empty mugs and there was a sudden silence in the kitchen while Esther served him. A couple of the women stared aggressively at the intruder, their chins jutting and lips tight with hostility. But the object of their disfavor was oblivious to the atmosphere in the firelit kitchen and just stood there with his mouth slightly open and his arms and legs akimbo, like a puppet whose strings have gone slack. After he'd shuffled out nobody spoke for a while.

Was this their oppressor – this man whom they'd known since he was a weanling; this poor sad creature with his baggy, ill-fitting jacket and flapping checked pants; this bumbling man with his lopsided smile and trembling hands?

"It's not their fault: nothing grows on this land. You can't blame a man for losing heart."

"They're ashamed, that's the trouble, ashamed of not being able to look after their families."

"It makes them mean, and angry – they want to escape . . ."

"And when they escape they never want to come back again."

"I thought things would improve when there was fertilizer and we were allowed to sell maize to the GMB – at least we could grow more food and maybe save a little money. But it all goes on school fees or to pay back the loan for the fertilizer. So the children are still hungry even if your husband doesn't drink the money away."

"If we had good land, things would be different."

"The men wouldn't have to go off to Harare to look for work; they wouldn't go with prostitutes and waste their money . . ."

"And we could grow enough food for the children and not have to sell half of it to pay school fees."

"If we had good land . . ."

Good land: enough to survive on, enough to grow food for the children and a little left over to sell. That was what they had fought for in the war. Everyone called it the "liberation struggle" – the struggle to break loose of the system that herded the black population like goats on to the worst land in the country, there to turn over the stony soil year after year, to scrape at it with their hoes, while the sorghum and maize crops dwindled and the children grew spindly and scrawny, like so many pot-bellied stick insects.

Well, they'd won the war. The suspicion and torture, the kidnappings and beatings, were over. There would be no more children forced to watch their mothers raped; no more charred bodies inside blazing huts. The faces in the government were black now, and it was black hands that drove the camouflaged tanks that roared down the tarred roads to Ndebeleland. The country belonged to the blacks, but the land, the good land . . . the land still belonged to the whites.

The anger in the room cooled to pity, then to shame, then nostalgia for long bygone days. Esther went outside to fetch more wood and Cornelia knelt to stoke the fire. Yellow flames brightened the room and lit up the faces of the children who had crept in through the door and wormed their little warm bodies in between their great aunts and grandmothers as the tipsy old women started telling stories.

As usual, it was grandmother Chengetai who started them off, sitting on the floor with her wizened legs straight out in front of her and Lovemore dozing against her bony old body. She began quietly and mysteriously, in the traditional way, and the children listened excitedly – silent and tense at the same time – as her cracked voice filled the firelit hut.

"Long time ago there was a family who had no food to eat. Nothing would grow on their land, so they lived only on whatever animals they could catch. If the father caught a hare they would have meat the day, but on other days they would have to fill their stomachs with water to stop them from feeling hungry.

"Now one day the father took his youngest son out hunting, but they went further than usual and came across a cave at the foot of a big kopje. And from deep inside the cave they heard a sweet-sounding voice. 'Come in my friend, and welcome,' said the voice –"

This was what the children had been waiting for. They knew all the stories by heart and knew exactly when to chime in with the ancient sing-song question-and-answer of Shona story telling.

Debbie Taylor

"Who's hiding in the cave?" they sang in a ragged unison.

"'I am the spirit of the cave,'" answered Chengetai in her soft, hoarse soprano. "'Take whatever you want from my treasures, but be warned: this is the only day you will be able to enter this cave, so be sure to take the most important thing away with you.'

"The father and son hurried inside and what they saw made their eyes pop out of their heads. There was every kind of meat, and fresh-cooked sadza; there were blankets and clothes and piles of money – all the good things they could imagine. Immediately they rushed to the plates of food and started eating the sadza –" Chengetai paused again for the children to play their part.

"Who does all this treasure belong to?" they sang again, staring raptly at the milky-eyed old woman.

"'It belongs to the spirit of the cave,'" answered Chengetai. "'Hurry, hurry. I will be closing the cave entrance soon. Hurry and take what you want as fast as you can – but don't forget to take the most important thing.'

"So the father stopped eating and began carrying armfuls and armfuls of things outside where he piled them all up in the sunshine, while his hungry little boy kept on tucking into the meat and sadza.

"'Quickly, quickly,' sang the voice. 'Get out of the cave, but don't forget the most important thing because I shall never open the cave again.'

"The father started rushing around madly, scooping up handfuls of coins and bundling them up in a blanket which he dragged outside the cave just as it was closing.

"Then he remembered his son, quietly eating sadza inside. But the voice had spoken the truth: the cave was closed for ever and he realized he had left the most important thing inside."

Esther and Cornelia slipped into the farm compound after sunset, like fugitives returning to the scene of the crime. The bus had deposited them by the gate, but they walked back up the road and waited in a little copse until darkness had fallen before making their way across the swampy foul-smelling vlei and sneaking into the compound from the north, away from the guards' normal patrol routes.

The welcome they received was muted: faces lighting up with surprised greeting, then darkening again as the shadow of fear passed over them and their minds began filling with images of the punishments that might be meted out if Esther were discovered back in the compound. She would be quick, she assured them, and careful. And she promised to be gone before sunrise the next morning.

With that her in-laws relaxed a little and sat the two travelers down by the fire with a bowl of sadza between them, while one of the children ran off into the night to fetch Beauty.

Within minutes there was a knock on the door and she was there, standing diffidently in the doorway with a puzzled frown on her face. Esther jumped up and tugged her into the room, pushing the door shut quickly behind her, then standing back and gazing at her pretty cousin. There was no mistaking Beauty's pregnancy now: a neat rounded swelling, like an inverted sadza bowl, pushed open the zip fastener on her skirt and her breasts strained at the buttons of her blouse. The two women tried to hug one another, but their two bellies made it impossible and they bounced apart laughing.

Then Beauty spotted Cornelia, standing stooped and ungainly, waiting to embrace her too. There was a split-second's hesitation, while the nightmare face of Cornelia-the-barren flickered over the dearly-loved features of Cornelia-the-cousin, and Beauty's fear-honed senses bristled with caution. She tried to banish it with a little shake of her head, but the suspicion stayed, stiffening her arms and fixing her smile as she reached out to greet her cousin.

"Do you think he'll be there?" Cornelia asked later, as the three cousins walked quickly through the dark compound towards the big house.

"How should I know?" Beauty snapped, her voice sharp with nervousness. If she were caught sneaking around the house like this, it would be the end of her job with Mrs. Johnson; perhaps the end of her time on the farm.

"Wait here," she whispered, as they drew nearer. "I'll go and knock on his door and ask if he'll see you – he might not be willing. You know he's practically retired now . . ."

She disappeared into the shadows and Cornelia and Esther crouched at the foot of a thick hedge and stared at the house. It was like an island floating in a sea of darkness: a huge cage full of light that burst out through cracks in the curtains, or from bulbs that hung above every door, and splashed bold bright patterns out across the surrounding garden. A guard sat in one of these pools of light, his chair tipped back against the wall of the house. Another circled slowly, submerged in the darkness, surfacing occasionally as if for breath in the bright spaces. Esther shivered as she recognized his face.

A small sound behind made them freeze and hold their breath. But Beauty's voice whispering "Come on, this way" unlocked their limbs and they followed her in a wide arc round to the back of the house and to the row of five doors, each slightly ajar and spilling out a thin stream of gold lamplight. Here they paused, unwilling to step into even this dilute puddle of light for fear of making themselves a target for the eyes of the ever-circling guard.

Immediately the door at the end opened and Seguro's bent gnome's body was silhouetted, beckoning, in the lamplight.

"You're safe now," he said, once they were inside and seated on the old sofa. "The guards are frightened of me" – he chuckled mischievously "– think I get up to all kinds of evil-doings in here at night. You won't get them poking their noses round the door investigating, I can guarantee. So" – he turned to Cornelia, without being introduced "– you want to have a baby, eh?"

Esther gasped and Cornelia nodded dumbly, while Beauty grinned and shrugged at her two cousins. She had warned them about Seguro's mind-reading ability. He looked at her hard for a moment or two, then frowned and shook his head slowly. "I will ask my father if we can help you, but I'm worried about you – I think your body is too damaged. Come, let's find out, shall we?" and he cut a circle in a big purple leaf and filled the gourd with water, as he had done for Beauty; then upended it so it swung heavily on its chain hanging from the ceiling. For a few seconds the leaf stayed in place, and they held their breath in awe. But then the swinging stopped and the water gushed out over the floor like a heave of vomit, splashing their bare feet and leaving the gourd hanging still and empty.

"There, I thought as much," said Seguro, in a soft voice. "I'm sorry, my dear –" Cornelia's shoulders were shuddering and her breath was coming in harsh hiccoughs of despair. "We can't help you conceive. But maybe there's something else we can do. Let me clear up this mess, while you start at the beginning and tell me all about it."

With that he knelt on the floor and began mopping up the water with a cloth and squeezing it out into a bucket he pulled out from under the table. Beauty tried to take the cloth out of his hands, uncomfortable to see a man doing women's work, but he pushed her gently back into her seat. "I'm used to it," he said, smiling. "Who do you think cleans the kitchen at the big house?"

So they sat, the three young women, while the old white-haired man wiped round their feet and Cornelia's unhappy voice filled the lamplit room. She told about how she had been married off, aged just fifteen, sacrificed by her father in return for the roora that would allow her younger brothers and sisters to eat. She said she had begun suffering from jeko after only a few weeks at her husband's homestead, and that it had never really been cured, though she'd been to the clinic at least four times. She did conceive once, she said, in the first year of her marriage. But she'd lost that baby after only three months and had never conceived again. Once her in-laws had even taken her secretly to have sex with her husband's brother while Mlambo was away. But that had not worked either. And now he was threatening to divorce her, throw her off the land and install a new wife there to bear children for him.

"Hah!" Seguro barked, banging the table in disgust. "So he thinks it's all your fault, does he? I know this kind of man: off working in Harare, messing with prostitutes, never sends money home – eh? Eh? Am I right? And what do you think? Do you think it's your fault too?"

"Of course it's not her fault," Esther broke in angrily, but Seguro silenced her with a long look from his piercing black eyes. "I'm asking your sister," he said quietly.

Cornelia didn't answer immediately. Instead she slumped lower against the arm of the sofa as if she wanted to sink inside its lumpy interior. She stared fixedly at her fingers picking desultorily at the frayed cover.

"I don't know," she said at last, in a small voice. "Sometimes I think . . ." Suddenly she looked up and met his eyes, like a wild animal whirling round desperately to face its attackers: "Do you think I'm a witch?"

The word was like a real presence in the room: a chill that tightened the skin and raised the hairs on their arms. Both

Beauty and Esther lifted their hands involuntarily as if to ward it off. Cornelia caught the movement from the corner of her eye and retreated still further into her corner, wrapping her arms protectively round herself and staring miserably at the floor. The only person unaffected was Seguro. He sat on the edge of the bed watching them, with his beady eyes twinkling and his head on one side in that bird-like way of his.

"Let me tell you a story," he said softly. "This is a true story. A woman I know went to the doctor one day, worried about her stomach. For the last six months she had been growing fatter and fatter, even though she hadn't been eating any more than usual. She knew she couldn't be pregnant because she was barren and her husband had recently divorced her. They had been married for eleven years and she had never had a child, so he had decided to take another wife.

"The doctor examined her carefully and smiled. 'Your child is growing nicely. You should give birth in three months' time,' he said. 'I don't understand,' the woman said. 'I can't be pregnant. I'm barren. That's why my husband divorced me.' 'Have you had relations with any other man recently?' the doctor asked, and when the woman admitted that she had, the doctor smiled again: 'Then I'm afraid your husband has made a terrible mistake,' he said. 'He is the one to blame, not you. He is the one who is barren.'"

The three women relaxed as he told the story, then laughed aloud as he reached the end. "What I am saying is that you should not blame yourself," he said, serious again. "Your husband is the one who has made you barren. You have been faithful to him, but he has betrayed you with other women. You wait and see – he will not have any success with his new wife either." He paused for this

139

information to sink in, then continued. "The question is what to do now to prevent him from abandoning you completely – if that is what you want . . ."

Mystified, curious, they watched him move the little smoky lamp over to the table where he pored over the haphazard heaps of dried leaves and roots there, fingering them reverently and weighing them in his big broad hand.

"I don't usually do this . . .," he said. "But it makes me so angry to hear of a husband discarding his old wife like a broken bucket to make way for a new one. Men these days have no respect; they ignore the advice of the elders. When I was a young man you wouldn't dare have sex with someone who wasn't your wife for fear of the old women. When they found out they would follow you round the village jeering and taunting you, making you feel ashamed. But men off working in the city are out of reach of the elders – they feel they can do what they like . . ." He took a twist of newspaper and handed it to Cornelia. "Write a letter to your husband and put a pinch of this powder in the envelope. This will pry him loose from that other woman of his and bring him back home in a different frame of mind, I promise." And with that he shooed them out of his little room, back into the inky black night.

"Are you still sucking up to that woman?" Esther asked Beauty. After a couple of near-misses with the guards they were back in the compound and sitting in the tiny thatched house Esther shared with Darwin.

Beauty drew back her slim shoulders and lifted her chin angrily, just like her mother. "Don't speak about her like that. She's a good woman; she treats me well."

"Well her husband didn't treat me well," Esther retorted. "Don't tell me she's any different. At heart they're all the same. She didn't stop him throwing me off the farm, did she?

That makes it her fault too. If she really cared about our health – like she says she does – she'd make sure we had enough food. She certainly wouldn't punish us for trying to look after our children . . ."

Beauty stuck out her lower lip in a pout and refused to answer.

"I'm sorry," said Esther, with a sigh. "We shouldn't quarrel. It seems such a long time since I saw you. Are you coming home to have this little one?" She patted Beauty's tummy, changing the subject. But before she could reply Darwin ducked his head under the low door-jamb and came into the room. Esther scrambled to her feet. "I want a word with you, husband," she said and steered him back outside, leaving the others to arrange the blankets ready for the night.

They talked for a long time, sitting on the raised mud step in the darkness under the eaves. Beauty disturbed them briefly to say goodnight before setting off for her own house on the other side of the compound, but it was very late and the rest of the compound was in darkness: there was no electricity here and no guards to watch over these sleeping families. After an hour or so it began to rain and soft warm drops, invisible in the dense blackness, pattered quietly down, surrounding them with gentle sound like curtains of enveloping fabric.

"Are you absolutely sure?" Esther asked in a whisper, straining her eyes vainly for the outline of her husband's face. "You'll have to tell your family. And once we've decided we can't change our minds. It wouldn't be fair."

Sitting beside him, with her shoulder next to his, she felt him move to nod his head.

"Yes, I'm sure," he said.

Cornelia had barely spoken after their consultation with

Seguro. She just hung her head to avoid their sympathetic eyes and lay down with her face to the wall as soon as she had unfolded their blankets for the night. She was silent on the journey home too, and Esther was painfully aware of her own pregnancy, flaunted bulky and shameless on her lap, as she sat beside the folded bony body of her sister on the bus.

What is a woman without a child? A sad, empty, hungry thing; a mockery of nature – and mocked by nature in her turn. Everywhere she looks, her eyes fall on the frenzy of life striving to renew itself: goats rutting by the roadside, their hard little buttocks thrusting; a thick-beaked roller – iridescent in turquoise and purple – proclaiming territory from the top of a dead tree; a cow lowing lovingly to the spindly, knob-browed calf that nudges and nibbles at her udder.

When the two sisters stepped down from the bus, even the warm mud at their feet teemed with ostentatious coupling. Grasshoppers, emblazoned with the red, yellow and green colors of lust, meandered dazedly off the path in clumsy piggy-back pairs, their secret parts secretly pumping; while ants and termites of every size issued like boiling liquid from their holes in ecstatic preparation for the virgin flights of their winged princes and princesses.

The very scent of sex was in the air: impossible to ignore. It filled the nostrils with a heady mixture of new-crushed grass, fresh-turned earth, a whiff of sour milk and the faintest fragrance of a kaleidoscope of small flowers peeping out from beneath the bushes where they sheltered from the tireless tearing of grazing teeth.

Out in the fields teams of women and children, with sacks slung round their necks, and hoes in their hands, worked their way slowly across the clotted ground, planting maize: one seed at a time, a thin stream, from one sack; a dribble of gray fertilizer from another; and, finally, a skillful swipe with the hoe to seal them in the earth. Every season the same: seed ripens, is harvested, then buried and reborn in the next year's crop. The cycles of humanity were no different: "Remember, child, that thou art dust. And unto dust thou shalt return." Alfred, poor child, had died; was buried. Esther's body, like the earth, carried the promise of replacement. But Cornelia was excluded from the infinite cycles of death and rebirth. No seed would ever grow in her womb now.

Still, there was little time to mourn. The two women were instantly absorbed into the complex work rotas of the growing season. Like a huge motor beginning to turn over, its duties were light at first, with only the strongest and fittest yoked full-time to its cogs and treadwheels. But later, when the shoots in the fields began to sprout – and the weeds along with them – every member of every household who could lift a hand, was put to work. Children no higher than a father's knee became custodians of their younger siblings; old women with trembling arms and rheumy eyes were set stirring sadza; schoolchildren rose before dawn to patrol the fields with hoes, slicing at the weeds between rows of new maize spikes before scrubbing the dirt from their nails and walking four miles to the schoolhouse.

It became more and more difficult to find spaces in the routine for anything other than work, or to save energy enough to stave off sleep at the end of the day. But one evening Cornelia did manage to resist the lure of her blankets and borrowed a pen and paper to write her letter to Mlambo. When she had finished she hesitated for a moment, with a pinch of the magic dust between her fingers, then dropped it in and sealed the envelope decisively. She gave it to Esther the next day and it burned in her pocket as she walked to the row of tin-roofed stores to post it on the way to the clinic.

The queues at the clinic were shorter than usual, along the

143

shady balcony and under the spreading syringa tree. And the ailments reflected the urgency of the season and the pressures on the mothers of Zimbabwe, who were unable to fullfil their normal task of mothering. There were toddlers with awful burns where, unattended, they had fallen on to the grate or tripped over a pot of boiling water; a few ancient great-grandmothers carrying infants on their backs to be vaccinated; worried ten-year-olds shepherding a bleary, feverish younger brother or sister; and a small bevy of bloated bellies, like Esther's, driven by their obviously impending due-dates to register – just in time – at the clinic for their deliveries. Many more who would normally be here were at home: the earlier pregnancies, whose hands were needed for weeding; the babies with diarrhea, or vomiting, or fever, whom no one dared spare the time to carry the three, four or five miles to the clinic.

Lovemore was one such ailing infant – sick, again, diarrhea, again, again; for the umpteenth time in his short hungry life. Esther had lifted him and tied him, as usual on to her back, to take him – again – to the clinic with her. But the thought of carrying even his slight weight, in addition to her eight-month belly, all the way to the stores and back, made her untie the blanket once more and pass his whining, swaddled body into Violet's willing five-year-old arms.

Esther's turn came at last and she clambered, with difficulty, up on to the examination trolley and proffered her prone body, with its criss-cross of surgeon's scars, to Sister Tekedi's probing brown fingers. Ten minutes later she was out in the sunshine again, with a handful of vitamins, a new medical card and confirmation of her fear that this baby, too, would have to be cut from her body. Her bones were too small: narrow and tight like a man's, with no space for her child's head to pass through.

She sighed and squinted up at the midday sky as she

turned wearily back down the road that led home: a tiny girl-woman, back hollowed, legs splayed with the effort to balance her belly beneath a pitiless burning white sun.

"Didn't you use masuwo?" Alita asked Esther as they quickly washed out the previous night's pots in the gathering twilight. There had been no time to do them before, and no need, since the leisured weeks, when the family ate three good meals a day, were behind them for another four months. Now there was only cold sadza or thin gruel in the mornings and a hasty hot meal thrown together at nightfall.

"Of course I did, mother. I'd try anything to prevent them from cutting me open again. But the nurse said my bones were still closed, so perhaps I didn't start the masuwo early enough." She knelt on a clean flat rock in the mud and used a sharp stone to scrape congealed sadza from the rim of a black pot while a flurry of baby chicks ran forward to peck at the dislodged white shards floating on the muddy puddles.

"Perhaps I should do what the Mozambican women do. Someone at the farm told me they stuff balls of dry grass in their vaginas to stretch the opening, putting in more and more each week until they're sure the baby will be able to get through."

Alita stood up straight, widening her eyes in disbelief. "Ugh!" she shuddered. "Imagine walking round with a lump of grass inside you all the time! I think the Shona way is better: a drink of masuwo every day to make your vagina soft, and a nightly massage to stretch the skin." She bent over again to rinse a stack of enamel plates in the remains of the water: "Do you know, I never once had a tear: not once for ten babies! But I suppose if it's your bones that are the problem, there's nothing you can do."

Esther piled up the clean cooking pots inside one another, like the skins of a great black iron onion, then struggled to

145

her feet with them in her arms. Suddenly she felt a surge of hot liquid between her legs.

"Oh no," she said softly, half to herself, "I don't believe it: not now, not tonight, it's too soon . . ." The liquid poured down the inside of her thighs and into the mud and soapy scum at her feet while she stood helplessly, in the fading light, with the dead weight of iron in her arms and the living weight of flesh in her belly.

In less than an hour, with Alita by her side, she was retracing her steps to the clinic.

Her contractions had started now: not too painful, but strong enough to make her stop sometimes, with a gasp, under the darkening sky, and hold on to her mother for support for a moment or two before stepping forward once more over the soft, weaving ruts on the road. They did not talk much, silenced as much by exhaustion and worry as by the sullen, gloomy beauty of the night. The moon had just risen and sat in a haze of moisture above the horizon like a fat, brooding pigeon on her eggs. Its dilute light touched trees and grass with the faintest silver sheen and smeared blurred black shadows on a monochrome underworld.

Once, while they rested for a few minutes on a grassy bank, Esther saw an owl appear out of the wound in a lightning-struck tree and float soundlessly on white wings down the road ahead of them. She touched Alita's arm and, with sinking hearts, the two women got to their feet and followed this ghostly harbinger of illness as it led onwards through the night.

The owl stayed with them all the rest of the way, stopping now and then, hunched and blinking, on a tree stump or termite hill, then opening its pale wings and sliding effortlessly into the air again, like a swimmer adrift on a current of water.

At last they arrived and – relief! – there were lights blazing at the clinic windows and a solid, reassuring yellow oblong of brightness tilted out through the open door: so another woman must be giving birth here tonight.

After the quiet moonlit menace of their long walk, the atmosphere inside the little building was a welcome assault on the senses: a mixture of hearty chatter and subdued grunts of pain, clanking instruments and running water, all bathed in harsh electric light. Sister Tekedi recognized Esther from earlier that day and her chubby face registered surprise and concern.

"I thought I told you to come back in a month," she admonished mildly, shaking her head. "Right, up you get, let's take a look at you." And she peeped and prodded and listened, then washed her hands and picked up the telephone.

"I'm coming with you," Alita said firmly, when the ambulance arrived two hours later to take her to hospital. "I know they won't let me stay," she went on, as Esther started to protest, "but I want to be nearby, just in case . . ." And Esther was glad to have her there because, when they climbed up the step at the back of the white Land-Rover, she was certain she heard an owl shriek from the shadowy depths of the syringa tree.

It was long past midnight when the Land-Rover crunched to a gravelly standstill by the jigsaw of buildings – part dingy old-colonial, part scruffy pre-fab – that was Kadoma District Hospital. There was a subdued hush about the place, an air of active waiting, like an army barracks between battles with only the sentries on duty. The driver conducted the two women through a pair of battered swing doors and down a long pitted concrete corridor that bisected one of the single-story buildings. He knocked at a half-open door and ushered them inside.

"I'm afraid you'll have to wait outside now," the nurse

said to Alita when she looked up from the newspaper she was reading and saw them standing nervously in the doorway. "You can come back tomorrow at visiting time."

Alita passed one of the bundles she was carrying to Esther and smiled reassuringly into her daughter's eyes. "Remember, I'll be outside all the time." Then she was gone.

Esther was alone.

Sure, there was the nurse who questioned her and wrote down her answers; and the other nurse who led her to the delivery room down at the end of the corridor, who gave her a gown to put on, then prodded, peered and listened while she lay shivering, half naked, on the hard examination table. And there were nameless other women, like herself, who slept or lay awake behind the doors that lined the corridor. But in truth, when it came to companion souls, she was alone.

Always, whenever she had a baby, she had to face the ordeal alone. Now, at her time of greatest fear, when she most needed a familiar face, Alita was kept away from her. This, the most frightening time – when piercing lights illuminated her most intimate places, when a needle would plunge her into unconsciousness and a cold knife would slit her open – this was the only time in her life she was ever parted from people she loved.

She lay curled on her side, like the fetus she carried, and placed her hands on her belly, seeking comfort in the movements of her unborn child. Yes, there he was, little sweetheart, sweetly shifting his pinioned shoulders and flexing his neck while his tiny heart thudded out a tremulous tattoo of life.

"Not long now," she whispered, as a clock ticked slowly on the wall above her. "Not long now . . ."

Suddenly there was a commotion and she heard raised voices and the rumbling of trolley wheels being pushed down the uneven corridor towards her. The swing door was kicked open and a man in a white coat backed into the room holding a drip in one hand and pressing down on the shoulder of a body on the trolley with the other. The two nurses she had seen earlier followed, half pushing the trolley, half trying to restrain the violent thrashing movements of their patient.

It was a woman, of course; a pregnant woman. But not like any pregnant woman Esther had ever seen before – more like a wild animal in a trap: eyes bulging and rolling, teeth bared and clamped on a piece of wood, flecks of saliva spotting her clenched, reddened face and her whole body writhing about as if the trolley was on fire. Was she possessed? Was she baby eating her alive? Esther, ignored on her bed in the corner, shrank back against the wall with her knees tucked under her, clutching the chifumuro charm she still wore, with every nerve fiber taut with fear.

Soon the woman's thrashings began to lessen, as though her limbs were suddenly too heavy to move, and the nurses began to undress her, stripping off her clothes to reveal an enormous striated belly and legs that still twitched slightly and lolled, out of control, off the side of the trolley like dead chickens' necks, so that the nurses kept having to heave them back on it again. She had soiled herself and the stench filled the room while they wiped and washed her like a baby, rolling her inert body heavily from side to side before finally inserting a catheter, dumping the attached polythene bag on the trolley, then covering her with a blanket.

Just as they finished another man rushed in, a young white man, in jeans and a checked shirt.

"Okay, we're ready," he said in guttural English. "Did she have any notes?" He frowned as he ran his eyes over the

149

buff card he was handed. "Blood pressure normal – taken just yesterday at Extension Eight! What are they playing at out there? Oh, come on, let's get her to theater."

"What about this one?" One of the nurses pointed to Esther. "CPD, waters broken. She needs an emergency CS tonight too."

The white man raked his fingers through his hair distractedly. "Is the baby all right? She'll just have to wait. Get her ready, will you? We'll be as quick as we can." And, unhooking the drip from its stand, he and the two nurses trundled the trolley back out again.

Esther was alone once more – in silence apart from the regular metallic ticking of the electric clock on the wall. The room was in disarray with the screens pushed aside just anyhow and a heap of soiled clothes by the door. Slowly she eased her body, with its flimsy cotton covering, back down to lie on the bed and winced as her leaking womb contracted on the little gasping amphibian inside.

She fingered her scars: one for each pregnancy. Here was Lovemore's: a neat vertical, just below her navel; and Violet's: a horizontal curve tracing the line of her pubic hair; and a third one, fainter than the others, at a slight angle crossing beneath Lovemore's bold exit point: the scar they left when they lifted her first child, a stillborn baby girl, out from the tensely clenched womb that had suffocated her.

It had been during the war, when everything was chaotic – telephone lines cut, roads booby-trapped – and no one dared travel at night. Her labor started and, though Miriam did all she could, there was no way to widen the gape of her pelvis' stiff jaws. Somehow they got her to the clinic, where, after more hours of fruitless augmenting agony, Esther was just one exhausted sobbing scream and a band of muscle, like a belt of solid flesh, began to form across her belly and to tighten on the baby inside.

They did not tell her, then, that her womb could rupture any second, nor that her baby was dead. By then she was delirious with pain and didn't know or care that their continuous hopeless jabbing at the telephone had at last made a connection with the hospital. She found out later that other women, less lucky than she, had to lie on their backs, fully conscious, while a knife was inserted up through their vaginas and their dead babies extracted, piece by bloody piece, through the stubborn white pelvic gateway.

The memory sent her fingers scudding over her scarred skin, searching for the movement that would mean that this child was still alive. No . . . no . . . yes! There he was, dear soul, plucky heart pumping, nudging her hand softly with his knee.

In time one of the nurses came back and peeled back Esther's gown to swab the fluid that still flowed in a continuous slight trickle between her legs and to listen for the baby's heart with a cold metal tube. Then she rummaged beneath a dark blue cloth on one of the trolleys for a catheter tube which she edged up Esther's narrow stretched ureter and into her bladder: a sharp hot pain to add spice to the duller ache of her contractions.

"Soon be ready for you," she said briskly, bending her head to listen again to the baby. "And not a moment too soon," she muttered quietly, making a note on the buff card she held. Sure enough, a brown-coated man appeared a few minutes later with a wheelchair to take her to the theater.

Dawn was breaking as he butted the front wheels out of the maternity ward and forced the wheelchair forwards over the clinker and gravel. Round they went, under the trees behind the main building, past the big garbage bins and the split black stain where the coal for the boiler was stored. At one point Esther heard her name being called and saw Alita's shadowy figure, shrouded in a blanket, standing

151

alone beside the path in the gray dawn light. But she couldn't reply because she was being hauled up a steep ramp to wait in the tall echoey hall, with its greasy gloss-painted walls, outside the operating theater.

Immediately Esther was thrust into an alien world, a world which had no links with her normal life but was familiar, nonetheless, with the chilling recognition that signals the start of a recurrent nightmare. The people – men? women? – wore green dresses that tied at the back, green hats covering their hair and white masks over their faces. Hidden lips spoke a language she only barely understood as their gloved hands pulled back her gown and sluiced purple disinfectant over her belly. She was surrounded on all sides by green strangers touching her body with a hateful impersonal intimacy. A needle sank into her arm; black rubber clamped down on her face; sheets of green fabric were thrown over her prone body as though to protect these alien eyes from the shocking sight of her naked and vulnerable flesh.

The speed with which they assaulted her – such a contrast to her long silent waiting in the maternity building – and the curt urgency of their indecipherable speech sent a surge of panic through her and she struggled against the weight of unconsciousness that was bearing down on her. For a moment she was icily aware of the hissing, humming and bleeping of the metal machines by her head and the sandy eyelashes of the white man who held the mask over her face. Then her eyes closed.

How the sins of the white fathers are visited on the black children. Like trees whose histories are recorded by the width of the rings in their trunks, so each year leaves its mark on the soft growing bodies of the children. Esther had been the child of a bad year: starved in the womb, stinted at the breast, and then stunted, irrevocably – as drought and

152

debt dragged on for a second, then a third year – into the child-woman that now bared her belly through the shrouds of green on the operating table.

The scars on her skin – deep purple weals that cut across her dusting of silvery stretchmarks – were the scars of a pitiless poverty that had fashioned a skeleton so skimpy no child could ever negotiate its narrow gateway.

Now the knife was inserted again, making a new red incision on the much-slit and much-mended skin. It sprung apart to reveal her womb, as wounded and knotted with scars as the brown skin that contained it. Metal tongs bearing fat cotton swabs mopped smears of blood, then the knife went in once more, slicing through a wall of muscular flesh that was now so stiff with old wounds it could no longer contract evenly. An ooze of pale liquid, swiftly swabbed, then a gloved hand was inserted and a child pulled out, by the feet, like a limp-legged rabbit from a hat.

How the sins of the white fathers are visited on the black children's children. This baby, born a month before his time, was an old man by the time his flaccid lungs filled with their first uncertain breath. His wizened little face was wrinkled, his buttocks crumpled and empty of flesh. Toothless gums sucked hungrily at his fist while his nostrils flared with the effort to inflate his puny chest. He was a travesty of babyhood, this scrawny red monkey born gasping and sucking at the air, his body streaked green with shit from intestines released by his oxygen-starved brain.

Over the gaping red gash that was Esther, the baby's cord was clamped in two places and cut, and a hissing vacuum tube pushed down his throat and down into each nostril, raking over the delicate membranes and sucking out the mucus. He tried to breathe, to choke; to cough, to cry: impossible. Gloved hands placed him head-down on a sloping table under blazing hot bulbs and covered his nose and mouth with a hard plastic mask attached to a bulb which they squeezed to pump air into his laboring lungs. His fists flailed in weak protest, then submitted to the light and the noise and the blasts of cold air down his windpipe. And when at last they lifted the hard mask from his face and withdrew the hissing tubes from his nose, he opened his tiny, hungry mouth and screamed out his rage and despair to the world.

Waiting somewhere on the threshold of consciousness, Esther answered her son's cry of anguish with a silent scream of her own and struggled to swim to the surface. But the mask and the needle held her back, while the placenta was eased out and slopped into a dish and wads of cotton were packed into her bloody cavity like lumps of stuffing into a cushion. Next her womb was lifted right out of her body and a damp cloth stuffed in the space beneath it and wiped thoroughly round inside her open abdomen. Streaked and clotted with gouts of blood, the cloth was pulled out and thrown into a bucket, followed by great red-stained wads of cotton wool, with the slimy flop of placenta – sacred life-giving flounder of flesh – tipped finally on top of the bloody garbage like a profane dollop of cream.

There were half-memories of her stretcher jolting back to the ward, of efficient hands heaving her immobile body, of curious eyes on her face and stripy-gowned figures moving in front of a bright square of morning window, as she slid into and out of sleep. Eventually it was a surge of nausea that roused her properly as the smell of sadza and chicken stew reached her nostrils from the lunch trolley that had just been wheeled in.

Without thinking, she rolled over on to her side to direct her retches away from the bedclothes and her eyes flew open at the cacophony of pain that bit into her: from internal stitches, deeply throbbing; from external ones, whiplashed across her abdomen; the milder, numb ache of the drip tether tugging at a vein in her arm; the itchy hot sting of the catheter draining her bladder. Each fruitless heave of her empty stomach ended in a grunt of agony as severed and bruised nerves spat out burning protests of pain.

Soon her helpless retching gave way to coughing – just as painful – as her lungs began to rid themselves of the shallow pools of fluid that had accumulated while she was unconscious. Tears of pain squeezed out of her eyes and poured down her cheeks as she subsided back on to the unfamiliar bulk of her pillows and tried to stifle her coughs. Slowly the worst clamors of pain receded and she was able to look around her.

Though most of the patients were at the opposite end of the ward by the food trolley, almost every bed bore some sign of its occupant: a discarded cardigan or the blanket-swaddled form of a baby on the pillow, buff files on a table at the foot of each bed, a woolly hat or an orange on a shelf, a pair of shoes beneath a cot. She saw that her own little bundle of belongings was on the table beside her head. Then her heart stopped. Where was her baby?

She must have cried out because there was a sudden flurry of concern down the other end of the room and soon a nurse was hurrying towards her.

"Your baby's fine, a lovely little boy, but he's in an incubator. We're keeping him nice and warm because he's so small. Don't worry, it's only for a few days. You'll be able to see him and feed him later on – as soon as you feel a bit better." And she briskly unhitched Esther's arm from the drip and thrust a thermometer into her mouth before whisking off down the ward again.

Weak with relief, Esther sank back again on her pillows. A movement caught her eye and she spotted her mother outside, peering in through the window. Their eyes met and

Esther smiled a crooked smile, mouthing "It's a boy" as well as she could with the thermometer protruding from her lips, before the nurse came back and Alita dodged out of sight.

The rest of the day was spent struggling, slowly and painfully, through an inadequate film of analgesia, to carry out the simplest of bodily functions. She sat up, sipped a cup of tea, exchanged greetings and names with her neighbors. She hobbled to the big dark bathroom to change her sodden red sanitary towel and ran water into a basin for a cursory wash. Visiting time came and went in a kind of dream, with Alita sitting quietly by her bedside for half an hour: just sitting, listening to the buzz of conversation around them, with her hand on the pillow by her daughter's head in a gesture like a sailor on a pier reaching out to hold his boat steady on the water. And while she was still sitting there, an anchor in a turbulent sea, Esther slid gently into an exhausted peaceful sleep.

Hours later, when the sinking sun slanted golden shafts of light through the window, and a surge of activity signaled the arrival of the supper trolley, she woke – ravenously hungry and in intense pain again. A nurse brought her some pain-killers and the woman in the next bed handed her a plate of food and helped her to sit up.

She ate slowly and steadily, concentrating on her food, and gradually became aware of something strange in the atmo-sphere of the ward. At first she couldn't identify what was wrong. Then it came to her: the quietness. Where was the chatter and laughter that usually accompanied a meal? These women seemed so somber and withdrawn. She looked at them more closely and, after a while, her eyes were drawn to one particular woman sitting alone on a chair beside her bed.

The woman was eating, like the others: pinching lumps of sadza and meat together in her fingers and pushing them into her mouth. But she was chewing absently, as though her jaws, and her hands, were being moved for her; being moved – not so much against her will as without it – to sustain a life she was no longer interested in sustaining.

Esther understood at once: this woman's baby was dead. Somewhere in this jumble of buildings, with its squeaky swing doors and echoey corridors, was a tiny cold corpse. Perhaps it was waiting in the morgue – a stiff little bundle marooned alone in the frosty depths of a huge man-sized meat drawer. Or perhaps it had been tipped without ceremony into the incinerator, a spirit sizzled to cinders along with the other bloody débris of childbirth, never to know the repose of the children who sleep by the river.

Esther pushed her plate away and slid gingerly out of bed. She had to see her baby.

"There he is, in there, the one on the left," said the nurse. "You can hold him if you like."

Esther peered through the smeary glass of the incubator at her son. He lay on his back with his arms flung out and his bony little chest heaving: a living skeleton in mottled red skin, no bigger than a plucked chicken. She could see the veins on his tummy – a tracery of blue – rising and falling as he slept. There was a flat, abandoned look about him, as though every ounce of energy that his fleshless little body could summon was working to expand his immature lungs.

Tiny, he was so tiny. All her children had been small, but none so small as this. And so painfully exposed, lying spreadeagled and uncovered in his glass cage for all to see; with his puffy eyelids and the porcelain curves of his nostrils; his neatly coiled ears and the soft rounded soles of his unwalked-on feet; the black gossamer ghost hair that covered his skull. As she watched him, he opened his eyes and looked at her: a solemn blue stare from his sad old-man's face and his limp and laboring body.

157

It was a look of such loneliness – from a scrap of humanity who had only air to caress his skin, only naked lightbulbs looking down on his naked flesh, only the smell of antiseptic in his nostrils. Esther lifted the glass lid and gathered him into her arms.

Within moments he was feeding and they were locked together like lovers in a first embrace: he sucking greedily, spluttering in his eagerness, and scratching at her breast with his nails as if he would devour her whole body; she sitting, bent over, cradling him away from her stitches, running a hand over his downy head and smiling, besotted, at his lustful frenzy. No child had ever clung to her like this, as if to life itself: perhaps because none had so tenuous a hold on it – the ghost hair on his back meant the ancestors had not yet decided whether they would release him into the world of the living.

After a while the nurse came back to prize them apart and settle him back – more a medical exhibit than a baby – in his inhuman cradle of glass.

"Will he be all right?" Esther asked.

"Oh, I expect so," the nurse replied airily. "He's having some trouble breathing – prem and CS babies often do – but that should sort itself out in a day or two. Meanwhile we'll keep him nice and warm and keep an eye on his respiration."

Esther stayed in the room for a long time after the nurse had gone and stared at her beautiful, scrawny monkey of a son through the glass: her little bug-eyed, red-skinned fish out of water, stranded on his hard white medical beach. Enough, it was enough. She had tempted the ancestors too many times by insisting that her unfit body was fit to bear children. One daughter was dead and one living; one son sick and ailing at home, one still half in the hands of the spirits; a belly as ripped and rutted as a country road:

perhaps it was time to concede defeat. But what if one of Lovemore's many illnesses should carry him off one day? What if Violet's husband-of-the-future took her to the other end of the country? What if this upturned red insect-baby of hers was reclaimed to the land of his ancestors? What a barren old woman she'd be.

"Goodnight, baby," she whispered through the glass, and turned to hobble back to the ward. Raised voices speaking in Shona stopped her as she reached the door.

"I told you to empty your bladder half an hour ago –"

"If you don't lie down properly on your back we can't help you –"

"Don't waste your energy crying out now, you'll need all your strength later on –"

She peered down the corridor and saw a young woman lying, in a tattered pink petticoat, on the very same bed she had waited on the previous night. Her teeth were gritted and her head thrown back in pain, while two nurses stood either side of her, like white-uniformed jailers, booming brisk and hearty instructions. Despite the woman's pregnancy, the nurses seemed enormous beside her, like billowing yachts in full sail by a tiny overladen pink fishing boat. Esther shrugged her shoulders sympathetically, then set off on her painful journey back down the corridor.

Later that night, when she tiptoed out of the ward to go to the toilet, a light was still blazing through the open door at the end of the corridor and voices were still raised in admonishment above the straining mother's cries of pain.

"How long has she been like this? What's the fetal heart-rate? Why don't you know? I told you to use the partogram. How else can we find out if the baby's all right? This is exactly what happened to that other one. Do you want us to lose this baby too? The doctor will be furious when he finds out . . ."

159

"Maiway, maiway, maiway . . .," moaned the pregnant woman, clutching at the metal frame of the bed. She was calling for her mother: outside, probably, with Alita; somewhere by the hospital gates, sleeping wrapped in a blanket, or peering anxiously through the chain-link fence at the one lighted window at the far end of the dark maternity building.

"Maiway, maiway . . .": the plaintive call of a daughter in pain echoed down the long concrete corridor with its layers of pungent polish streaked by trolley skidmarks.

Esther couldn't sleep when she got back into bed: for hours the sounds of the other woman's lonely drama flooded the corridor and seeped under the closed door of the ward. Then, at last, there was silence.

Wide awake and curious, Esther slipped out of bed once more. Framed in the open doorway, the woman was naked now, and shivering convulsively, on her side with her arms crossed protectively over her breasts. While Esther watched, one of the nurses appeared and thrust a big white sanitary towel between the woman's legs. She then hauled, with both hands, on the sheet covering the bed and ripped it from beneath the woman's shuddering body so she was lying on the bare cold plastic. It was as though, having cooked and eaten the meal, the nurses were gathering up the dirty pots and bowls and doing the washing up. And the woman, now dazedly donning her crumpled petticoat, was just another soiled utensil to be washed and cleared away, ready for the next meal to be served.

Esther waited to see the woman edge slowly down off the bed and stoop awkwardly, one hand on the towel between her legs, to retrieve a pair of panties from the floor. Then she turned and went back to bed.

Over the next few days Esther seemed to spend half her time padding on bare feet, with her stitches pulling painfully, up

160

and down that long pockmarked corridor: to the cavernous bathroom for the luxury of splashing in the sporadic supply of hot water she had not had to fetch herself; to the toilet where the wasteful miracle of the flush never ceased to astound her; and to the nursery, where her son fought his lonely battle for life next to other wrinkled infants in their heated glass cradles.

A doctor came each morning and sailed down the ward, stopping briefly at each bed to flip open a buff-colored folder and smile vaguely and benignly in the general direction of each patient's face before passing on to the next. Sometimes he spoke to them, with Sister translating, directing brusque rhetorical questions at them like a member of royalty addressing a humble subject.

"It was the muti the traditional midwife gave you that caused the problem wasn't it? Go to the clinic next time you're pregnant," he said to one women who had been in labor for twenty-four hours by the time she was admitted.

"Quite a patchwork, isn't it?" he commented, in English, when he came to Esther, surveying her latest line of stitches. Then, seeing her uncomprehending smile, in broken Shona he explained: "Three children is enough, yes? Operations no good. No more operations, okay? Must use family planning now."

Esther was too shy to answer. But when he had gone she spoke to the nurse. "I did use family planning, but it didn't work and I got pregnant anyway. I heard there was an operation you can have to stop you having any more babies . . ."

But the nurse interrupted her: "Do you want your husband to divorce you, woman? That operation's for older women who are sure they've had all the children they want."

"But my husband understands that it's dangerous for me to have any more children," Esther protested. "He agrees to me having the operation."

161

But the nurse only laughed. "Ah! Men say one thing when they really mean another. No man wants a wife who can't give him babies. Take the pill instead. But take it properly this time – no missing days . . ." And with that she patted Esther's arm and walked briskly out of the room.

Meanwhile, the baby seemed a little stronger. Gradually the rapid heaving of his chest had slowed and the little grunting noises that accompanied each labored gulp of air had nearly faded to nothing. His skin began to lose its transparent redness and the terrible long moments when he lay limply, not breathing at all, grew ever fewer and further between. Soon he was turning his head towards Esther when she spoke to him through the glass, gazing with rapt adoration into her eyes as he fed and reaching out a skinny arm to touch her cheek.

"Feed him as often as you can," said the nurses. "He needs to grow fat and strong so that he'll be able to keep himself warm when we take him out of the incubator." And Esther was happy to oblige, though the tug of the stitches in her womb, which contracted whenever he sucked, spiced every sweet contact with her son with a bitter tang of pain. Meanwhile the soft black thistledown on his back, which showed no sign yet of disappearing, acted as a constant gentle reminder that this child's life should never be taken for granted: he was a gift of the ancestors, and his soul might be snatched back any second.

So she named him Chipo, the gift, to ensure she would never forget that this precious baby had nearly been withheld from her. And at last, after seven days, it was time to go home.

* * *

Somehow, in the short time she had been away, spring had turned to summer and the shallow puddles of green grass had overflowed their margins and spread across the ground until almost every inch of the veld was covered with a thrusting spiky carpet. The sun beat down on Esther's bare head and filtered through her thick thatch of hair as she walked slowly down the road from where the ambulance had deposited her outside the clinic.

The noises of summer filled her ears as she plodded through the shimmering mid-morning heat haze: crickets whirring their summer lovesongs, a flock of tiny blue-breasted finches fluting and twittering from bush to bush, the chattering chaos of a weaver-bird colony whose nests hung like knitted gourds from the branches of an acacia tree. In the distance, when she shaded her eyes, she saw the big fork-tailed silhouette of a black kite spiraling slowly upwards in a current of warm air high above her home.

But when her feet eventually took her aching body with its tiny fragile cargo down the path that led to the homestead, only Violet and Lovemore were there. Esther hesitated for a moment and watched with pride as her daughter heaved her son up under the arms, from where he was poking his fingers into the dirt, and struggled with him into the shade by the hut where she began pushing lumps of sadza into his mouth.

"Violet!" Esther called across the sun-baked courtyard. "I've brought you another little boy to look after for me."

"Why did you name him Chipo?" asked Cornelia later, when the family were gathered together round the fire at the end of the day. It was quiet now in the sleepy kitchen and they were relaxing at last, basking in the warm light of the dying embers. They had been besieged by visitors all evening, everyone eager to pay their respects to the newest member of the community and pass comment on his likeness to this or that, living or dead, member of the family. But now the visitors had all departed to lay work-weary heads to rest in their own homes.

Esther leant against her mother, with Violet nestling under her arm, and sighed a big sigh of contentment: to be back amongst this familiar huddle of bodies, with the glow of firelight on her cheeks and the smell of woodsmoke in her nostrils.

"I called him Chipo because he nearly died," she explained, reaching out a hand to touch her baby's head as he slept in Cornelia's strong arms. "I wanted to give him a name that would remind me of how close I came to losing him and how grateful I should be to the ancestors for letting him live."

At that all eyes turned towards the sleeping child, now anointed by his great-aunt Miriam with a halo of black to protect his tender head from harm. Cornelia bent her long face down over the tiny bundle in her arms and cradled him closer to her big bony body. And if anyone thought – for a moment – that this childless woman was rumored to be a witch, no one spoke their thought aloud or tried to take the baby out of her hungry arms.

It was a blazing, beautiful night with the moon riding high in a glittering indigo sky and the scent of sweet grass in the air. A chorus of quiet "goodnights" in the kitchen doorway sent each person out on soft moonlit feet to their sleeping place in the circle of thatch-roofed houses squatting companionably on the warm summer earth. With her new baby on her back, Esther threw back her head and drank in the blue air and the stars and the feeling of being back home.

Cornelia was sweeping out their old sleeping hut, the one they had shared since they were children. There was no need for a candle: a sharp blue-white square of light leaned in through the open door. Esther sat outside and lifted Chipo round off her back, waiting while her sister skilfully whisked a little pile of dust out through the moonlit doorway and began laying out their blankets on the clean floor.

"There," she said when she'd finished. "Not a soft hospital bed, but the best I can do." She reached out her arms in the moonlight. "Here, let me hold him while you get ready."

Esther looked at her sister's face, open and loving in the soft white light; and at the big generous arms, waiting to hold the baby for her.

"Take him, Cornelia," she said suddenly, holding her child out to her sister. "He's yours; a gift. I want you to keep him and bring him up as your own son." She put him gently and firmly into her sister's arms. "There, Chipo, little one: meet your new mother."

PART FOUR

Tendai

*I*t was her habit to wake up at night: a nocturnal creature with huge eyes bulging above bony cheekbones – like an owl, or a bush-baby, or any one of the myriad prowling animals who inhabit the twilight zones, where sounds and scents create pictures on the brain as clear and vivid as any image seen by the daylight eye. She would wake and stare into the inky darkness with her myopic eyes, barely noticing the warm salt liquid against her eyelashes.

To her that liquid was like air: surrounding her, penetrating her, flowing into every opening. She gulped it down when she opened her mouth to draw back her vestigial lips in a grimace or make-believe yawn. She tasted it in her snub-nose nostrils and on the tongue she pressed to the roof of her mouth when she began her first dreamlike attempts at sucking. She pissed and dribbled into it, that cloudy pale amber bath that filled her ears with the echoey underwater sounds she had heard all her short life.

They were touch-sounds; not so much heard as felt. A sonorous symphony of bubbles and gurgles rippled through her liquid atmosphere and tiptoed across her skin, while a rhythmic bass pounded, pounded, in the background: a deep double-beat – half hiss, half thud – pulsing heavily in the languid, lapping liquid.

Tendai: child of the night, infant offspring rocking in a red and black twilight with a roaring sound filling her sweetly coiled ears. It was a kind of bliss, though she knew no other world with which to compare this bubbling warm under-world that cradled her folded limbs and cushioned the impacts of her bobbing body.

Sometimes she would wake with energy fizzing in her veins and would fling her bony head from side to side on its slender stem of a neck and try to stretch out her cramped legs, pushing convulsively with pale feet and tangling her flailing arms in the fat white tether that floated beside her in her murky sea. At other times she slept, soothed by rhythmic rocking and the faint rumble of conversation that filtered in with the soft red light which was all she knew of the world outside. Or she would float in a soporific half-dream, letting her thumb slide into her mouth and feeling the contours of its translucent new nail hard against her tongue, experimenting lazily with raising her faint-feather eyebrows or resting her forehead against the warm pulsing wall that was both her paradise and her prison.

Poor Tendai, scrap of humanity, skin furred with dark down like a caterpillar, smeared with waterproof wax like the undersea swimmer she was. She could not know that the slimy sponge-limpet that anchored her, tether and all, to the wall of her blushing pink prison – she could not know that the blood pooled there for her nourishment was a miserable thin soup, a mean gruel which starved her growing body and made it develop in miniature. She was a tiny bonsai baby, starved at source, with only a thin stream of goodness flowing from the red roots in the placental pad through the floating white tube of a trunk to where it blossomed in the blue-marbled ball of her belly.

She did not feel hungry – her stomach was always full of the liquid she swallowed. Instead there was often a vague lethargy weighing on her little wrinkled body, a kind of numbness while her small stores of energy were eked out in the work of pumping her heart. Just that: opening and closing the tiny clenched fist that sent the thin blood rushing through the web of blue vessels that fed every part of her body.

And so she grew, day by day. Cells multiplied in intricate preordained patterns: adding, here, another layer of bone, there a lining of waving cilia; here a yellow spattering of fat cells, there a new fingerprint whorl. All so perfect, miraculous; but all a touch skimpy, like a dress cut too small from a patchwork of remnants. Baby Tendai, every cell hungry, blissfully floating in a roaring red twilight, blissfully ignorant of her hunger.

It was raining. Beauty straightened her back gingerly and stood upright for a moment, wiping the drips from her eyebrows with the back of a wet hand. All around her were women's backs, plastered with wet cloth, and bent – as hers had just been – over rows of bushy young tobacco plants. Heedless of the rain, their hands were busy reaching into the glossy green leaves and wrenching off all but the central shoot, while their bare feet shuffled slowly forwards in the soft mud.

Some of the women had babies on their backs, who wailed as the rain seeped chilly through their shroud of blanket or plashed rudely on the tops of their heads. Others were pregnant, like her, and needed to rest more often to ease their aching backs, to stand splay-legged with bellies thrust forwards and both hands behind, kneading at the knots of burning muscle at the base of their spines: wasting precious time, losing precious money, as their total of pruned plants grew gradually smaller with every passing week of pregnancy.

Elsewhere in the great expanse of field, lushly green under a glowering gray sky, were the smaller shapes of children, the contours of their thin bones raised like the weals of a whip through their clinging wet clothes as they crouched beside their mothers, and burrowed, likewise, into the dripping depths of the sodden plants.

Beauty had never known such rain before – such regular, sweet rain: like a blessing from God, or a gift from the ancestors. It did not rain like this at home. A line had been drawn on the map of Zimbabwe, marking where the rainclouds lightened from gray to white after losing their burdens of water and gave this, the good wet land, to the whites and that, the poor dry land, to the blacks. Home was on the wrong side of that line, where the teasing promise of rain stayed in the air all summer and the scent of it floated tantalizingly on the soft winds that blew over the fences that divided the black land from the white.

She wrung out her scarf, then retied it over her curls and bent once more to the fragrant bushes. Home: what would they be doing at home today? Staring at the sky and praying for rain, that was certain. And it would be time to start weeding the maize and thinning out the cotton and groundnut fields. Esther's child would be nearly a month old; Cornelia would have dispatched her letter to Mlambo; Miriam, her mother would be caught up in some fresh battle; and baby Alfred's grave would be invisible now beneath a sheet of clear running water . . .

Home: how she missed it – the dear familiar faces that each bore some resemblance to each other; the family jokes, and the feuds, that would fade and die down but were never quite forgotten and could burst into life again with just one "do you remember?" round the kitchen fire. It was nearly a year since she last sat by that fire in her mother's big kitchen and watched her tending some child or riffling through her crackling dry store of herbs and roots. Nearly a year, while one baby died and another was born; while Beauty, the daughter, became Beauty the wife and would soon become Beauty the mother.

The jab of a fist or foot just beneath her diaphragm made her catch her breath and stand up again with a hand on her seven-month belly: a slender sapling woman, swaying in the rain, with her neat mound carried high and hard beneath her swollen girlish breasts. She gazed over the fields to the compound in the distance, where the ochres and russets of the squatting huts were wet and glowing in the rain as if newly painted.

This was her home now; she must remember that. She was a wife now and her place was here, with her husband. It was all decided, all arranged; there was no room for doubt. She was caught in the grip of tradition and there was no question of resisting. Tradition was a tutor that left little to chance. It both posed the questions and provided the answers. If she stepped out of line, the long arms of tradition would whip out and tug her gently back again.

So, she had cheated her elders and married a man they had not sanctioned or seen? Tradition had furnished the solution. Her new in-laws were to dispatch a messenger to her village with gifts to wheedle a blessing from her family and placate them for stealing their daughter. And so it had been done, over six months ago, and a first link between the two families had been forged.

So, she pined for her mother and grandmother? So, she harbored fantasies of running back home when she was rebuked once too often by her husband or when her chores seemed to stretch endlessly into the night when everyone

173

else was resting? Omniscient tradition dealt with that danger too. It decreed that a daughter, when she marries, must forsake her old family and cleave to her new one, must finally wean herself away from her mother. And it cruelly enforces her separation by forbidding the new wife to visit her home until the masungiro ceremony is held near the end of her first pregnancy.

Masungiro – it meant "tying" or "binding." It was the ceremony by which the young wife was released from her old family ties and fastened securely to those of her husband's clan. Before that symbolic untying and retying was completed it was considered too dangerous, too tempting, for a daughter to return home to her mother. And Beauty had been warned – as every new wife is warned – that flouting this rule of tradition would bring punishment upon her mother in the form of an agonizing, incurable backache.

After two weeks of this work in the tobacco fields, Beauty knew all about backache. She would not wish this pain on her mother, however domineering and infuriating she might sometimes be. She bent again and immersed her hands in the dripping green sea of foliage.

Home: it was no good – the village still felt like home. Was it raining there too? She would soon find out, would soon be returning in triumph, bearing her tender trophy – the proof of her womanhood – exultantly beneath her breasts.

If only her father were still alive. How proud he would be to receive the small retinue that would accompany her: her new uncle-in-law, perhaps her father-in-law too. Perhaps they would manage to buy a heifer as well, and a young filly-goat – plump virgin animals signifying their recognition and appreciation of the virgin who had been taken into their family. And a new blanket, whole and entire, with no tear, to acknowledge the wholeness and purity of the unspoilt young woman they had received.

Then her heart contracted, gripped by a sudden doubt, and a hot surge of blood brought a sheen of sweat to her forehead. Was her secret safe? Could anyone have found out about the teacher? Might Esther have whispered a hint of her shame into somebody's ear? Could she trust Seguro, the old cook, to keep quiet? No, no one else knew, she was certain. And her heart beat normally again and the sweat cooled on her brow and mingled with the fine mist of rain that fell unceasingly down over the field.

To return to her family in shame was unthinkable. If a wife was discovered to be spoiled she could be publicly humiliated: her in-laws might select their oldest cow or an ancient nanny-goat to bring as a gift of mockery to her family. Sometimes they would deliberately slice a great hole in a blanket and unfold it tauntingly in full view, angrily accusing the bride's parents of failing to raise their daughter properly, and bringing disrepute on the whole family. She might even be divorced.

Seguro was right: divorce was so common these days – some men just discarded women like broken buckets. But sometimes the punishment seemed fair: if a wife was lazy or disobedient, for instance, was insolent or disrespectful to her in-laws; or if she was discovered to be sleeping with another man, like a common prostitute. Some women were sent home in disgrace for not preparing themselves properly for marriage: for failing, as young girls, to ensure the beauty of their vaginal lips by massaging them with oil and pulling them twice-daily until they were ripe and plump as two succulent slices of fresh mango.

Mango: her mouth watered and her stomach lurched at the thought. Soon it would be the mango season, when every child's face would be smeared and their hands caked with the dirt that congealed to the sweet juice that ran down their chins and between their fingers. The intensity of the image made her almost dizzy with hunger for a moment and she stood upright once more to steady herself.

She looked at the sky, trying to estimate the time. The rain had stopped and over on the far horizon breaks were appearing in the dense banks of gray cloud, letting shafts of white light fan out over the land. This time as she glanced round the field, there were more women standing, made restless and uncomfortable by their gnawing hunger, and some of the younger children were whining to go back to the compound. Soon someone would make a move – having weighed her desire to stop work with her need to continue, and deciding in favor of the former – and then, one by one, all but the poorest women would follow.

Beauty walked back slowly with her mother-in-law and two of Peter's sisters. Too tired to talk, the four women picked their way between the puddles behind the other groups of women in a companionable silence, inhaling the heady scent of wet foliage and syringa blossom. The trees by the path were heavy with the big mauve sprays and the red mud beneath was already starred with fallen flowers. Clouds of mosquitoes danced under the overhanging branches and zig-zagged raggedly out of formation as the women's warm bodies passed.

The sound of a motor behind made them turn and step out of the way as a tractor ploughed down the road towards them, its trailer laden with men. Beauty waved and smiled when she recognized Peter's face among the others standing rowdy and laughing in the back, holding on to the iron railing, with a tank of pesticide slung over his shoulder and a mask hanging carelessly round his neck. Here they watered crops with poison that splashed on the men's skin and was washed by the rain into ditches where the children played. When the sun shone it hung in a shimmering mist over the fields and the women breathed it in in great lungfuls as they bent over the tobacco plants. And when it rained, like today, their arms and legs were soaked with it up to ten hours at a time. They weeded with poison too, so the maize spikes pushed cleanly up through a bare soil that was eerily empty of life.

Another tractor passed – going much faster – plunging headlong through the puddles and sending groups of women squealing out of the way, their legs streaked red with flying mud. Beauty stared down at her filthy skirt in dismay, then laughed to see that every other woman was doing the same. The disturbance had broken through their exhaustion and a chorus of good-humored grumbles filled the air.

"That driver should buy us some soap for our clothes!"

"If men did the washing they'd be more careful."

"Who will fetch the water to wash all of these?"

"Do they think we have nothing better to do at the end of the day?"

Beauty knew all of these women by name now; knew who was friendly and to be trusted – and who was hostile and suspicious. She knew where they came from, how many children they had, who lived with who – even what illnesses they suffered from. She knew whose husbands beat them, or were drunkards, and more or less what each earned. And they knew her too: this pretty gazelle of a girl with her Grade Five education, who had captivated the most eligible young man in the compound and stolen him from under their noses. Some still resented her good fortune and muttered angrily when they saw her striding jauntily up to the big house for her early-morning sessions with the boss's wife. But others were coming to respect this shy, fresh-faced young woman with her quiet voice and ready smile. There was something strong there – a solid steel core to her pliant girlish body.

177

Beauty felt it too. These long hard months away from home had honed away some of her innocence, just as they had whittled away every ounce of spare flesh from her lean limbs. She still lowered her gaze respectfully, or knelt, when addressing her in-laws. But she had also learnt to meet a stare head-on with steady eyes, to parry an attack with a sharp tongue, to argue with tact and sensitivity, and to tune in unerringly to every change in the volatile hothouse atmosphere of the compound.

It had been such a difficult year: learning to be a wife, a tobacco grader and a health worker all at once; facing hunger and homesickness and the terrible threat of witchcraft; feeling a child growing in her womb for the first time; watching her closest friend driven off in the back of a police van; seeing more cruelty and sickness and pain than she'd ever witnessed in the village. Somehow she'd come through it all.

Back at the compound the women dispersed, without pause or thought, into the chores of the evening. Beauty picked up a canister and walked quickly to the standpipe. As she walked her eyes critically scanned her surroundings – checking, judging, calculating – in a way that had become automatic since she had finished her course. At one house she stopped to help a little girl who was struggling to hang a tattered blanket over a bush to dry.

"The roof leaks," the girl explained unnecessarily, hauling on one frayed corner.

"All the roofs leak," Beauty said grimly, flinging the blanket deftly and picking off the wet bits of blackened thatch that clung to it.

All over the compound every bush and tree was festooned with colored blankets hanging out to dry in the evening sunshine. It looked like a festival, with enormous flags flying, but Beauty knew better. Those blankets had not properly dried out for weeks. Tonight, still damp, they'd be taken down again and wrapped round bodies that had probably been working in wet clothes for most of the day.

She walked on, skirting a heap of muddy rubble where someone had begun digging a refuse pit, before the rain – and the work on the farm – had forced them to abandon the task. As a health worker, these pits had been her major success: not surprising really, since they were almost the only things people could achieve without some extra money or help from the boss. There were over twenty pits now, each as far away from the houses as people could manage – though that was difficult when the houses were crowded together as closely as they were.

Her body stiffened angrily: Mrs. Johnson thought they were ignorant, dirty people – she could tell by the way the white woman's long pointed nose would wrinkle when she was forced to touch one of the sick children who came to the house in the morning. Did she think they chose to live crushed together like this, so that every family argument could be heard by neighbors in the next house, so that the stench of garbage filled their nostrils while they were eating their breakfast? Couldn't she imagine how a mother feels to watch a cloud of flies crawling on her child's hands or in the corners of its eyes and to see those same flies buzzing ecstatically on a gob of green chicken shit? Beauty had glimpsed the sparkling clean toilets in the big house. Did Mrs. Johnson ever consider what it must be like to share one smelly hole in the ground with six hundred other people?

They hated dirt, loathed it more than anything. Even the crudest mud floor in the compound would be swept then wiped with a cloth at least six times a day. Some women even scrubbed their arms and legs with water before beginning to cook, in an effort to discourage the flies that might otherwise be attracted to the scent of their sweat. When they went to fetch water they would scour their big buckets

179

spotlessly clean with sand before filling them and then tap the side with their hands so any minute bits of chaff or dead insects would float to the top where they would be scooped out on to the ground. But Mrs. Johnson would not know about that: her water came rushing clear as crystal from a tap and she had a cook to prepare her food.

Beauty reached the standpipe. Now that she knew it was unprotected and unhygienic, she could not watch the women and children scooping up the water from the open trough without wincing. Chickens and pigeons scraped in the greenish slime round the base of the concrete trough and their white droppings stained its top. Little girls in filthy, muddy rags lolled against it and dipped their hands in for a mouthful of water between scoops of an older child's cup. Beauty hoisted her full bucket on her head and turned back to the house.

How could people keep themselves clean when they were herded together like zoo animals, with just one standpipe and one toilet between them? She knew something now about the spread of disease: how the summer rain made a perfect mud-and-shit playground for parasites; how their eggs and hook-mouthed young lay lurking there waiting for a bare foot, or a finger to adhere to; how tiny animals – so small they were impossible to see – could pass so easily into a child's stomach from the teeming brown breeding grounds they walked through every day.

The worst place was the vlei. The rains had made a nightmare of that simplest human function. Few people could face the toilet now, but the vlei was nearly as bad, with scads of flies rising at every footstep until the very skin of your bare feet shrank from the necessity of that daily muddy walk among the trees.

Beauty remembered the day her course tutor had read out a list of "basic amenities" he thought each farmer should provide on their compound. Even now she wanted to laugh: a ventilated toilet for every household, a standpipe for every ten families, plots of land for people to grow food and vegetables, new brick houses, a school for the children . . . The list went on and on. He had told them about something called a "minimum wage" too – the smallest amount of money an employer was permitted by the government to pay his workers. That was even more laughable. She had never earned that much in her life, no matter how many hours she worked. It seemed that seasonal workers, like her and the other women, were not included in this piece of legislation. But then neither were many of the men, it seemed. She knew of several in the compound earning far less than the legal minimum. And, from talking to trainees from other farms, she now understood that the Johnsons were among the more generous of employers. At least beatings were rare here, and there was Mrs. Johnson's "surgery" in the mornings. And though the schooling provided was derisory – with one Form-Three-educated boy teaching a single unruly class of raggle-taggle children of all ages in the beer hall – the crèche had begun last month and was a big success.

Her arrival at the house broke into her thoughts and she braced her knees to lift the heavy bucket from her head, tipping its contents into a clay pot and two enamel bowls before turning back to the standpipe for another load. A little breeze had started up, pushing the clouds aside to reveal a soft pastel sky. Beauty shivered in her damp blouse, then looked round quickly as she heard someone calling her name.

A skinny seven-year-old boy was running towards her.

"Can you come, please, Mrs. Kanyemba?" he gasped, skidding to a breathless standstill. "My mother is having a baby and she wants you to go to the big house with her."

Beauty frowned momentarily and stared at the little boy

in dismay – she was so hungry, and tired, and there was still so much work to do before she could rest. Then she took a deep breath of resignation.

"Yes, yes. Of course. Tell her to wait at home until I've finished fetching the water, then I'll go with her."

Beauty knew she ought to be pleased. This was a woman who'd had every one of her other six children at home, deeply suspicious of her neighbors and refusing all offers of help. Somehow Beauty had managed to persuade her to go to the mobile clinic for her anti-tetanus jabs and now here she was asking for transport to take her to hospital to give birth. But she hated going to the big house outside normal "surgery" times; hated the long wait at the kitchen door, while one of the servants went to tell Mrs. Johnson she was there, and the familiar look of exasperation on the tall white woman's face while Beauty politely explained the latest medical emergency.

This time the Johnsons had visitors for dinner and loud laughter echoed down the long polished corridor when Seguro went to announce Beauty's arrival. While they waited, the pregnant woman sank to all fours at the foot of the concrete steps and gritted her teeth in an effort to bite back her grunts of pain. Beauty put a hand on her shoulder and squeezed it reassuringly, eyeing the four big saucepans bubbling on top of the stove through the kitchen door and the tiers of gleaming china piled up ready on a tray. The smell of roast pork filled her nostrils and she could see an enormous fat brown joint sizzling through the glass of the oven door.

"Typical! Just when the meal's about to be served . . ." Mrs. Johnson's high voice, acid with irritation, came floating down the corridor accompanied by the tip-tapping of high-heeled shoes.

"Can't it wait for a couple of hours?" she asked as she

burst into the room and stood at the top of the steps peering out into the twilight.

"I'm sorry, madam," said Beauty, putting on her prettiest apologetic smile. "I think she's quite close . . ."

As if to emphasize the urgency of the situation, the woman let a little moan of pain escape through her clenched teeth. Mrs. Johnson stepped back quickly as if bitten.

"All right, all right . . . tell her to hold on, will you? I'll just go and get my coat." And she disappeared, trailing a cloud of cigarette smoke and perfume.

A few minutes later she reappeared, accompanied by five other white people, talking and laughing loudly. They crowded into the kitchen behind her.

"There goes our Florence Nightingale – off on her errand of mercy," said one of the women, waving a glass of white wine.

"Mind she doesn't have it in the car!" warned one of the men and they all laughed again.

"They do, you know," said the first woman, when the uproar had died down a bit. "One of mine had hers behind one of the barns – it just popped out in a minute or two: no trouble at all! Where is the lady in question, anyway?" she asked, and peered down the steps to where Beauty stood beside the woman who was still crouching on the ground.

"Look at this!" she called to the others over her shoulder. "What did I tell you? She's squatting just like an animal. Hurry up, Joanie, that baby'll be here any minute!"

With that they all pressed forwards into the doorway and stared down at the woman, while Mrs. Johnson went to fetch the car. Hearing their voices, the laboring woman struggled to rise to her feet. Beauty tried to shield her from their curious gaze with her body and glared at them with her dark eyes blazing, willing them to show them sign of pity or respect. But the group of white people barely glanced at her.

183

"They have one every year, you know – just like every-thing else on the farm," said another of the women.

"No wonder they're so overcrowded. Do you know, some of them sleep ten to a room! I don't know how they stand it."

"And they won't use birth control. It's hopeless, they just can't control themselves."

"I don't know why they don't just sterilize them at the hospital after they've given birth. I heard of one doctor who used to do that – just tied their tubes when he was doing a Cesarean section. No one was any the wiser!"

The pregnant woman was standing now, gripping Beauty's arm and staring fixedly at the ground. Beauty could tell by the strength of the pressure from her fingers that she was having another contraction but was determined not to let their white audience witness her pain.

Someone flicked a switch and suddenly they were all illu-minated by the porch light; three men identically dressed in pale pants, belted low on their hips beneath the swell of their bellies. Their short-sleeved shirts strained open over folds of flesh and there were darker patches where the material stuck to their perspiring bodies. The women, on the other hand, were corseted like sausages in their skins, inside shimmering floral sheath-dresses with narrow little shoe-lace belts where their waists should have been and thin bleached hair sprayed to candyfloss stiffness. Their naked arms and legs were blotched with freckles and matching splashes of red picked out their finger- and toe-nails. Their lips were red, too, and the wine-glass each held was marked with a greasy red smudge where each had sipped. Beauty noticed again the dense mats of coppery hair on the men's arms and wrinkled her nose at the strong smell of these people – a powerful mixture of clashing perfumes and aftershave lotions, of soap and deodorant and hair-spray, all overlaid by the more familiar smells of cigarette smoke and alcohol.

Mercifully a crunch of gravel heralded the arrival of the car.

"Now I want you to come with me, just in case something happens," Mrs. Johnson insisted firmly.

Beauty knew it was useless to object so she obediently slipped into the back seat beside the woman.

"Tell her to lie back and put her feet on the front seat," Mrs. Johnson instructed. "I don't want that baby born in the car. Right, off we go . . ."

Beauty tried to make the woman comfortable and untied her scarf to wipe the perspiration from her brow. The woman smiled a brief, grateful smile, then clutched at her arm again as the car lurched forwards. Beauty looked at Mrs. Johnson's competent freckled hands on the steering wheel. Her gold rings and slender gold wristwatch glinted faintly in the lights from the dashboard.

"Transport to hospital in times of emergency" was another of the "basic amenities" the course tutor had listed. Did that imply that some farmers just let their employees bleed to death if they had an accident or problems in childbirth? Well, perhaps allowing an adult to bleed to death was not so different from paying them so badly that their children died of starvation. No, that was not strictly true: it was almost unheard of for a child to starve to death in Zimbabwe. But Beauty now understood that a sturdy, clean, well-fed baby never died of diarrhea, or measles, or malaria – or any one of the numerous ailments of childhood that sent mothers half crazy with worry. It was the scrawny underweight ones who succumbed, crushed as easily as blades of grass underfoot, like her own little cousin Alfred.

In just over an hour they arrived at the hospital. Mrs. Johnson stalked imperiously across the foyer and handed her charge over to a bemused man behind the reception desk. Then they were on their way back home again, with

Beauty in the front this time, surreptitiously rubbing her bare arms and trying to stop her teeth chattering with cold – Mrs. Johnson had gone round the car before setting off, ostentatiously opening the windows to disperse the intimate smells that had accumulated on their outward journey.

"I suppose I'll be driving you here soon as well," the white woman remarked after a while.

Beauty took a deep breath: "Thank you, madam. But no, actually I'll be going home to have the baby. It is our Shona tradition to have the first child at your mother's house."

The response was just as she feared.

"Well, really, Beauty. I think that's very selfish and inconsiderate of you – going off without so much as a 'by your leave,' after all I've done for you too. How am I supposed to manage in the clinic with you away?"

"I'm sorry, madam. I won't be gone very long and I've found someone to take my place. She speaks very good English." Mrs. Johnson sniffed angrily and drove the rest of the way in silence.

Next morning there was a marked chilliness in her employer's manner when Beauty arrived, as usual, for her daily stint of interpretation.

"This place is a mess," she complained, running a distasteful finger along the shelf where the medicines were stored. "Stay and clean it up after we've finished, will you? Oh yes, and I've been thinking about your payment. I think it's about time your people started paying some of your salary – it is for their benefit after all, isn't it? I don't see why I should keep on forking out all of your money . . ."

Beauty opened her mouth to protest, then shut it again.

"Yes, madam," she murmured submissively.

She couldn't really complain: each farm health worker was supposed to be paid sixty-five dollars a month by the

186

people in his or her compound. But she had been lucky up till now to receive fifty dollars direct from Mrs. Johnson. Many of the others on her course got no money at all – either from the farmer or the farm workers. She hardly dared ask the people on her compound for money: she knew how hard-pressed they were just to make ends meet, without having to find extra money to pay for her services. And she couldn't blame them either. The comments they made at the meeting she called when she first graduated said it all.

She had been dreading it, of course: lecturing to a group of people she still barely knew, most of whom were far older and more experienced than she. But once she had started, she forgot her shyness and something of her mother's reckless eloquence took hold of her tongue as she explained the importance of hygiene and nutrition to the motley audience of men, women and children who had gathered, curious, in the beer hall, to hear what this pretty young upstart had to say.

They listened quietly, politely, as she tried to impress on the women how vital it was to bring their children to be weighed at the mobile clinic so that their growth could be monitored, and how they should make sure that their families always washed their hands properly after going to the toilet and before sitting down to a meal. Then, when she had finished, a woman put up her hand.

"Will you give us soap to wash the children? And mealie meal to feed them if they are found to be too thin?" she asked sarcastically – and the meeting erupted into angry complaints about their lack of money and the squalid conditions in which they were forced to live.

It had been the same with almost everything she suggested: they were not being deliberately obstructive – what mother would deliberately hold back from any reasonable effort that might improve the health of her children? – but many of her suggestions were simply beyond their means. Even ORS – oral rehydration solution: a drink made from sugar, salt and water and said to cure diarrhea, one of the most feared diseases in Zimbabwe – even making ORS was impossible for some households in the slack season. During those long months some families had practically no money coming in at all and could barely afford to buy mealie meal, let alone keep a regular supply of salt and sugar in their homes. How could she even consider asking people like this for money?

A tentative knock on the half-open door signaled the arrival of the first patient: a blind girl of about eleven, led by her younger brother. Beauty had seen this girl on the compound, being tugged passively here or there by one or other of her siblings, or sitting in silence in the shade of a mango tree with her knees drawn up to her chin, gazing blankly and sightlessly while other children bounced and swung wildly from the lower branches, narrowly missing her little hunched body.

No one knew why she was blind – her mother said her eyes "just went funny" when she was about three years old – but Beauty remembered being taught that a lack of green vegetables can affect a child's sight. And where were they supposed to find green vegetables on this farm, except in Mrs. Johnson's lushly watered and perfectly tended vegetable garden behind its tall wire-mesh fence?

On the white woman's instructions she reached for a little tube of ointment, some of which she smeared on the child's eyelids.

"I know it won't do any good," Mrs. Johnson sighed, "but I feel I've got to give her something. I'd like to get her into a special school near Harare, but her mother won't let her go – Lord knows why, the child's no good to her here . . ."

There were only two more patients: at this time of year all

but the most serious or painful complaints were ignored by people anxious to take every opportunity to earn a few extra dollars on the farm. The two were both women with jeko, that unmistakable feminine scourge of stinging urine, dragging cramps and discharge that so many women suffered on and off: a dreadful nagging illness that makes a woman ashamed and disgusted by the smell and the feel of her own body. Apart from backache, it was the most common of the women's complaints, gnawing away at their vitality with a continual vague discomfort, then flaring up now and then into a fever or a burning pain. Never really serious – no one ever died of jeko, or was even ill enough to stop working. No, jeko was more insidious than that: like termites secretly eating away at the roof-poles of a house, weakening the structure with a labyrinth of holes, invisible but for a sprinkling of wood-dust on the mud floor beneath.

The symptoms were as familiar to Mrs. Johnson as they were to Beauty and, before the young black woman had even finished translating what they said, she had begun writing letters of referral for them to take to the clinic.

"Now don't forget what I told you," Mrs. Johnson said to Beauty after they'd left. "Seguro will show you where he keeps the cleaning things. I want this place spotless. Hygiene is vital for health – as I'm sure they taught you on that course of yours. We must set a good example, mustn't we?" And she smiled her tight-lipped smile before hurrying out into the morning sunshine.

Beauty sighed: she would be even later than usual at the tobacco fields and from now on she might not even be paid for this work. She trailed across the sunlit yard towards the kitchen, breathing in the scent of jasmine and the damp earth smell from where one of the gardeners was watering flowers with a hose. Cascades of purple and magenta bougainvillaea blossom nodded dazzlingly against the white walls of the house and three sunbirds – little flashes of iridescence – hovered and darted into the scarlet throats of the hibiscus flowers.

Seguro was sitting on the step, with a bucket of soapy water and a cloth at his feet.

"Good morning, Mrs. Kanyemba. I believe these are what you are after."

Beauty cupped and clapped her hands politely in greeting then grinned down at his mischievous deep-wrinkled face, cocked quizzically on one side as usual.

"Did she tell you I was coming or did you know already?" she asked.

He tapped his temple enigmatically with his forefinger. "What do you think, my young friend? Am I a powerful, all-knowing nganga or am I not? Are such things difficult for someone of my extensive talents?" He thrust out his puny chest in mock bravado and she laughed as she reached for the bucket.

"Wait," he commanded in a different voice.

She put down the bucket again and looked at him. His face was suddenly serious.

"You have not been following my instructions, have you?"

Like a little girl caught with her fingers in the cooking pot, Beauty stopped smiling and hung her head.

"I can't help it," she said hopelessly. "There's always so much to do. Last night I had to go to the big house with Mrs. Rwisi and then Mrs. Johnson insisted I went to the hospital too – there just wasn't time for supper. And you know no one stops for lunch in the tobacco fields. Mrs. Johnson says she's going to cut my money next month, too, so I'll have to work even harder in the fields to try and make up. But I'm strong," she assured him, lifting her chin proudly. "You don't have to worry about me."

He grunted disapprovingly. "The sooner you go home to your mother the better. She'll know how to look after you – feed you up a bit, cosset you. The ancestors knew what they were doing when they insisted on that."

She grinned again as she hoisted the brimming bucket carefully on to her head.

"I'm serious," he said sternly. "Your child is suffering. You know what they say: 'look after what you have – because the ancestors may not give twice.' Have you forgotten how close you were to losing this baby? You are strong, yes. But do not take your strength for granted. Your child is suffering. It's time you went home. Now, go away, and don't speak to me again until you come to say goodbye."

The chamber where she lay was bounded by bones: white arches curved like the rafters of a church or the spreading roots of an acacia tree washed bare by summer storms. At first she knew them only as shadowy bars, dense black bands silhouetted on dark red, vaulted over her bobbing body in its corporeal capsule. Later they were real prison bars, crowding in ever closer as her body expanded, until almost every movement she made brought her up against an unyielding hard edge.

For several weeks it was possible for her to gain some kind of slippery purchase, and she could use this bony boundary like the rungs of a climbing frame, scrambling against them from the inside with her elbows and knees and wrenching her little body around into this position, or that, until the mood of restlessness left her.

Then, one day, she found she was stuck and no effort she made could shift her from her tip-tilted upended position.

She could still make some movements, of course. She was not wedged too tightly to arch her back and thrust her knees forwards, or pass a waving hand clumsily in front of her

191

myopic eyes. But her days of floating and swimming, of whirling, diving and somersaulting, weightlessly in her heavenly warm bath – those carefree days were over. Tiny Tendai – all bone and brain, with the flesh spread so thinly on her spare little frame – baby Tendai was coming in to land.

The girl suddenly dropped to the ground and began yelping, with her tongue out and her head thrown back. She scratched convulsively at the earth with both hands then danced sideways on all fours, carving a great swathe through the crowd, which shuffled back nervously out of her way. One of the three men on the drums looked up at the sudden commotion, nodded with satisfaction, then bent with renewed vigor to his drum – a hollow carved tree-trunk with goatskin stretched over the top – quickening the tempo till his hands were no more than a blur in the humid evening sunshine.

Half-standing, half-crouching, he held the drum steady and hard between his thighs, as though it was a rabid animal that would escape and run amok if he relaxed his iron grip for one second or let a single pause interrupt the hysterical tattoo of his hands. His blue shirt was unbuttoned and its cuffs hung loosely from his elbows like the trailing feathers of an exotic bird while the flesh of his chest and arms, ridged with muscle, shone golden with sweat. A tall man of twenty, black curls matted into rough-tousled tufts and a blaze of concentration in his eyes, he was the obvious leader. Occasionally the other two glanced at him, changing their rhythm or speed at his slightest sign, the sinews of their bare feet taut as blades in the mud as they braced their lean bodies over the drums.

Beauty's heart, like those in the rest of the crowd, kept pace with the drums and she backed off with the others when the Mozambican girl lurched in her direction.

"It's the spirit of a baboon," someone whispered in awe. "Look at the way she's moving. Can you see the white beads on her wrist?"

Fighting the hypnotic imperative of the drums, Beauty wrenched herself away from the crowd and stood apart until her breathing slowed to normal. How glad she would be to get away from all this: from the stifling press of strange bodies, the sticky squalor, the mesmerizing power of foreign drumming and this cacophony of competing spirits. Sometimes the air seemed so thick with alien ghosts it was hard to draw breath without feeling your body invaded.

But at least this summer drumming seemed joyful, as it should be: a passionate celebration of power – so different from the remorseless viciousness of those long hungry winter months. And the cheeks of the chanting children had plumped out to cover the gaunt masks of their November faces.

So the seasons came and went, breaking like waves over the people on the compounds, bearing them up on a surge of relative prosperity when there was work in the fields, then letting them sink once more into the winter troughs of scarcity that left their mark on every body: sapping energy, dulling eyes, stripping flesh from bones, etching desperation into hearts.

But from today, for a few short months, Beauty would be able to forget all this. She hurried towards the big house, dressed in her best dress, the one she had worn when she went for her interview with Mrs. Johnson all those months ago, and a cardigan to cover where the zip gaped open at the side to allow for the bulge of her belly.

The kitchen door was ajar.

"Come in, Mrs. Kanyemba," Seguro called from inside. "I hope you have come to say goodbye."

"Not only goodbye: goodbye and thank you," she said. "I

am going on the morning bus, with my husband's uncle and his son."

Seguro was perched on a stool peeling potatoes into a bowl. He wiped his hands on his apron and waved her to sit down.

"There is some advice I want to give you before you go," he said, leaning forward and peering searchingly into her face.

"My father came to me last night. He told me that your mother is troubled – very troubled. No, don't worry – " Beauty had gasped with anxiety and had started getting down off her stool – "She's not sick, or in danger – at the moment. But she needs your support, just as much as you need hers. She is a strong, powerful woman. But she has enemies, my father tells me."

"My baby cousin died a couple of months ago," Beauty said, a worried frown creasing her pretty brow. "There are some people who blame her. They are saying she's a witch because she uses traditional medicine."

"Do you think it's her fault too?" he asked, staring still harder at her.

"I don't kn . . . I mean, no, of course I don't."

"Aha! I knew it," he crowed, slapping his knee. "You have doubts, don't you? You think maybe we old ngangas should give up and let you smart young health workers take over, eh? Eh?" He prodded her arm with his finger and she winced.

"At the course they said we should be discouraging people from taking too much traditional medicine," she muttered, not meeting his eyes. "They say some people have been poisoned by ngangas."

"Did I poison you?" he asked, prodding her again. "Answer me. Did I poison you?"

"No, no, you helped me. You know you did."

"Right. Well, you remember that," he said in a gentler voice. "You have the makings of a fine healer yourself. Don't spoil it by being arrogant. The best healers are those who listen with respect to their elders. Our hair did not go gray and we did not lose our teeth for nothing, you know."

He smiled then, showing his bare pink gums with their few crooked yellow stumps.

"Learn from your mother: she has much to teach you. Then one day perhaps you will be fit to teach her too."

"This is the bush," said Miriam, stopping beside a shrub studded with small red flowers. "It's the root that you need. But look carefully at the flowers and the leaves – so that you can do this for yourself next time." Glancing round to make sure no one else was nearby, she squatted and began hacking carefully at the ground beneath the bush with her hoe.

Beauty watched as her mother unearthed a length of wizened root and severed it from the mother-plant with a single deft slice of the hoe-blade. The wounded flesh shone white for a moment before she scraped the earth back over it and tamped it down reverently with her hands.

"You must only take one piece from each plant," she said, rising to her feet. "Come, you find the next one." And they walked on, out of the village: a mother and a daughter, with the rising sun warm on their backs and their long blue shadows leading them along narrow red paths beaten flat by generations of bare feet.

Twelve years ago, as a child, Beauty had danced along these same tracks, listening wide-eyed to grandmother Chengetai's stories, half forgetting to look for firewood as her attention was continually caught: by a resplendent butterfly flapping like torn paper over the waving sea of grass, or the knife-edge flash of blue as a swallow skimmed and skidded through the haze of tiny insects that hung in the cool

195

morning air. And sixty years ago it was Chengetai herself, still a loose-limbed young wife, who scanned these same bushes for a telltale glimpse of red, her body heavy with the child, now ten years dead in the ground, that was to be husband and father to the two women who now searched the morning landscape for those very same bushes.

"There," Beauty said, pointing. "Over by the tree with the weavers' nests." She turned off the path and started hurrying towards where a host of black and yellow birds fluttered and chirruped round their hanging basketwork globes, like outsize bees buzzing round tiny green hives.

"Why don't you dig?" she asked, puzzled, when they arrived. Miriam didn't answer.

"Isn't it the right one?" Beauty asked again, impatiently. Then: "Mother, is anything wrong?"

Miriam was gazing silently to where, in the middle distance, the land dipped slightly and faint tendrils of white mist hugged the ground, skulking as if afraid of the sunshine, embracing the bushes with cold white arms and entangling themselves in the lower branches of the trees.

"It's the river," she said in a dull voice. "I didn't realize we were so near. I can't dig here."

They stood a while longer, staring at the softly swirling vapors winding and unwinding above the invisible seam of sweet water, until the mist seemed to reach cold fingers right out across the sunlit clearing to stroke shivers from the surface of their skin.

"I tried everything, you know." Miriam spoke as if in a trance. "But he was so weak. There was so little life there to work with. And it's true, I was proud. I wanted to prove I was powerful." She laughed bitterly. "Remember what I've always taught you? There is nothing the ancestors hate more than arrogance. So this is my punishment.

"Are you satisfied now?" she cried out, shaking a fist

towards the ephemeral white wisps that reeled in a slow-motion dance among the long morning shadows. "Have you made me suffer enough?"

Beauty touched her mother's shoulder and the older woman subsided, as though an electric current coursing through her body had been suddenly switched off. She wiped her eyes roughly with the back of her hand and heaved a great sigh.

"You have good hands, Beauty. Good, strong, healing hands. Come on, I must take you away from here. A pregnant woman should not linger near the graves of children."

And they turned away from the sacred mist-shrouded place and waded back to the path, knee-high through sparse plumes of long grass, disturbing clouds of floating insects like dust as they passed.

"Ever since they started training people, it has been more and more difficult for the ngangas," Miriam was explaining. "They have begun saying we are witches. Well, that's nothing new – we have always been vulnerable to that accusation. But it's much worse now. If anything goes wrong, people are much quicker to blame us, because the new training teaches people that our traditional medicine is always harmful and that all ngangas are dangerous. And when people are selected for training, the ngangas are hardly ever chosen. I was only trained because I was a midwife – a nyamakuta – as well as a nganga. So people are forced to decide who they are going to trust – the ngangas or the new health workers – and fewer and fewer trust us any more."

They were walking across open land now, where the grass straggled its long pale runners gamely over the stony ground and platoons of red and black ants zig-zagged in head-to-tail sorties across the path.

"I was chosen just because I spoke English," said Beauty

shrugging. "But there were some on the course – from different farms – who were elected by vote. None were ngangas though," she added thoughtfully. "You're right about that. And they told us to warn people away from traditional medicine."

"So what happens now is that people only consult ngangas in desperate cases, when they have given up hope. But by then it might be too late for us to help – then we get all the blame if a child dies. It's the same with the old midwives. Most of the younger women think the clinic or the hospital are the only safe places to give birth, so they only go to a traditional midwife if there is an emergency and they can't get to the clinic in time. But the emergencies are sometimes the most difficult births. Then the midwife is blamed if there are problems. And now they've been trained they daren't turn people away, even if the woman is not a relative. That makes it even worse for them if something goes wrong."

"Do you get money from the government now you're trained?" Beauty asked. "The woman who delivers the birth control pills to the compound gets a hundred dollars – and a bicycle as well. But I'm supposed to be paid by the people in the compound – and I can't ask them for money. Those people are so poor."

Miriam snorted. "The government thinks it's more important to stop people having babies than to bring those babies into the world safely," she said. "No, traditional midwives are supposed to be paid by the villagers too – even when they've had training. But we have a much more responsible job than the people who give out birth control pills. Our work is a matter of life and death. No one blames the birth control worker if the pill doesn't work!"

Beauty spotted another bush and knelt down beside her mother as she hacked away the impacted earth from its roots. The sun's slanted rays shone in Miriam's face, picking out every ridge and furrow, so that Beauty was suddenly aware that her mother – her indomitable, immortal mother – was growing old.

"Yes, your crotchety, bad-tempered mother's getting old and tired," Miriam said, reading her thoughts and glancing sideways with a mischievous gleam in her black eyes. "You know the saying: 'All plants that grow tall must eventually bend.' I'm just waiting for my youngest daughter to take over my work, then I think I'll retire and spend the rest of my days relaxing under your father's favorite mango tree."

Beauty threw back her head and her peal of laughter made a turtle dove start into the air with a hysterical shriek and clatter off into the distance.

"You'll never retire, mother. Not until you join the ancestors – and not even then. You'll come back and stir up trouble for your long-suffering descendants for ever!"

Miriam laughed too. But then her face changed. Their eyes met and locked: two women kneeling in the red Zimbabwean earth.

"I mean it, Beauty. Would you like to learn? Shall I teach you the nganga's art the way your great-aunt Eustina taught me?"

Hand in hand; hands of the living, hands of the dead: by the light of the kitchen fire, Miriam parted her daughter's slender thighs and tried to fit a closed fist into the narrow space at their apex, encircled left and right by twin arcs of pelvic bone. Eustina's hand too, washed in water boiled with leaves of the devil's thorn bush, tested the width of that opening, grinding bone against bone and foreshadowing the day when it would be the bones of Tendai's baby skull that would be crowned by that hard white coronet.

The fit was tight, as they both knew it would be, and they

twisted the fist round slowly, searching for the widest diameter, pressing Beauty's legs further and further apart till the light tawny skin of her inner thighs was stretched tight over straining tendons and a sharp cartilage edge showed either side of her hoarded folds of plump purple.

"Not good, not good," whispered Eustina in Miriam's ear. "The bones may give a little, but it will not be an easy birth."

"You must start taking masuwo right away," said Miriam briskly, hiding her anxiety as her daughter sat up and pulled down her skirt, then folded her long legs sideways under her body like a resting calf.

"The passage is narrow. We must do all we can to widen and relax it. I'll prepare the mixture right now, here in the kitchen while everyone's asleep." And as Beauty edged the charred sticks further into the heart of the grate and crouched low to blow a flame from the fading red embers, Miriam reached for her pestle and mortar.

Eustina shuffled nearer to the fire and watched approvingly as the two women worked long into the night. In all there were three different mixtures to prepare: one from the roots they had gathered earlier that day; another from the leaves of a yellow- and white-flowered shrub, torn into small pieces then beaten to softness. These were boiled in water over the fire and the liquid, to be brewed fresh each day, was made into a dilute sadza porridge for Beauty to eat every morning. The third mixture was pulp from an aloe to massage into her vaginal petals and into the tough ridge of muscle at their base.

"That's to prevent you from tearing," explained Miriam. "The mixture makes the skin supple and pliable so it will stretch over your child's head like the neck of a woollen jumper."

"And what if the passage doesn't open wide enough?"

Beauty asked, staring at the bubbles that rose in the two big black pots on the fire.

"Then you will have to be cut open, at the hospital, like your cousin Esther. But don't think about that: concentrate on happy things. If your mind is at peace when you go into labor it will be much easier for you to open up for your child to be born."

"Will there be much pain?" she asked then, in a small voice, wrapping a blanket round her shoulders and tucking it under her bare legs to protect them from the chill of the floor.

Miriam put down the pestle.

"Yes, there will be a great deal of pain," she said simply.

At first, when she woke in the mornings, it was with that rude jolt into anxious alertness that characterized her wakings at the farm: where she was up and walking to the standpipe, rehearsing her timetable of chores in her head, before the sleepy warmth of her body had cooled. In the compound she seemed always to be rushing. But here, at home, though the same sudden intrusion of consciousness interrupted her dreams, she could stretch out luxuriously under her blanket while the twins chattered to each other in soft voices, stepping carefully round her head as they folded their blankets and stacked them beneath the rope, knotted to the rafters, on which their few small dresses hung.

They had pinned some magazine pictures to the wall: of white women, smiling maniacally through shining red lips, tossing long tresses of red or blonde hair back from naked pink shoulders and thrusting rose-colored nipples pertly at the camera, introducing a blaze of California sunshine to the brown dung-and-mud-lined walls of the hut. Beneath their ecstatic blue-eyed gaze each morning, the twins spread a ragged white crochet cloth over the neat pile of blankets and tugged the old wooden door open to admit the pale gray light of dawn.

A year ago Beauty's own pictures, stained with the rust from old drawing-pins, brightened these walls. They were probably still here somewhere, with her old school books: food for termites burrowing up through the floor.

School books; school teacher: the doubt still gnawed away at the back of her mind, like the termites nibbling secretly at the crumbling yellow pages somewhere beneath one of the small heaps of belongings ranged round the circular wall of the hut. Would her bones yield to her baby if she had not come as a virgin to her husband? Would the jostling crowd of ancestors who would preside over this birth – would they turn a blind eye to her impurity? Or would she be punished for her sin?

"Eustina," she prayed, staring up at the cobweb-strewn thatch. "Please look after me, please make it all right."

But there was no real need to pray. Eustina was always beside here these days: smoothing the frowns away from her forehead with a gnarled hand as she slept and trying to banish the troubled dreams that caused them; or placing her old head with its faded red-patterned scarf on Beauty's belly to listen for Tendai's tender heartbeats.

Fierce old matriarch: why should she care who fathered this baby? Or whether another father had been here before? Let the fathers of the fathers worry about fatherhood. All she really cared about was the baby, and the mother whose body was carrying it. Until Tendai was claimed by the fathers and the roora payment was made, she would remain under Eustina's watchful old eyes in the custody of Beauty's ancestors.

It was evening and the complex of chores that brought the long day neatly to an end were under way all over the village. No scolding was needed to send the young boys out to round up the animals and drive them home to the barns for the night; or to dispatch the young women with their buckets to the well. Bidden only by necessity, each adult and child followed, without thinking, their own lines of duty, weaving a seamless pattern of co-ordinated activity.

A woman would reach round to lift a weanling babe off her back and would find, without having to call, that an elder child's arms were waiting to take the baby from her. As she bent to dismantle the piles of dirty dishes and pots, another child would appear with water to tip into the bowl. Elsewhere dirty clothes were collected, and one daughter washed, crouching in the mud and stretching the wet material over a big flat stone so she could scrub off the worst of the stains, while another rinsed and draped the clean clothes along the wire fence, like faded, dripping bunting from a long-forgotten festival. Near the well, another sister and her brother would pluck handfuls of succulent leaves from the few ragged rows of cowpea plants. While inside the kitchen, the floor was swept again with a bundle of twigs, and a damp cloth wiped over it so the flames of the fire were reflected in the gleaming black soot and candle-wax glaze, and women stretched out their tired legs in an orange oblong of evening sunshine that flooded in through the open door.

"Uya, uya, uya kuneni," Cornelia crooned to the baby swaddled in her arms. "Come, come, come to me, little one."

She lifted him out of his blanket and held him up facing her, so his feet pressed down against her thighs and his knees flexed under his weight as she danced him up and down.

"Beautiful bird, where are you off to? Come, come, come to me, little one," she sang, smiling, as he tried to balance his lolling head on his shoulders.

"Are you going to climb high in the sky, little bird, so you can fly right up through the clouds?" And she bent her head and pressed her smile into his forehead so that when she lifted her lips away he was smiling too.

"See, he loves you already," said Esther, kneeling up to tip a bowl of white sadza flour into a pot of water on the fire. She tapped her son's soft brown elbow gently with a wooden spoon.

"Look after your aunt, do you hear me? Make sure you bring her up to be a good mother."

Everyone in the kitchen burst into laughter. Esther rounded on them scowling in mock indignation.

"I don't see what's so funny," she said. "You know how hard it is to raise a mother properly these days. Chipo – don't listen to them: this is a serious business."

She plunged the spoon into the pot and began stirring, then beating the mixture as it thickened and bubbles began erupting, making craters on the glutinous surface.

"What man is going to pay the roora for this child?" Miriam asked with a sly smile – provocative as always. "Will it be the father who has so many children he can afford to give them away, or the father who has no children at all and must accept the kind offerings of his brother-in-law?"

"Ah, we must wait to see whether the father with no children has decided to divorce his wife. There will be a price for him to pay now if he wants to remain married . . .," said Esther, tipping more flour into the pot and holding the spoon with both hands to beat into the heavy white porridge.

"What do you think, Cornelia? Will your dear husband, Mlambo, come home now his wife has a baby?"

Cornelia tore her besotted eyes away from Chipo's pink toothless grin. "You know, I don't really care any more," she said quietly. "So long as the ancestors allow me to keep my child, I don't mind if he stays in Harare for ever and marries a hundred new wives!"

"I have a better idea," said Esther. "Why don't you pay the roora for Chipo yourself?"

There were gasps of delighted shock at this outrageous suggestion – for a woman to seize the man's prerogative and gain such complete control of a child.

"Yes, yes," Beauty broke in excitedly. "Like Chikombo, our ancient Shona queen. She founded her own dynasty by paying the roora for all her children. You remember – they carried her totem name instead of her husband's so they stayed linked to her ancestors instead of his."

"Behold the great queen Cornelia!" cried Esther, brandishing her spoon and spraying globules of sticky white porridge round the room. "Mother and founder of a new dynasty!"

This was playing with fire and the women knew it. Their eyes sparkled for a moment or two with a light of reckless rebellion as they contemplated the uproar such an action would cause. Then, as quickly as it had ignited, the light was snuffed out and Alita, a calm voice as always, breathed their collective sigh of resignation into the evening air.

"Don't talk nonsense. It could never happen. The men, the ancestors – they would never allow it. It is against all our oldest traditions. The child carries the father's totem and belongs with his family."

"Yes, but which father?" Miriam asked again, with an irreverent chuckle.

They fell silent, looking at Chipo, who bounced and smiled in his aunt-mother's strong hands: Chipo, precious gift, for whom no cattle nor cash had been given.

"I could never find the money, anyway," said Cornelia. "The only time I ever get money is when Mlambo visits – so it would be his money in any case. Besides he hardly ever comes home. You know sometimes I worry how I'm going to feed this little one."

"Oh, he'll be home when it's time to collect the check from the Grain Marketing Board for your maize," Esther commented sourly. "That's a tradition I'd like to see broken. Sorry, mother–" Alita was taking a breath to make her usual protest – "but I don't see why Mlambo should get any share of what Cornelia earns."

"It's his land," Alita began.

"Oh, his land, his cattle, his money, his child . . ." Esther spat out in exasperation. "Why should the men control everything? I know, I know – don't tell me . . ."

"It's tradition!" they all chorused together, laughing.

"Well, I have a hunch that our brother Mlambo might come home sooner than you all expect," Miriam said mysteriously.

The weeks passed. Early summer became late summer and the young things born in the springtime began emerging from their juvenile hiding. Scruffy fledglings clung to twigs like fluffy fruit, squawking and gaping for food. The five piglets born to Miriam's mud-nuzzling sow left their lumbering mother's black-caked dugs and scattered, squealing delightedly, to search out new mud patches to snuffle and squelch in. Caterpillars who had steadily chomped their way through the summer green, bursting umpteen new layers of skin, and had searched out their crannies for an extended post-prandial rest, now embarked on their final disrobing.

Tendai, too, was growing impatient inside Beauty's womb. Her lungs, like the wings of a butterfly still trapped in its chrysalis case, waited crumpled and deflated in her chest. She was now wedged so tightly that she was forced to sit cross-legged – upside-down like an inverted Buddha – with her head bent and her arms pinioned to her sides. In her lap was the umbilical cord – the pumping lifeline of her underwater weeks – coiled like a pulsating snake and shuddering as she pummeled, with her fists and her feet, on the walls of her pink-padded cell.

This drumming could occur any time, taking Beauty by surprise: as she stood on tiptoe by the henhouse platform and reached for eggs in the depths of empty straw-lined oil-cans; or as she slowly worked her way across one of the maize fields, slashing down at the weeds with her hoe. At night, after the twins were asleep, when she knelt by the light of a candle and rubbed oil into her breasts and belly, she could sometimes see her own flesh jerking with the movements of her restless passenger.

Miriam had given her the oil: "to help your skin expand smoothly without stretch-marks and to prevent your nipples from hurting and cracking when your child first starts to feed." Despite the oil, Beauty could already feel these creases in her skin with her fingertips and see their faint purple tracery running down each breast, like streams down a mountainside.

Eight months ago these were a girl's breasts: high and firm with perky little tip-tilted nipples. Now they hung and swung, until the flesh tore itself with its own burgeoning weight; and her nipples, shiny with oil in the candlelight, stood up hugely dark and swollen, leaking liquid: stubs of flesh as fat as her finger, rising like volcanic islands from mottled brown areolar seas. Her belly, once flat and flawless as silk, now moved without warning and had ballooned out so much she could no longer see her pubis. Even her navel – once a deep little dimple – pouted rudely up at her as if dismayed by its sudden prominence.

Gone was the willow-lean girl with her graceful gait and boyish figure. This was the body of a woman: a strange, bloated, pregnant woman, whose back ached and whose breath came in gasps when she ran. Sometimes she would catch sight of her shadow, waddling sway-backed and bulky-black beside her, and would glance round for the woman it belonged to, scarcely able to believe it was hers.

Yet hers it was. Somehow her miraculous body, after months of hunger and hard work, had managed to fashion itself into the shape of a mother. True, there had been some plundering of old flesh – from her arms and her thighs, and the rounded cheeks of her buttocks. And her new flesh was barely sufficient for the demands that were being placed upon it. But here it was, nonetheless: glorious, mountainous, gleaming with oil; striated and stretched by its own swelling weight; awesome, enormous, glowing gold in the candlelight.

"What shall I do with them, aunt?" wailed Esther one morning, walking slowly across Miriam's wide courtyard with Chipo in a blanket on her back and Lovemore hitched up on one hip.

"The little one won't suck properly – and this other one's still got diarrhea. Cousin, help me, what's wrong with my children? Come on you two, what does your fine training recommend?"

Beauty and Miriam had just come back from a morning's weeding and were sitting in the shade with the twins, digging hungrily into plates of cold sadza with their fingers. One of the twins jumped up immediately and hurried inside the kitchen for another roll of bamboo matting for Esther to sit on. She collapsed on it with a sigh of relief.

"You know it still hurts me to carry things," she said, patting her tummy. "I don't think it took this long to heal after I had Lovemore – talking of whom . . ." And she stood the little boy up on his unsteady legs and pushed him over to her aunt.

Miriam put down her plate and reached out to tug Lovemore on her lap. She smoothed his forehead with one hand

and stroked the other soothingly up and down his dusty bare back.

"He's hot," she said after a moment. "And his skin is dry – with no sweat." She held his face gently in both hands and tilted it up towards her. "Are you thirsty, little chief?"

The other twin scrambled to her feet and returned with a big mug of cool water, which she placed carefully in Lovemore's two hands, then smiled, as encouragingly as any proud mother, as she helped him raise it to his lips.

"Have you tried ORS?" Beauty asked. "That's sugar and salt in water," she explained quickly. "It replaces the liquid he's lost from the diarrhea. I've seen it work lots of times. Sometimes that's all the cure children need."

Esther raised her eyebrows skeptically: "They suggested that at the clinic, and it works for a while, but then he gets sick again almost straight away." She sighed heavily. "I just wish he was healthy – you know –" she gestured at the twins "– lively, bright-eyed, clever, funny. But he's always got something. If it's not diarrhea it's a cough, or a cold, or fever. And it makes him so miserable, poor kidlet . . ."

"I think you should take him to the clinic," said Miriam.

The two younger women stared at her in surprise, then spoke at the same time: "I thought you didn't trust the clinic?" "Can't you give him something yourself?"

Miriam smiled at their consternation, then her face darkened.

"Sometimes I don't know any more," she said in a sad, haunted voice, quite different from her usual brisk no-nonsense tone. "Perhaps they would have been able to save your little brother. I just don't know. But I do know that a child's life is too precious to play games with."

She caressed the nape of his neck under his grubby chifumuro necklace. "My hands tell me his spirit has been weakened. That's why he can't keep the bad airs at bay."

209

Esther opened her mouth to interrupt but Miriam raised a hand to stop her. "All right, all right. I will give you something for him – but on condition you take him to the clinic first."

"And what about Chipo? Must I take him too?" She untied the blanket and cradled the tiny baby in one arm, unbuttoning her blouse with the other. He opened his mouth readily for the nipple and sucked greedily for a moment or two, grunting and snuffling like a little red-faced piglet, then spluttered and let it slip from his mouth.

"See?" Esther cried despairingly. "He hardly takes anything and when I try to force him he just cries and cries till I stop. What's the matter with him? Could it be my milk? Or are his father's ancestors angry that I'm going to give him away to Cornelia?"

Miriam knelt closer and pressed two fingers gently on a spot at the back of his head. "Good, good, that's much better, its gone. Did you notice he had a second nhova at the back when he was born? Just a small one, but they can be very dangerous." She pushed the tip of her little finger into the corner of his mouth and he sucked on it obligingly. "Come on, little one, let's relax and try again."

Esther smiled admiringly as her son settled peacefully back to his feed. "Will he be all right now? He's so tiny . . . And there was an owl that flew ahead of us all the way to the clinic the night he was born. I'm worried that it was a bad omen. Do you think it's wrong for me to give him away?"

The twins began piling up the enamel plates with a clatter that drowned all conversation.

"Patience, Margaret, stop that a minute," Miriam told them. "Come and sit here next to me and listen. Now, tell me, what is the most precious thing that a person can have?"

They giggled and nudged one another. "A child," they said together, their eyes earnest and round with the effort to please.

210

"Good. And what is the most important lesson for a child to learn?"

This was harder. They frowned and stared perplexedly at her. Then Margaret's – or Patience's – brow cleared. "Obedience and respect for her elders?" she asked hopefully.

Miriam smiled and put an arm round her grandchild's bony little shoulders. "Yes, that's very important. But I was thinking of something else."

Patience – or Margaret – leant over and whispered in her cousin's ear.

"Sharing!" they chorused triumphantly.

The three women clapped their hands and laughed.

"Now, explain to your aunt Esther why sharing is so important," said Miriam.

"Well, if there is a famine and two people are hungry, but only one of them has a bowl of sadza . . .," began one, " . . . the other will die if that person keeps all the food for herself . . .," the other continued, " . . . but if they share the food out between them . . .," the first one took up the tale again, " . . . then they'll both survive until the next harvest!" they finished together with a flourish.

"That's why children have to eat two-two or three-three to a bowl," Margaret – or Patience – informed Esther patronizingly, as though addressing a less able classmate.

"I see. Thank you very much for explaining it to me," Esther replied gravely, swallowing her smile. "I think I understand now."

They decided to go together next morning. Beauty insisted on carrying the infant Chipo so Esther would only have Lovemore to manage. They made good progress and, for once the weather was kind, with a fresh breeze fanning the perspiration from their foreheads and fat white clouds scudding in front of the sun. They stopped once: to drink from a standpipe at the side of the road and for Lovemore to crouch, whimpering, by a bush to ease the recurrent cramp in his guts. Then they were off again, walking as quickly as they could, mindful of the cotton and cowpeas, the maize, melon, groundnut and bean fields, waiting for them back at home.

"Soon be time for the green maize," Esther remarked as they passed a field where the spiky green stands were already nearly head-high. "Do you remember, when we were children, how we used to check the fields everyday, peeling off the outer leaves to see if the cobs were big enough to eat yet?"

"Oh, yes. Those weeks seemed to go on and on: I was so sick of sadza, sadza, sadza – every day for months. And always the same relish." Beauty laughed. "Now I'm just grateful if there is sadza every day. I didn't realize how lucky we were. You know some families have to start on their green maize before it's ready because they never manage to harvest enough ripe maize to see them through the year. But that just makes things worse: there's even less left over to mature in the fields and dry out for storing in the granary."

Esther shook her head with its unruly mop of hair. "It only takes a few months of hardship to make you appreciate your good fortune."

She sighed, then. "I suppose I should be thankful that my three beautiful children are alive at all – even though they are suffering."

They walked on in silence. What were the figures? Beauty couldn't remember exactly, but she knew that fewer and fewer children were dying in Zimbabwe – thanks, so the course tutor told them, to things like ORS for diarrhea, and injections to prevent diseases like tetanus, whooping cough and typhoid. She had felt so excited when she found out how simple it was to prevent a child dying. Now she was not quite so sure. What about a child like Lovemore? He had had his complete quota of injections by the time he was nine months of age – the mobile clinic that came every month to the farm saw to that. And if Esther was telling the truth, he'd drunk pints and pints of ORS for at least some of his bouts of diarrhea. Yet still he was suffering. He was alive – oh, yes. They'd manage to keep the poor child alive all right. But what kind of living was this?

She glanced over at her nephew's soft curly head nodding drowsily on Esther's back as she walked. How many days free of illness had he had in his short life? Why, his body was so occupied with recovering from this or that minor infection it had barely enough energy left over for growth, let alone for chattering and chortling and getting into mischief. Looking at him now, Beauty was aware of how often she had seen him like this: lolling half-asleep, sucking listlessly at his thumb, or just staring vacantly at his surroundings as though even moving his eyes was too great an effort for his battle-weary little body.

And Chipo, the gift: what gift of life would be his? Already – barely ten weeks out of the womb – he'd had more than his fair share of suffering. He was so light on her back she could almost forget he was there. Quiet, too, and so still: with that same lethal lethargy that characterized his elder brother. Now here they were taking him for the first of the injections that would keep him alive too: alive, like his brother; safe from killers like diphtheria and measles; preserved in some kind of half-life limbo, where he would succumb to ailment after ailment but would be unable simply to die.

"What do you mean 'food's the key'?" Esther asked, raising her eyebrows quizzically.

"What? Oh, I didn't know I'd spoken aloud. I was just

thinking about how difficult it is to keep the children healthy if you can't afford to feed them properly," she said. "But I don't suppose that's news to you – come on, we're nearly there. If we hurry we'll be at the front of the queue!"

In fact there were several queues, and they were directed to join separate ones as soon as they arrived. Beauty sat on the clinic steps among a group of other expectant mothers, while Esther took Chipo and Lovemore over to where a white-uniformed nurse was trying to coax a screaming infant into a hanging harness to be weighed.

Beauty looked round at her fellow patients. Some of them she knew from school and she was soon drawn into conversation: catching up on gossip, and vowing – as always, whenever they bumped into one another – to visit each other's houses more often.

"Is it your first?" one woman asked. "Oh, you will really respect your mother after you've finished giving birth!" she teased. "Only then will you understand the pain she went through with you!"

"But I already respect my mother," Beauty protested, grinning.

"Is that why you dropped out of school and got married without her permission?" asked another. "There! You see we hear all the news."

"Oh, she doesn't mind about that," Beauty said airily, nose in the air. "And my school fees weren't wasted because I've got a job as a health worker on the farm where I work. They wanted someone with good English," she said smugly.

A sudden ripple of curiosity broke into their conversation.

"Look over there!" hissed the first woman. "There's someone whose school fees were definitely a waste of money. I wonder what her mother thinks about that!"

The girl could not have been older than thirteen: massively pregnant, in a dress that must have belonged to a mother or an aunt and which trailed down to her ankles at the back. She approached them with her eyes on the ground and sat, without greeting anyone – enveloped in her silence and her shame and her absurd, voluminous dress.

"She must have stayed too long listening to the boys' radios one night," commented one woman in a low voice. "They tell the girls they want to play music but they always have some other game in mind!"

"I reckon it was one of the school teachers," whispered another. "They are always seducing their pupils – you know, saying they're in love with them, promising them good grades. But it always ends with the girl getting pregnant and having to leave school – so she doesn't get any grades at all."

"Maybe she has a diploma in love!"

"But that only qualifies her for prostitution . . ."

"Be quiet, all of you!" Beauty exploded. "How can you be so cruel? However it happened, it can't possibly have been her fault. If she was spoilt by an older man, you should be sympathetic. After all, it might have happened to you, or to one of your daughters . . ."

She stopped then, breathing heavily, and an uncomfortable silence fell on the group.

"Maiway, maiway, maiway . . .," the unmistakable cries of a woman in labor came from the clinic's little two-bed maternity ward, breaking into the silence and reminding the waiting women why they were there.

Beauty's turn came soon enough and she scrambled up on to the trolley in the examination room next door.

"You've had your TB jabs already, you say? Good. Now are you sure about the month of conception. Your baby's still rather small for his age . . . still, I'm sure he'll be a lovely healthy boy."

The nurses – the tall, kind one with glasses – prodded her belly and vagina with hard, experienced fingers.

"Hmm – borderline CPD. Your pelvis may be too narrow for a vaginal delivery. We'll try, but you may have to have a Cesarean section. Right, down you get, Mrs. Kanyemba, and we'll see you back here in a couple of weeks' time."

"Maiway, maiway, maiway-ay-ay. . . ." Another bout of wailing made Beauty hesitate on her way out and peep quickly through the half-open door of the next room. A pregnant woman of about her own age was kneeling on the floor, rocking her body to and fro, with one hand pressed to the small of her back.

"Maiway, mother, help me," she moaned. "Something's eating away at my back . . . It's a curse – oh, mother, where are you?"

Beauty turned and hurried away, not wanting to hear any more. Curses, school teachers, Cesarean sections, under-weight babies: this visit was turning into a nightmare. She went to join Esther instead and found her retying Lovemore's array to chifumuro charms around his neck, wrist and chest.

"Honestly, I'm sure they don't weigh that much," she grumbled. "It's that Sister Tekedi – she just wants to prove she doesn't believe in traditional medicine. Now I'll have to bathe them both in chifumuro water as soon as I get home in case they've been harmed by any of the other children."

"What did she advise? Did she give you anything for the diarrhea?"

"What do you think? She did what they always do: weighed him and lectured me on not feeding him properly – then told me to give him ORS for the diarrhea. She weighed Chipo too and told me to feed him more often, and to bring him back every month until he's had all his injections."

Beauty gazed round at the scene: pregnant women, women with babies on their backs, with babies in their arms, with toddlers on their knees. Many would have walked for two hours or more to get here. They still had that walk back

216

home ahead of them, through the sternest heat of the day –
all for something, anything, that might protect the health of
their children: a series of injections, cough syrup, aspirin,
antibiotics – or just another weighing, another lecture,
another dot on the remorseless graph of hunger on their
child's weight chart.

"There was a woman in labor at the clinic," Beauty said.
"She was all alone, kneeling on the floor."

They were walking home, slowly, with the midday sun
beating down through their scarves so their heads throbbed
with the heat. The children were clammy against their backs
and the crazed and cracked mud of the road burnt into the
soles of their feet. They screwed up their eyes and frowned a
little to protect their eyes from the glare as they plodded
onward through the shimmering air. Here and there they
passed a group of cows, heads hanging in the shade of a tree,
flicking flies with lazy tails while the crickets buzzed and
whirred endlessly in the grass.

"That's what I hated most about the hospital," said Esther
after a while. "I felt so alone – and some of the nurses were
so rough and impatient. You want to be brave, to behave
like a strong mother, but they make you feel like a trouble-
some child."

"It's safer at the clinic, though, isn't it? It's better to give
birth there, just in case something goes wrong."

"I suppose so –" Esther did not sound very convinced. "It
depends what kind of things goes wrong. There was one
woman who lost her baby at Kadoma Hospital and I over-
heard the nurse saying it was because they had not checked
often enough to make sure it was all right. I think it just died
inside her – even though they had all the equipment there
ready for an emergency. So it's not necessarily safer . . ."

"Do you mean they just forgot about the baby – just let it die?"

Esther shrugged. "I don't know for sure – I'm just telling you what I heard."

They walked on in silence, submitting to the pounding heat, placing one foot after another along the hard-baked mud road, feeling the children growing heavier and hotter as they slumped and sweltered inside the bulky blankets on their backs.

A familiar row of tin-roofed buildings – the bottle store, grocery and beer hall – told them they were nearly home and they turned gratefully off on to one of the myriad sandy tracks that wound between the trees and thorn bushes to where they lived. Beauty heard someone call her name and looked up across the sun-bleached landscape. Two women in the distance, with hoes hooked over their shoulders, stopped and raised their hands in greeting.

"There is trouble at your home!" one called out, gesturing extravagantly down the path behind them.

"You can hear them shouting a mile away!" cried the other. "I should stay away, if I were you – wait until it's all over. Esther! Your sister's there too . . ."

"What's going on?" Beauty shouted, her voice high with anxiety.

"We didn't wait to find out. Well, don't say we didn't warn you!"

Beauty and Esther quickened their pace and half ran the rest of the way, ignoring the peevish cries of Lovemore and Chipo, jerked rudely out of their soporific heat-drugged stupors. When the two homesteads came into view – two clusters of thatched huts divided by a stretch of open ground and a four-strand wire fence – they slowed down, squinting into the sun and trying to make out what was happening in the middle of Miriam's courtyard.

Miriam was there, of course: unmistakable in her red-patterned scarf. She was leaning forward, with both hands on her hips, every sinew of her tall body expressing anger and defiance. Behind her cowered the twins, nervously holding hands, their shoulders hunched as if expecting a blow. Daniel, her twelve-year-old-son, stood beside her, looking at the ground and shifting his feet uncomfortably in the dust as if unsure of whose side he was on.

Beauty could see why. Facing Miriam, ranged against her under the fierce afternoon sun, were two men: Samuel and Mlambo. Though Samuel's back was towards her, Beauty could tell by the way he squared his shoulders in his baggy checked jacket that her uncle was intent on provoking some kind of showdown. Beside him, his son-in-law Mlambo seemed equally spoiling for a fight. He was gripping Cornelia hard by the arm, as if she was a criminal under arrest, and her big bony body wilted unresisting at his side like a broken stalk of sorghum after a hailstorm.

The sound of quick feet behind made them turn and Alita was there, hurrying towards them, her face stricken with panic.

"It's terrible!" she gasped. "I couldn't stop them. They want to kill her – they blame her for everything!" She pulled at her skirt agitatedly with her fingers while her eyes darted from one face to another, searching for reassurance.

"What can we do?" she cried desperately.

"Calm down, mother, please." Esther took hold of Alita's restless hands, squeezed them tight, then shook them gently. "Now, tell us what's happened – slowly . . ."

Alita took a deep breath and smiled shakily at her daughter. "I'm sorry – but it's so awful . . ."

Esther shook her hands again, more roughly this time. "All right, all right, don't be angry. I'm calm now. It was when Mlambo came home – on the morning bus. He came straight to the house looking for Cornelia. He looked dreadful

219

– as though every evil ngozi in Zimbabwe were after him –
and he just started hitting her, without even greeting her
first. He just slapped her face over and over, calling her all
sorts of dreadful names – accusing her of putting a spell on
him and sending a ngozi to torture him. A black goat, he
kept going on about a black goat . . .''

"I don't understand," Beauty interrupted. "How did
Samuel get involved? Why do they want to kill my mother?"

"I don't know, I don't know. It all happened so quickly."
Alita tugged her hands free and began twisting them distractedly again in the material of her skirt.

"Somehow Samuel managed to convince Mlambo that
Miriam was behind it all – that she had some kind of control
over Cornelia. You know he's always hated your mother,
especially since Alfred died –" she shrugged her thin shoulders helplessly at Beauty.

"The letter!" Esther broke in. "It must have been the
letter she sent!" She grabbed Beauty's arm excitedly.
"Beauty, it worked, the letter worked – Seguro was right.
He said it would bring Mlambo home. And your mother
knew – do you remember what she said yesterday? She said
he'd be back sooner than we expected – and here he is!"

The three women stared over at the little group in time to
see Mlambo push Cornelia to the ground and raise his hand
to hit her again. They saw Miriam step forward and they saw
Mlambo hesitate. For a long, still moment they stood like
statues, petrified, in the shimmering air: a man with his arm
raised ready to strike; a woman cringing like a dog on the
dusty ground; a nganga with her black eyes blazing under
the blazing white eye of the sun.

"If you hit her again, you will regret it, I promise you."
Miriam spoke quietly, but her words cut cleanly as knives
through the heat-thickened air.

"The ax may forget, but the tree always remembers.

When she dies a shadow will fall on her coffin and you will not be able to lift it to carry it to the grave. She will refuse to be buried in peace. She will remember the wrong you have done her and she will make sure you never forget it."

He froze while she spoke, mesmerized by the menace in her voice. Then, when she stopped, he raised his arm again.

"I warn you, Mlambo," she said, in the same quiet voice. "If you believe I sent the black goat to haunt you; if you believe I have cursed you with barrenness . . . And –" turning to Samuel – "if you believe I murdered your son and bewitched your wife and your daughters . . . If you believe I have the power to do all that . . ." She paused, flashing shafts of white fury at them both: "Then believe this, believe this: believe that I have the power to make you suffer."

Even from where they were standing, the three watching women could see that Miriam's words had pierced the men's balloon of bravado. They seemed to shrink inside their clothes for an instant and, when Samuel reached out a restraining hand, Mlambo's arm slowly dropped to his side.

Seizing her opportunity, Cornelia crawled quickly out of his way, scrambled to her feet behind Miriam, and stood, cowed and awkward, gingerly touching the side of her face and trying to wipe the dried blood from her nose and mouth.

"You're wrong, Miriam," Samuel hissed through his teeth, backing reluctantly away from her. "You are the one who will regret this. I will make sure that everyone recognizes you for what you are. I'll make sure you never work as a nganga again. Come on, Mlambo – we have people to see, business to do." And with that the two men turned and strode away.

He was true to his word. By nightfall the news had spread round the village and the talk rumbled ominously in every homestead, like thunder in the hills. Men clustered in groups round the fires in the darkness outside the kitchen huts and leaned forward eagerly on their stools. Teenage boys squatted nearby, listening attentively as the older men waved their hands to emphasize some point, sketching wide arcs of red light in the air with their cigarettes.

"You can't hide a pair of horns under a paper hat – she had to be found out sometime."

"She killed her husband too; just smothered him one night while he was asleep."

"I never liked her treating my children. You could tell there was something evil about her."

"Someone told me she does abortions as well – murders unborn babies and eats their hearts, then makes them her slaves."

"It must have been her – the black goat, I mean."

"You know I'm sure I've seen a big black goat out in the bush near her homestead – she's probably been doing it for years –"

"And we never knew . . ."

"Well, I've always suspected it. She brings trouble to everything she touches."

"So they're calling in a muuki from across the river. He should sort her out once and for all."

"Yes, sort her out once and for all . . ."

Inside, by the kitchen fires, the talk among the women was more divided.

"Since that baby died I've always wondered . . ."

"I wouldn't let her touch me if I got pregnant again."

"Well, I don't know. I'm sure my child would be dead if she hadn't been there when he was born."

"And just look who's accusing her! Who's the saint and who's the sinner, just tell me that?"

"You know the saying: 'The man most afraid of the hyena

is the one who has smeared himself with fat.'"

"So why did that baby die then?"

"And what did the black goat mean?"

The talk went on and on, like a malevolent wind, stirring up dead leaves of suspicion and making them crackle and dance. Conversations, conducted in whispers, dredged through the dusts of memory for old hurts and humiliations which were shaken clean of cobwebs. In this febrile atmosphere, where few spoke without first glancing round, the rank plant of innuendo flourished. It sucked in the dry, dusty air and grew well, despite layers of murk clogging its leaves. Like a hairy gray weed it was, forcing up through an expanse of gray concrete, seeming to draw its sustenance from the heart of the dead concrete itself and from the dusty wind blowing across it.

It was as though all the times in the past, when Miriam had faced up to her detractors – as a nganga, as a widow, as a woman claiming rights for other women – all those times had been but a rehearsal for this.

Not because this occasion was any more serious than the others. But because somehow this time the timing was right. The precarious harmony between the men and the women had been disturbed once too often, and a jealous god had been roused. An ancient, ugly god, that had slumbered fitfully through the ages, drugged on the narcotic of tradition, had been nudged at and needled and finally shaken into awareness. And now the god had awoken, it was hungry. Its nostrils flared and twitched as it scented the sour smell of sacrifice on the dusty malevolent wind. And its greedy eyes alighted on Miriam.

The speed with which it happened was astounding. Even on the compound, at the height of the winter drumming, Beauty couldn't remember anything like it. One day her mother was striding off to the store to buy soap, calling out cheery greetings to the people she passed, flanked by her usual escort of scampering curly-haired children. But the next time she walked through the village it was through a wide corridor of silence. When people saw her approaching they ducked their heads back through their doors, dragging their bewildered children in behind them. And when she returned to the homestead afterwards, Beauty could see that perhaps this time her mother was beaten.

"It will pass, mother. They'll soon forget. Next month there will be something new to worry about and it will seem as though this never happened."

Miriam sat down wearily on the door step and slumped back against the wall. She untied her red scarf and wiped it across her brow.

"Five years ago I might have agreed with you. But now I'm not so sure. Times are changing; people are changing. They treat our traditions like so many mangoes on a tree, thinking they can just pick the ones they want and leave the rest rotting on the branches. And I'm just one of those mangoes. But I'm sour and I'm bitter and I set their teeth on edge: I don't melt sweetly on the tongue so they want to destroy me.

"People these days want their medicine to taste sweet. They don't want to worry about their duties to the old ones, their promises to their families, their responsibilities to their neighbors and their children. If the clinic says their children can be made healthy by a simple injection, why should they listen to a cantankerous old nganga who rubs black oil on the heads of their children and says that wives should get a share of the maize money so they can make sure there's enough food in the house?

"It's too difficult, you see, my way to health – so confused and confusing that sometimes even I can't find a path through the leaves and the roots and the nagging of your great-aunt Eustina, and the hunger and the jealousy and the impossibility of scratching a living from this mean, mean land we've inherited.

"You know after your cousin died in my arms, I was ready to give up. I even began burning my herbs. But Eustina wouldn't let me. She cursed me and said I was lazy. She kicked me and told me I had work to do. She even laughed at me for thinking it would be easier; for thinking that being a nganga and a nyamakuta – the healer and the one who receives babies into the world – for thinking that path would be a straight one. Then she reminded me of our bravest nganga of all, of Mbuya Nehanda – of how she had to fight a war against the white men to bring health to her people . . ."

She sat up straight for a moment, her black eyes ablaze and her fists clenched. Then she slumped back again and the light went out of her eyes.

"But I'm not Mbuya Nehanda. And I haven't the strength to fight this war. I just want a rest from it all."

"And your work? You were going to teach me. . . What about your work?"

"Dear Beauty," Miriam sighed fondly, her voice laden with defeat. "Do you really think it would matter if I never delivered another baby?"

"It would matter to me and to my baby," Beauty said quietly.

If she had been a breathing thing, she would have gasped as the walls of her padded cell closed and squeezed her tight. She could feel the firm embrace of an octopus's grasp as muscular arms wrapped themselves round her folded inverted body like so many coils of sinuous rope, and squeezed her, and squeezed her, in a hold that was part massage, part hug, and part – something else: an awakening, a quickening, a rehearsal for a gala performance.

225

For perhaps half a minute she was held, let her body be gripped in that fearful, exhilarating bondage. Then it was over and she was released once more: beached and abandoned to butt into and nudge at the suddenly quiescent boundaries of her submarine world.

They had been happening for nearly three months now, these sudden upheavals that forced fluid into her gaping mouth and made it gurgle and roar in her ears. At first, when she was smaller, their grip was much lighter; more a casual stroking caress. But now there was no doubt about the seriousness of their intent: they were passionate, urgent, arousing. They made her aware of her body, of its solidity; of its ability to resist each crushing grasp. And now, when the waves of upheaval receded, she had less of a sense of loss: because the arms never released her entirely, but remained wrapped loosely around her, like the arms of a sleeping lover, so however she moved to squirm into a more comfortable position, she could always feel their warm weight on her skin.

That skin was smoother now, thicker; had lost some of its painful transparency, so the network of pulsing blue vessels were now barely a shadow on her belly, and the black silken down, that once clung to every crease of her crumpled little inverted body, had sloughed off like seaweed from a rock, to leave her glowing peachy-bare and naked, glimmering palely in her underwater twilight.

"Are you ready, little one?" Eustina whispered, peering through the lattice of bone and muscle to where Tendai nodded in her padded pink cradle. "Sleep sweetly, my dearest. There's a long, hard journey ahead."

Then she reached out her gnarled old hands and gently parted the plump folds of flesh that Beauty oiled and massaged each night. Using the direction of the folds as her guide, she allowed her questing fingers to slide slowly inwards and up to where the blushing vagina wept pearly tears like the dripping walls of a subterranean cave. There she stopped and felt for the hard knob of flesh – like the pout of a lemon or pear – that pushed down into the roof of the cave.

When she found it, and touched it, she smiled.

"Oh, get ready, little one," she chuckled gleefully. "Your prison is opening up."

And it was true. The hard pout had softened, as a woman's lips do when they yield to a lover's first kiss, and had parted a little, langourous and swollen, in the shy expectation of more.

"Oh, easy, this part should be easy," she crowed, slipping a finger into the kiss-shaped space and loosening a little plug of blood-stained mucus.

"Yes, we'll soon have you out of your cradle, my sweet slumbering water-baby." Then she frowned and her eyes became serious.

"Then comes the hard part," she said.

And she reached out her hands once again. And she made her measurements one last time. Here: cupped over Tendai's tender skull with its slick black tendrils of hair. And here: knuckled into the white open jaws that guarded the gateway to life.

In her dream she saw her great-aunt Eustina lifting down the fat painted clay pots, one by one, from the neatly stacked towers in the kitchen.

"It's this last one I want; the smallest one right at the bottom."

And, strangely, the smallest pot was indeed at the bottom, with the larger ones balanced miraculously above it.

"You'll have to break it," Miriam warned when the last of

the towers was dismantled. And she held up an ax whose blade gleamed red in the firelight as though smeared with fresh blood.

"It's such a pretty pot, though. It would be a pity to smash it open," the old woman pleaded. "Let me try with my hands first."

Beauty woke with a strange sensation between her legs and slipped a sleepy hand under her blanket to find that her underwear was sticky with slime. She opened her eyes then and stared for a long time at the shadowy, cobwebby thatch, listening to the twins' even breathing on the floor beside her, and letting the small piece of knowledge expand and spread out in her mind.

This was it: the first sign. Just as her mother had explained.

Any day now her child would be born.

"You'll have to start packing your things," Miriam said later when she told her. "It's a long walk to the clinic. You don't want to waste time when you're in labor."

"I'm not going to the clinic," Beauty said firmly.

Miriam sighed: she had heard this before.

"You have to go. It's your first child – every first child should be born at the clinic. Just in case something goes wrong. Your bones are narrow, you know that. What if you need to be cut open?"

"And what would the village say about you, mother, if your own daughter refused to let you deliver her baby?"

Miriam's eyes flickered. "I don't care what they say. I just want my daughter and my grandchild to be safe."

"And will I really be safe at the clinic? Don't they ever lose babies there?"

"Yes – no – I don't know. Please –" Miriam begged. "Don't make me do this. I couldn't bear it if . . ."

"But I had a dream, mother," Beauty interrupted, her

eyes shining with excitement. "Aunt Eustina was there and she was saying that we have to try."

Miriam hesitated a moment, looking into her daughter's beautiful eager flushed faced. Then she shook her head quickly, decisively:

"No. I won't let you take the risk."

Beauty tried again. "Tell me honestly, mother. Is my pelvis really too narrow? Are you certain I'd have to be cut open?" She gazed at her mother with a mixture of challenge and hope in her brown eyes.

Slowly Miriam shook her head once more.

"No, I'm not certain," she said with a smile.

For days now their household had been virtually cut off from the rest of the village. No one came to consult Miriam and the twins ran home saying the other children had refused to play with them. Daniel, with the sullen withdrawal of adolescence, neglected his chores and shut himself up in his hut with his school books, or disappeared into the bush for hours on end without saying where he was going.

But perhaps hardest to bear was the absence of the other women – of Esther, Alita, Cornelia: forbidden, on pain of a beating, to cross the boundary to Miriam's homestead. The lack of that contact was like bereavement. One day the two households were braided into one by the weaving, to and fro, of five women: carrying children to be tended, a gift of cowpea greens, a pestle and mortar for loan, mugs of sugar and soap powder, a foaming pot of fresh-brewed beer; gossip, laughter, voices raised in argument. Then the links were severed and there was silence. The dust on the paths between the two households, once scuffed thirty times a day by hurrying bare-soled feet, lay flat and undisturbed in the sunshine.

229

There was a sense of waiting during those long hot summer days: waiting for Beauty's labor to begin; waiting for a final confrontation with the men; waiting for the maize to ripen. They no longer waited for rain – that urgent expectation had passed and what rain there would be had fallen. Now, in the stillness of late summer – when the green spikes of maize rustled softly in the fields and the golden mopheads of sorghum and millet bent and swayed under the fluttering weight of feasting finches – now, when the worst of the work was over, they were waiting for fruition.

The pains began gradually one hot night, advancing slowly into Beauty's awareness, so that she woke herself with her own moans and found her hands pressing up under her belly and her blanket thrown sideways on the floor. She lay tense for a moment, while the tightness gripped and a glaze of sweat started upon her forehead; then breathed again as the waves ebbed away, leaving her heart beating wildly in the darkness. Quietly she struggled to her knees and, wrapping the blanket round her waist, slipped silently out through the door.

The air seemed fresh and cool after the stuffiness of the little hut and she breathed in deeply, hugging herself with excitement and fear, half willing the next pain to come, half dreading the ordeal in store. She walked a little way from the hut and stood, legs apart, with her blanket hitched up and her underwear pulled aside, relieving herself in the dew-soaked grass and gazing up at the stars.

"By this time tomorrow," she whispered, "I shall have my child in my arms." Then, because the stars were so beautiful and the night so cool and clear, and because she could feel the spirits clustering, solicitously, around her –

"If the ancestors allow it," she added quickly, smiling secretly to herself, never doubting for a moment that they would.

"It's not too late to change your mind," Miriam said later that morning, arriving back from the bush with an enormous bundle of firewood on her head. She hefted it off against the outside wall of the kitchen and rubbed the back of her neck to ease the stiffness away.

Beauty looked up from where she was kneeling by the open door.

"What after you've collected all that wood for the fire?" she teased. "I couldn't possibly go to the clinic now, thinking you'd gone to all that trouble for nothing."

Miriam shook her head grimly. "Stubborn, too stubborn for your own good," she muttered, a smile lurking beneath her scowl.

"Yes, I know. It's a great fault in a woman," Beauty said, with an exaggerated sigh of contrition. "Perhaps I take after my mother." Then she drew breath in sharply as another wave of pain welled up under her belly.

"See? At least your child has some manners," Miriam retorted with satisfaction. "She will teach you not to be so rude to your mother."

Bent over, with her hands on the ground, Beauty didn't bother to reply. Then, a bit later, when she was sitting up straight once more:

"How do you know it's a girl?" she asked.

This time it was Miriam who didn't answer. Beauty followed her eyes and saw Alita walking purposefully across the open ground towards them. Mother and daughter exchanged puzzled looks: Alita, of all people – the good and faithful wife, the mildest and most timid of all the women. What had happened to make her come to them now?

"I had to come," she said simply, in reply to their questioning faces. "I had to warn you. They've just left – Samuel and Mlambo – they've just gone to fetch the muuki. They say they'll probably be back before nightfall and they took

231

the last of the maize money to pay him with . . ."

She raised her hands in a vague gesture of exasperation. "Oh, it's crazy, crazy, all this . . ."

She trailed off then, noticing the pile of firewood and the preparations taking place in the kitchen – bamboo matting and blankets on the newly swept floor, a pile of empty fertilizer sacks, pots and buckets brimming with water –

"Oh, no! Has it started?" she cried in dismay, falling to her knees beside Beauty. "I'm so sorry, my dear. What a time to have your baby."

"That's right," said Miriam. "Tell my daughter she's crazy to stay here. Tell her she's better off at the clinic."

"And tell my mother," retorted Beauty, "that, whatever happens, I'm staying right here with her."

Alita looked at the two women – each with her chin tilted aggressively and her arms folded implacably over her breasts. She shrugged.

"I never had any complaints," she said to Beauty. "Your mother was always good enough for me. Now, don't argue," she said, raising her hand as Miriam started to protest. "You may not have any faith in yourself. But I have faith in you. And, what's more, I intend to stay here with you both until this terrible day is over."

Four hours later, when the sun was a high hot ball and twelve minutes was the width of each landing on Beauty's long staircase of pain, Esther and Cornelia arrived too. They had taken advantage of the men's absence to scuttle across the clearing between their two homesteads, glancing round nervously in case they were seen.

"I'm sorry," Cornelia said, hanging her head dejectedly, a purple bruise splashed across her cheek. "This is my fault, isn't it? If I hadn't sent that letter, Mlambo would still be in Harare . . ."

"Oh, be quiet," Esther said sharply, made irritable by her

anxiety. "It could be my fault too, for giving you Chipo, making Mlambo ashamed of the kind of husband he's been."

"If anyone's to blame, we all are," said Alita. "It's a wonder we've not all turned into hyenas the way we talk about our men behind their backs. Do you think they don't guess what we say about them? They're not stupid. They know how a husband should behave. They know when they wrong us. That's what's behind this. They blame Miriam because she's the one who speaks out to their faces. But they want to teach us all a lesson."

"Well, we'll try to keep them away – at least until the baby's born," Esther promised as they turned to leave.

After they'd gone it seemed suddenly quiet in the kitchen. Beauty knelt on the mat staring at the sticks in the unlit grate, listening to the sounds outside: a chicken clucking fussily in the doorway: the endless soft buzzing of flies; a rustle as a little gecko skittered across the thatch. She raised her head and saw a message she couldn't interpret pass silently between her aunt and her mother. Miriam nodded imperceptibly and rose to her feet, while Alita crawled forward and began lighting the fire.

"What are you doing?" Beauty asked, suddenly afraid, as her mother began taking down the bulbous claypot towers.

"Time's running short. You'll be needing me soon and I've work to do, things to prepare, medicine to make for you. But first –" she grunted, heaving the largest pot away from the wall, out of its clinging shroud of cobwebs – "first I'm going to build a fence – a good, strong, invisible fence to keep evil-doers away."

She rummaged around in the pot and slipped something – Beauty couldn't quite see what – into the pocket of her skirt. Then she plunged out of the dark hut into the blinding solid heat of the afternoon sun. Moments later Beauty heard the rhythmic chopping of a hoe cutting into the hard ground – there; there; there; there – at four points around the hut. And, as the last hole was completed, and the dust scraped back over the last magic thing buried there, another contraction flexed its fingers and took hold at the base of her womb, wringing pain from her flesh like water squeezed from a newly washed blouse. And, for the first time – bent double as she was, cradling her pain in her arms – Beauty began to comprehend the enormity of the task that lay ahead.

A little groan of despair escaped her lips and she dug her fists into her belly, as if she would fight the force that gripped her, that would hold her prisoner now until her baby was born. Indeed it was as if she really were trapped, chained for ever to the floor in this murky dungeon of a hut, sealed in a dark tomb of pain by the magic barrier Miriam had erected, while outside – in the slabs of solid sunlight – other people, lucky people, walked free.

She could see the clamoring black tunnel of pain stretching out in front of her and there seemed to be no end to it; no pinprick of light in the distance; no promise that she would survive; no sense at all that, somewhere in that endless black catacomb, her laboring knot of a body would untie itself, would be released and resolved into two so that a new Beauty would emerge, whole and entire, with a new life kicking in her arms.

All at once – after twelve hours of labor – she was certain it would never happen; that she would be caught for ever in a howling darkness, while the ratchets of pain tightened remorselessly in her womb and her child refused to be born. How could she ever have thought it was possible? The men, the muuki, the spirits would never allow it. She would be punished: for being touched by the teacher, for lying to her husband, for marrying without permission – for hoping against hope that she could somehow deceive her ancestors.

The pain ebbed slowly and she sat up, wiping her forehead with the back of her hand.

"A bad one?" Alita asked sympathetically.

Beauty nodded dumbly, her eyes wide with terror, hoping for some word of reassurance.

"Well just try to relax, there's much worse to come," Alita blithely advised. "You shouldn't tire yourself out trying to fight them." And she bent over, unconcerned, to blow into the fire.

Beauty bit her lips and stared miserably at her aunt, then coughed as she was suddenly enveloped in billows of thick gray smoke. She tried to catch her breath, but the smoke and the lump in her throat and the thudding of her heart made even breathing impossible. Panic began seeping into her mind as the airless smoke-filled room began to close in and her swollen womb seemed to expand from inside, pressing up into her stomach and lungs so that she, Beauty, began to disappear altogether, crushed between them, suffocated from within and without.

Avalanche of adrenalin; cascade of fear. Like hot lava it started to flow, burning all it touched, readying every muscle for flight. Beauty's eyes blackened as their pupils surged open to suck in the scene of danger. Her blood abandoned its meander through her skin and pulsed headlong into deeper vessels, propelled by her racing heart, leaving her skin clammy and icy cold. In her womb, red cocoon, whose puckered mouth had been slowly relaxing – to a kiss, then a smile, then a slack little "o" of surprise – the rhythm of unfolding was halted.

Like a tide on the turn, with waves colliding, running sideways, in a confusion of conflicting forces, the drug of fear chased its ripples of chaos through the onward-flowing stream of her labor.

235

The opening, the unraveling, the unwrapping was arrested, as the flood of fear fed on itself, renewing itself and augmenting into a towering tidal wave of terror that engulfed all her faith and her courage, possessing her completely. It bound her to the pain in some ghastly infatuation, so she waited for it now in a ferment of horror, shrinking at every nuance of sensation so that when the contractions gripped she could experience nothing but pain, and when they let her go she could think of nothing but pain to come.

Once she looked wildly round the kitchen, expecting that somehow the very substance of her surroundings would be altered to match the tumult in her body. But no, everything was just as she remembered: the rough brown walls curving round either side of the door; the molded mud dresser with its rows of plates and bowls; the black polished floor with its drifting litter of wood ash; Alita kneeling, stirring a bubbling pot; Miriam crouching, laying out objects on a spread of plastic sacks.

Didn't they realize what was happening to her? It was as if she was invisible and the fear had spirited her away to a different world. Or perhaps she was already dead and it was her ghost that now gazed in dazed disbelief on this tranquil and untroubled scene.

She must have made some sound because suddenly the two women looked up. Immediately Miriam came and knelt beside her, gently prizing her hands away from where they were still buried in the flesh of her belly.

"You must try to relax. Let your body open up. The more you tense yourself, the longer it will take."

She moved round behind her daughter while she spoke and began massaging her shoulders and the base of her spine. "Don't think about the pain. Concentrate on what I'm doing instead. You know, once you've had your baby you'll be able to start learning my work."

She spoke soothingly, her strong healing hands smoothing away the worst of the panic, like wrinkles from a blanket on the floor, and all the while talking, talking:

"I remember the first time I ever delivered a baby. I was still at home after having my second child and my mother – your grandmother – was away visiting relatives. My younger sister – your aunt Lydia – went into labor and I didn't know who to call for help. Everything was fine at first and I was just starting to feel confident when the baby's arm appeared out of her vagina. An arm! I nearly fainted, was so dizzy I could hardly move. That was the first time your great-aunt Eustina spoke to me. She'd been dead nearly three years, but suddenly I could hear her voice – as clearly as I'm speaking to you now – telling me exactly what to do."

"Is she here now?" Beauty asked, peering curiously into the shadows.

"Oh, she's always around when a child's being born," Miriam assured her. "Looking over my shoulder, interfering like an old busy-body, shouting if I do something she doesn't approve of. She's a lot less patient these days that she was when I was younger. If you listen hard I'm sure you'll hear her grumbling at me now – just as I'll grumble at you when I'm a spirit and you're a nyamakuta . . ."

Forgetting, for the moment, to concentrate on tensing her body for the next contraction, Beauty strained her ears for the cracked wheezing voice Miriam had described so often. She tried so hard that Alita, watching her intent face, burst out laughing.

"It's no good. I've tried to hear her too. Sometimes when I see your mother talking to the air, I can just feel her presence. And once when I was in labor I'm sure I felt two pairs of hands on me. But she's elusive, that old one. She only talks to your mother."

"You're lucky I'm here at all, you ungrateful wench,"

Eustina muttered in Miriam's ear. "If you're not careful I'll leave you to cope with this on your own. Then perhaps you'll treat me with a bit more respect. Now pay attention, this will not be an easy birth, you know that. She's narrow, but there are other problems too. There's something worrying her; she's frightened. It's stopping her womb opening. And there's trouble with the shape of her back – you've seen this before – so the baby's not pressing down properly."

Miriam sighed. She should have foreseen this. Again she wished her daughter had gone to the clinic so she would not have to see her suffering like this, not feel so responsible for her safety. But would the nurses cope any better? Would they tell Beauty stories to distract her, or knead her spine to ease some of the pain? And what could they do that would undo the lifetime that had made this slender body so unfit for childbirth?

Day by day, year by year: subtle, remorseless. A little girl, barely able to walk, would search out something to tie to her back: a doll, perhaps – passed from an aunt to a mother to a sister, till only rows of pink holes marked where yellow curls once sprouted, and only one plastic eyelid, with its stiff fringe of black lashes, flapped shut over one staring blue eye; or an old shoe, patting it and swaddling it lovingly, and hoisting it up to nestle between her sharp shoulder-blades, arching her back and protruding her pert little buttocks in a parody of womanhood.

A year later the rehearsal would be over and it would be the weight of a real baby that would bend her soft skeleton and would mould it, like the wind moulds a sapling, into a permanent "s" of a curve. While her brothers scampered freely, their bodies unburdened, growing straight as telegraph poles, her bones would already be bending: under buckets of water, each day a little fuller; great loads of firewood that crackled and rocked as she walked – and always the baby, the baby, whose body she could barely encompass in her loving and willing brown arms.

Miriam could see Beauty now, as a child, gamely staggering under the weight of her baby brother, planting her feet proudly in the dust and grinning triumphantly up at her mother. But the Beauty that turned to her now was not smiling. Stretched on the rack of another contraction, a hunted animal stared out from her face, and its eyes bulged in dumb terror at the incomprehensible pain of its wounds.

For hours they tried everything to gentle the poor wild beast she'd become. Alita brewed a sweet ale for her to drink, but she pushed the mug from her lips. Miriam held her tightly in her arms, whispering soothing words in her ear, but she just knelt stiffly unmoved, staring straight in front of her. They draped a blanket round her shoulders and urged her to lie down and rest, but she flung it off as soon as it touched her, as though the rough cloth was burning her skin. They even sang a lullaby from her childhood, trying to reach a rock of calm memory in the depths of her turbulent sea.

All in vain. Nothing they did seemed to touch her, or blunt the bright blades of pain that slashed into her terrified flesh. She just knelt rigid, staring blindly at the fire, her thin shoulders shuddering, her whole body trembling, her hands clenching and unclenching as if to fend off each coming assault.

But there was no stopping these attacks. They were as merciless as an army of mercenaries, striking unerringly, again and again, just at the moment when her defenses were down, buffeting her body over and over as the evening sun slanted in through the door and stalked slowly in a wide arc across the floor.

Once her control broke completely and she yowled with anguish, begging Miriam to put an end to her misery.

"Rapfumo," she pleaded, gripping her mother's arm. "Anything to get rid of this baby."

And, although it hurt to do it, Miriam had to refuse, explaining patiently that it was too dangerous to speed up the birth at this stage:

"You're not open enough. It would only make things worse."

But Beauty wouldn't listen. She just clamped her hands over her ears and turned away, blocking out her mother's voice and rocking to and fro moaning miserably to herself.

And so it went on, hour after hour, while the light dimmed to a cool blue outside. From the bush came the mournful clonking of cowbells as the cattle were herded to their barns for the night. And as the women began banking up the fire for their long vigil and readying their stock of candles, first one cricket, then two, started chirping from the depths of the woodpile. But still Beauty trembled, with her eyes as blank and her body as paralyzed as a dead bird vibrating on a live cable.

Miriam decided to examine her again and nodded to Alita to close the door. Together the two older women unbent Beauty's fear-stiffened limbs and laid her out, like a plastic doll, on her back on the blankets. Alita lit a candle, while Miriam washed her hands, then knelt at her daughter's feet: a prostrate worshipper at the shrine of a fallen idol.

Miriam sat back on her knees. "It's no good. Eustina's right. There's something stopping her opening up. Beauty –" pulling her daughter's dress down and rolling her over gently on her side towards the fire – "Beauty, listen to me. You must let us help you. You can't do this on your own. If you close your heart to us, there's a danger your womb will stay closed too. Is there something you're afraid of? Anything you're holding inside? Beauty, trust me. You must let it out or your child will refuse to be born."

240

She stroked Beauty's forehead, running her nails gently through the damp fringe of black curls on her temple and, after a while, she saw tears begin welling up under her daughter's thick lashes and start running helplessly in a golden stream down her firelit face. And following the tears came the words:

"It wasn't my fault. I tried to stop him . . ."

The confession was like orgasm: the same frantic tensing of muscles; the same helpless peak of release; the same great sigh of relaxation afterwards.

"But you must have known," she said at last, when she had dried her tears and was lolling back weakly against Alita's soft breasts.

"Of course I knew," said Miriam. "But what I know isn't important. It's what you know, and what you feel, that counts."

"And will you tell Peter?" Beauty asked then, her face clouding at the thought.

"I shall do my duty, naturally," her mother pronounced, puffing her chest out pompously. "After all, a nyamakuta is one of the main guardians of morality."

Beauty and Alita stared at her in sudden alarm. But the black eyes were twinkling wickedly in the firelight.

Perhaps there had once been a time of peace, of floating weightless and unencumbered, of swaying and somersaulting in an open sea. But it was like a dream now; or the dream of a dream: faintly flickering on some screen at the back of a mind that was hardly a mind at all at the time that the dream was first dreamt; or locked in the marrow of bones that were barely bones at all when tadpole Tendai frolicked freely in her bloodlit pond.

Now her pelagic past had been replaced by a present so monstrous and all-pervasive that it seemed to stretch back to her very beginnings, so that she could not remember a time when her body was not balled like a wad of clay in a fist, and kneaded by fingers that seemed to want to remodel her into a new shape: a shape without arms or legs or even a face.

The pressure came in waves, closing gradually like swaddling bands wrapped tighter and tighter, till her knees nudged her nipples and her chin was tucked into her chest. And there was only minor respite between these regular crushing crescendos because, though her spine was allowed to unbend a little, there was now so little room in her capsule that even her nose – snubbed already to near flatness by nature – was splayed still flatter against the enveloping walls.

The worst of it was that there seemed to be no direction or purpose to these assaults – unless it was destruction, annihilation; a reversal of all her months of careful growth, making her shrink and shrink, with all the substance squeezed out of her, until she was once more a mindless hollow bobbing ball, bouncing again among fallopian fronds.

So she submitted – what choice did she have? – and, having never known fear, nor the pain of a promise betrayed, she did not imagine – with a mind that was unpracticed at imaginings – what horrors the future might hold; and could not predict – with a mind not adept at predicting – that this crushing would continue augmenting till for every two minutes of partial relief there would be one of impossible pressure.

For hours it went on – relentlessly, violently – pinioning her pretty limbs to her body. Yet it was oddly comforting, this annihilating embrace, because it allowed her no space to resist. And if she were to be crushed? Obliterated? So be it. She would yield without struggle to her fate.

Then something changed. At first it was barely perceptible

– just a suggestion of method in the madness. But soon it was unmistakable, as the random wrangling of the arms that clasped her began to resolve into a recognizable rhythm. And its purpose, at last, was so clear that it roused her from her snug swaddled stupor: of course – *down*, she was meant to go down.

Down: it was a force on her buttocks and an answering force on her head. Down: it was an imperative bearing down on her upended end. Down: it was all her reality, not some crude all-encompassing vise. Now here was a force she could grapple with, and she flung herself into the fray.

Suddenly she was a mole scrabbling in a tunnel, pushing backwards with bare pink-toed feet; grimly groveling through solid red soil; butting blindly, head downwards in the dark. Or a turtle paddling madly, beating frantic flippers – now against sly shifting sand, now against surging surf as the waves of each contraction spewed her out then sucked her back from the shore. Down, down, she scrambled; digging, delving, driving ever downwards; gaining, inch by slippery inch, a wriggling progress through her contracting cocoon.

Until –

What was this? Was she to be stopped now – when her heart thundered and her blood pounded in her veins?

Bone – there was a barrier of bone: a hard halo, a white crown, rammed cruelly on to her head by the force of her downward descent. And no – she couldn't pass through it: though she twisted and turned, it just mocked her with its toothless white grin. Nor could she avoid it, for when she tried to retreat, she found her way back implacably barred – by stiff bands of muscles, massed bunches of biceps, advancing down hard on her heels.

Now she felt fear – now her life-lust was ignited and her will to survive had been roused. But there was no going

243

forward, and no turning back, as the white jaws bit into her skull.

* * *

The light from the fire flickered on her spreadeagled legs, but her face was lost in the shadows. Only the glimmer of white teeth, biting back groans, showed where Beauty tossed her head from side to side on her back in the gloom.

It was past midnight and the storm of pain was nearly directly overhead. For twenty hours it had been slowly gathering and advancing, until its climactic thunderclaps were coming less than three minutes apart and hot white sheets of lightning threatened to split her storm-tossed body in two like the trunk of a blasted tree.

Miriam straightened up and washed her hands again, then met Alita's questioning eyes with a look bordering on despair:

"I can't understand it. I knew it would be tight, but I've delivered women narrower than this. It was going so well too – her womb's nearly opened completely. It's just her bones that are holding the baby back."

"Should I try to find someone with a tractor to take her to the hospital?" Alita asked. But she didn't even wait for an answer. It was too late, she knew, even if she could discover someone willing to help the witch's daughter in labor.

Then she saw a light – in the distance, over at her homestead – and heard men's voices coming faintly towards her on the still night air.

"They're back," she announced quietly to Miriam as she shut the door.

But the nganga wasn't listening – at least not to her. Instead she was having a muttered argument with someone kneeling invisibly in the shadows by Beauty's head.

"How can you be so sure it's wrong? It's the way I was

244

taught. Every hospital and clinic in the country has women lying down like this."

"Because I can see for myself," Eustina burst out in exasperation. "When she lies like this, her bones can't hinge open properly. That's why our calculations seemed wrong. They *are* wrong if she lies on her back. But they're right if she squats in the way we know."

"But I vowed I wouldn't take any chances; that I'd do exactly as I was taught this time. Everything's at stake – my daughter, my grand-daughter, maybe even my own future. If this birth ends in tragedy because I disobeyed the clinic's teachings . . . No. They were right about baby Alfred, and I was wrong – stubborn and wrong. This must be the best way to give birth. All the doctors in Zimbabwe can't be wrong."

"But they can't feel what's happening inside. Those people can't see with their hands the way we can, like the blind reading faces with their fingertips. You know I'm right. You can feel it as well as I can." And she shuffled towards Miriam on her knees and grabbed her string of red beads in her fist, tugging and twisting it savagely until it bit into Miriam's throat as surely as the white necklace of bone was cutting into Tendai's soft scalp.

"If you don't follow your nganga's instincts, you don't deserve to wear nganga's beads," she said, and the necklace suddenly snapped, sending beads cascading over the floor like drops of solid blood.

Alita gasped and darted forwards in a vain attempt to scoop up the spilt beads. Had she imagined the necklace jerking and breaking of its own accord, or was it Miriam's own hands, now dazedly fingering the limp dangling cotton round her neck, that had ripped the red necklace apart?

"Leave them," Miriam told her, brushing the hard red droplets from her skirt and off the plastic sacks that were spread out beneath Beauty's bare legs. "I'll make another when this is all over – if I'm still fit to be a nganga, that is," she added bitterly as her daughter's face convulsed once more into its familiar mask of anguish.

* * *

A merciful deadness began to spread through her cramped and compacted body, dulling the pain in her head and making each new excess of compression recede from her waning consciousness like a fading echo. Where before every greedy grasp of her crushing cocoon had been met by a surge of her own tenacity, making her squirm and struggle to free herself from its constraining clutches, now the pressure was so great that it constricted her umbilical cord, closing that fat pulsing lifeline so she was cut off from her sources of energy at the peak of every contraction.

And if she had been a breathing thing, she would have coughed and spluttered in paroxysms of panic, lungs laboring, mouth gaping for air. As it was she simply languished, in a torpid limp lethargy, as her heart slowed and her blood crawled, sluggish and dark, with its load of poisonous gas.

For Beauty there was no such deadly narcotic; no merciful blunting of awareness. She was there – with the hard floor under her head and the smoke stinging her eyes; with the rough blanket against her cheek and the heat of the fire on her legs. She was there. And the pain was there too.

What was this wetness on her face? Tears of agony or just water from the smarting of her eyes? Sweat running down from her forehead? Or blood from her bitten lips? Perhaps it was from Alita's cool cloth, wrung out in fresh water and wiped soothingly across her forehead. Her aunt's sweet face was there, gold and copper in the light of the fire, bending over, murmuring meaningless words of comfort.

But Beauty was beyond the reach of mere words; beyond

being in labor; beyond even being Beauty. She was back where she started, nineteen years ago, when her own flame of life-lust was ignited – grappling with unnameable forces in a pitiless all-pervasive present.

She no longer knew about the child in her womb. She only knew about the pain of expelling it; only knew about the deep, rending, inner wrench, as though some great blunt-taloned vulture was tearing away at her flesh; only knew about the vicious cold gnawing at the base of her spine, like a grinding stone rasping against her bones; about the uncontrollable trembling of her limbs; about the sudden shameful stench between her legs; about the strange guttural noises forced past her gritted teeth, sounding more like a cow or a pig than the voice of a grown woman.

And she knew about exhaustion: about a yearning for sleep that was like hunger – that cruel craving for rest that a prisoner feels when being questioned in a blank-walled cell, and kicked in the solar plexus when her head nods with weariness, or slapped round the face when she dares close her eyes. She was there, spreadeagled, on the floor of that cell; exhausted, unable to resist, while hard boots pounded away at her flesh.

Miriam looked at her daughter: a slender young woman felled by the weight of her pregnancy, pinned down helplessly on her back, dwarfed by this great striated mass that seemed to squat over her like some gluttonous beast feeding on its prey. She saw a woman in the posture of defeat, a dying woman lying flat on her back, legs akimbo, labia exposed in the firelight.

"Help me, Alita," she said suddenly. "Help me lift her up. I can't bear to see her like this."

Alita flashed one of her rare dazzling smiles and the two women heaved Beauty up on to her knees. Alita edged round behind to support her buttocks and back with her own knees and body, as she had with so many other nieces and daughters. And as Beauty arched back in relief against her aunt, who braced herself to take the weight, some subtle shifting of pressures inside made the thin membranes break.

In a sudden warm gush, that pale golden sea – that was both air and water to Tendai – spilled out on to the crumpled plastic sacking, dislodging hidden red beads from its folds and floating them towards Miriam. She stared at the beads as they formed a curved line at the edge of the advancing pale tide, and it crossed her mind that they looked for all the world like a necklace.

For a second a little thrill of awed pleasure passed through her. But there was no time to dwell on it and she flung herself forwards, thrusting her hand past Beauty's shining wet labial folds to make sure the cord had not been forced past the baby's head by the surge of the breaking waters. For the first time, now the membranes were broken, she could feel the slicked slime-covered scraping of hair that was plastered to Tendai's little bruised scalp and, slowly, her careful fingers traced the rims of flesh and bone that encircled it. No, all was well; no sign of the cord. And – she traced round the margin once again to make sure – yes! The space was bigger, rounder, wider, than it had been before.

She extracted her hand, now streaked with silver and red, and sat back on her heels with a sigh.

"It's going to be all right, I know it," she said, smiling into Beauty's eyes.

But Beauty's face showed none of the relief her mother felt. With teeth bared, cheeks flushed and eyes glittering, it was set in an expression of sheer fury. With a violent shake of her shoulders, she shook off her aunt's soothing caresses and rounded on her mother.

"All right for who?" she snapped. "All right for you maybe. But what about me? It's so long since you had a baby, you've forgotten what it feels like. Well, I'll tell you. It's agony. I don't ever want another child."

To her surprise and chagrin, Miriam nodded knowingly at Alita and both women chuckled delightedly.

"What are you laughing at?" Beauty asked petulantly, jutting out her lower lip and scowling. "I'm cold. I want to go to the toilet. I feel sick – and all you can do is snigger. It's not fair," she wailed resentfully, angry tears streaming down her cheeks. "I hate you, hate you for laughing at me."

Miriam composed her face. "I'm sorry. It's just so good to see you up and fighting at last – it means things are moving; that your baby's about to be born. Now listen to me very carefully: any moment now you will feel an unbearable urge to push. But you mustn't push until I tell you – do you understand? Otherwise all those months of massage and masuwo will be wasted and you will tear. Beauty? Do you hear me?"

But Beauty's eyes had begun to glaze over with inner concentration and her face was suddenly contorted and engorged with blood. She was holding her breath and grunting and her whole body was shaking in uncontrollable wild shudders. Miriam pinched the inside of her thigh as hard as she could and repeated her warning.

"Don't push yet, not until I tell you. Breathe, Beauty, breathe. Don't hold your breath yet."

Slowly Beauty's eyes began to focus again and the hectic color ebbed from her face as she subsided against Alita. She was panting – they were all panting – staring at each other with sparkling eyes.

Then, above the thudding of their hearts and the crackling of the fire and the chirping of a cricket by the door, they heard the sound of a drum beating and men shouting in the distance.

Merciful deadness snatched away by merciless life, by a living nightmare far worse than any dying dream could have been.

Her sluggish blue-blooded crawl towards oblivion was halted and fresh red blood was flushed through her body. The thick numbness that congealed in her nerves was pierced by shafts of the purest pain. And for a moment, as she hovered on the threshold – between known death and unthinkable life – oh, her abandoned drift into death seemed so sweet.

But no, she was to survive. Cruel life had her in its teeth again and she was being mauled and gouged at and battered back into being.

The jaws that had trapped her and taunted her and left their purple bruise, like a wreath of violets, on her head, had opened a little wider. The brutal bands bearing down on her buttocks pressed a little harder. And slowly the movement began.

But no, she would not be released readily from this crushing dark cell; would not be allowed to slip easily past the white bars that had kept her prisoner for so long. No, every inch would be an agony, as her head was rammed violently – violently but gradually – gradually but remorselessly – through the opening.

Gradually her face was defaced; her skin skinned; her scalp scalped; her lips ripped. Her forehead, pretty pale mound with its smooth flawless peach-petal skin, was pounded to flatness and the skin pinched raw-red as it was ground past the hard savage gape.

Even her skull – perfect porcelain patchwork, with its precious plump cargo of brain – ruptured along its newly knit seams and collapsed like a mere mangled mouthful: a flesh-and-bone bolus to be crunched, wrenched and chomped, then swallowed up by the gulping red gorge.

A part of her mind could hear the drums coming closer; could even hear the men shouting to one another as they began building a fire in the courtyard. With some cold sliver of rationality, she also noted that, though there must be at least twenty men out there, they had not yet stepped over the invisible shield that Miriam had erected round the hut.

Of all this she was aware, in a helpless detached way, just as a woman at the peak of love-making is aware of someone knocking at the door: aware but not aware; afraid but beyond fear; distracted but utterly undistractable.

She was pushing and nothing else mattered: not the men outside, not the smoke in her eyes, not her mother's voice, not her aunt's arms under her breasts.

She was pushing and she did not care: if her heart was bursting, her skin tearing, her bladder spurting its golden contents in a triumphant arc across the floor.

She was pushing and there was no stopping her: she was powerful, passionate, drugged on adrenalin; she was contorted, congested, grunting with the effort; she was kneeling, braced backwards, thrusting with every sinew; exalting, expanding, hurtling towards her deliverance.

The pain had stopped. The crushing had stopped. The brutal blackness had relented and released her. At last her head was freed from its clamp and her neck from its cramped inward arc. With a great groan of relief her spine uncurled, flexing her head backwards and downwards through a more yielding red throat of flesh.

And suddenly there was a chill on her poor mangled skull and firm fingers easing a last tight band of skin carefully down over her face. And there was light – gentle orange, warm brown, soft black shadows – pressing in past her swollen bruised eyelids. And sound – ragged breathing, a fire crackling, a drummer drumming.

Then something else: a surge of urgency that flared her tiny nostrils and made her mouth gape open to gulp in her first breath of air. And what air it was – loaded with smells and tastes that were brighter than the colors in her eyes and louder than the sounds in her ears: salt-blood, sour-urine, sweet-shit, spice-smoke. If this was life, she was glad to be alive.

Miriam bent and gently wiped the baby's nose and mouth with small pieces of clean cloth. Then, when Beauty began straining again, she grapsed the head and tilted it, so that first one and then two shoulders were shrugged out of their clinging red shroud.

The rest was easy, as the child's narrow body, with its slender coronet of pelvic bone, slithered through the mother's narrow body, with its slender coronet of pelvic bone: a circle through a circle; a cycle recycled; an ending, an unbending inheritance.

THE END